IN FINE FORM

Caitlin Press Inc.
8100 Alderwood Road,
Halfmoon Bay, BC V0N 1Y1
www.caitlin-press.com

Text design and cover design by Vici Johnstone
Cover image by Robert Wnuk. Sourced from UNsplash under Creative
Commons License Zero.

Library and Archives Canada Cataloguing in Publication
        In fine form : a contemporary look at canadian form poetry / Kate
Braid, Sandy Shreve, editors. — Second edition.

    Previous edition has subtitle: The Canadian book of form poetry. Pub-
lished
        by: Vancouver: Raincoast Books, 2005.
Includes bibliographical references and index.
ISBN 978-1-987915-02-0 (paperback)

        1. Canadian poetry (English)—20th century. 2. Canadian poetry
(English)—21st century. 3. Literary form. I. Braid, Kate, 1947-, editor
II. Shreve, Sandy, editor

PS8279.I49 2016   C811'.6   C2016-
903271-X In

edited by Kate Braid and Sandy Shreve

In Fine Form

2nd edition

A Contemporary Look
at Form Poetry

Preface by
Molly Peacock

CAITLIN PRESS

CONTENTS

PREFACE TO THE SECOND EDITION

Routine is the means by which we achieve our destiny — and by which a poem fulfills its inspiration. Just the way you almost cannot believe that breakfast, lunch, dinner and eight hours of sleep will eventually energize a person to cultivate an entire life's work, it is hard to credit that the simple counting of stresses or the almost child-like capturing of rhymes will help an evanescent inspiration flower. But inside inspiration a musical regime flows and, like three square meals and a night's rest, it makes for a marvelously flexible, healthy poem. Call this *form.*

Form is not the outside of a poem. It is the inside. A poem comes into being as it is built — or, to be more organic about it, as it is grown. The poem's structure develops inside its words even as the words grow the poem, just the way a bud grows inside a stem.

Fences train vines. Does form *train* a poem? The way my trainer at the gym urges reps for fitness? There *are* gymnastics in traditional form. And like virtuosity in anything, basketball or piano solos, formal dexterity is built on routines. The imagination leaps because the poet urges it again and again. These leaps themselves become rhythmic.

Form does something else vigorously physical: it compresses. Because you have to meet a limit — a line length, a number of syllables, a rhyme, you have either to stretch or to curl a thought to meet that requirement. Curiously, as the lyrical mind works to answer that demand, the unconscious is freed to experience its most playful and most dangerous feelings. I have always thought of form as safety, the safe place in which we can be most volatile.

Emily Dickinson famously wrote, "After great pain, a formal feeling comes — " and technique is a great comfort, perhaps even an antidote to pain. I think of a story a poet once told me, how, when undergoing an excruciating medical procedure as a child, he would count sequences of five on his fingers till it was over. That count is iambic pentameter … or the heartbeat line, *lubdub, lubdub.* It's no accident that we think of form as structuring the body of a poem, or that we think of poems as *having* bodies.

And formal bodies are fun. The enchanting idea that human beings are not so much defined by knowing as by *playing* comes to us by way of Johan Huizinga, the Dutch philosopher, a thinker now embraced by game theorists. Huizinga said in *Homo Ludens* that "All poetry is born of play … the nimble play of wit and readiness." But to be truly ready, we must rehearse. Musicians rehearse to perform, as do dancers. Athletes of all stripes practise to be ready for the interplay of rules and inspiration. Form is the beauty of play. What is beauty, by the way? Let's say it is the sudden encounter between unlikely entities — like "fun" and "regimen." For me, the beauty of form is the sudden union of boomeranging-ingly free inspiration with disciplined language.

Difficulty and discipline scare some people. But they excite poets who tackle formal patterns. I am always trying to get others to read more poetry, and when I find myself saying to reluctant readers, "It's not really that difficult," I half wince. I might try to deliver poetry as simple, but I know that a formal poem is as satisfyingly complex as an illuminated page from the *Book of Kells*. To go back to sports: a great game stunningly played can be breathtakingly compli-cated. Think of cuisine: it's exciting to try to sort out the layers of spices in a mouthful of something a dazzlingly experienced cook has constructed. The human activity of making *enjoys* these complications. Not when you start out, of course; then you need simple instructions, a recipe, and formalists adore provid-ing those, too. This anthology, now in its second edition, supplies explanations with its beautiful examples.

Just ten years after the first edition of *In Fine Form* appeared, Canadian poets happily find that they no longer have to apologize — much less justify — the use of form in poetry. There are twenty-first-century sonnets, triolets, villanelles, roundelays so colloquial they are transparent to the naked eye of the ordinary reader. No longer is free verse fiercely contrasted to form, partly because of the work of Kate Braid and Sandy Shreve. They and all who practise, or experiment with, the defined repetitions that are the playground of poetry let us understand that no poem exists without its shape and sound. Intrigued by the varieties of form and seduced by the paradox of the liberation from con-straints by constraints (patterns do seem to liberate thoughts we've kept hidden from ourselves), most poets have stopped thinking about formal poetry as jail. Why think of a formal apparatus as exterior bars for containment? Form is an inside.

Because contemplation and emotion are interior, we can think of their means of expression, poetry, as the inside of an inside.

Molly Peacock
Toronto, December, 2015

PREFACE TO THE FIRST EDITION

Anna Akmatova, writing in an age of experimentation, chose classical metres — suggesting, as Joseph Brodsky points out, that "her raptures and revelations were no greater than those of her predecessors." Curious, the idea that formal verse is a leveler.

From my own experience it is a liberator — like the nut cracker that frees the kernel from its prison. But that is not quite right. No analogy is ever quite right.

I had a sculptor friend who worked in clay until she felt she was getting too sloppy, whereupon she turned to marble because the medium itself imposed its own discipline. "Free verse" and "formal verse" might be substituted for her "clay" and "marble."

As readers, the variety and intricate patterns of formal verse surprise us. Sometimes, by not surprising us at all. Like Mozart, for instance, and rhyming verse: one anticipates the note or the rhyme and then, when it comes, it is a consummation. It was what we expected but *more than we expected*: a deep satisfaction.

Also as readers, formal verse can teach us how to read. Like dancing with a professional, we are given no option but to acknowledge the pattern, fall in and become a part of the art. By paying strict attention, form can even provide a poem with additional meaning. Listen to the stresses in a stressed poem and the meaning will become clear.

This much-welcomed anthology shows us what Canadian poets from the sixteenth century to the present day have done with form. Poets and readers alike will be grateful. Form is part of our heritage — free verse, an upstart. Not an unwanted or untalented upstart, but a newcomer nevertheless.

P.K. Page
Victoria, 2004

INTRODUCTION

"The impeded stream is the one that sings."
– Wendell Berry[1]

The seeds

This book sprang from three roots — curiosity, necessity and a love of rhyme, repetition, metre and rhythm. In the ten years since it was first published, we have been happily surprised at the enthusiasm of responses to the first edition and the increasing numbers of Canadian poets now writing in forms. But as always, poetry has continued to evolve and change so when a new publisher (Caitlin Press) asked if we would consider a second edition, we realized that yes, it was time.

But first — what is form? It's a question we will return to, but in short, it's structure. A form poem is one in which predetermined details of composition, including rhyme, repetition, metre and/or rhythm, are accepted as givens. Often these affect the poem's shape on the page, so a formal poem can sometimes be recognized at a glance — the fourteen lines of a sonnet, the three lines of a haiku, the somersaulting lines of a pantoum.

In the 1990s, both of us had been writing form poems for some time and were finding that when we assigned them as exercises in writing classes and workshops, student work shone. But it seemed a contradiction — shouldn't being asked to write within tight restrictions limit a poet's free expression?

And therein lies the delicious paradox of form poetry. Ask any parent — constraint can generate freedom. So too, in poetry. Just look at a child's delight in rhyme and (what seems to the reading parent) endless repetition that becomes almost chant-like. And it's a pleasure we never entirely lose, though we may become more sophisticated and more subtle in our taste.

T.S. Eliot wrote: "Every revolution in poetry is ... a return to common speech."[2] In the early 1900s many North American poets saw the traditional language of formal poetry as too often staid and limiting, and instead embraced the colloquial tone of free verse (sometimes called open form). By the 1950s free verse had become the norm, and many tended to pooh-pooh the elements of formal poetry (especially metre and rhyme) as being old-fashioned.

---

1   Wendell Berry, "Poetry and Marriage: The Use of Old Forms," in *Standing by Words* (San Francisco, CA: North Point Press, 1983), p. 205.

2   T.S. Eliot, "The Music of Poetry," the third W.P. Ker Memorial Lecture, delivered at Glasgow University in 1942 and published by Glasgow University Press, 1942. From *On Poetry and Poets* by T.S. Eliot in Gary Geddes, *20th Century Poetry & Poetics: 4th Edition* (Toronto, ON: Oxford University Press, 1996), p. 817.

But in our own work we were finding that closed and open forms each had their own challenges and delights. To write free verse well still required understanding the craft of poetry, and there were times when subject matter or mood called for a closed form — the obsessiveness of a sestina, for example, or the thoughtful depths of the glosa, the second look of the palindrome. Closed forms in particular reminded us how poetry is rooted in sound — the sensuous pleasure of repetition, the music of rhyme. We felt there was not only room, but a need, for both.

In 2000 Kate was asked to teach a course on writing poetry in form, but couldn't find an anthology with Canadian content. Meanwhile, Sandy was diving yet more deeply into writing in form, and growing frustrated at the absence of Canadian poetry in books about the subject. In lamenting this lack over coffee one day, the two of us discovered we each, independently, had been thinking of putting together a book on form, featuring the high calibre of Canadian work we knew existed. Glad that we didn't have to tackle such a project alone, we decided to do the book together.

Historically, Canadian poets have written a great deal in given forms and many contemporary poets continued to include formal poems in their books. So when we began searching for poems for the first edition, we checked the individual collections, anthologies and literary magazines on our shelves, and scoured the Canadian poetry section of the Vancouver Public Library. By the time we were finished, we'd set aside what we considered was an astonishing total of 1,400-plus poems (and had read countless more) dating from the 1800s (and in one case, the 1600s) to the present.

But, we wondered, if this many poems had been published, how many more were still languishing on poets' desks? With some concern that we were about to be flooded with limericks, we put out a limited call for submissions, hoping for perhaps 200–300 poems to fill the gaps in our research. Within weeks we were elbow deep in high-quality form poems; by the time they stopped arriving, we had almost 1,000. This was an abundance we had never, in our wildest dreams, expected.

In the decade since the publication of the first edition of this anthology, there have been even more poets writing in form — and formal poetry has become more visible in books, literary journals and classrooms. We wanted to reflect this interest by integrating new work into this second edition, but again decided not to put out a general call for submissions. Instead we've selected from the many form poems we each collected from Canadian books and journals over the past ten years. We were, however, concerned that Aboriginal and Black poets, in particular, might not have accessed these traditional outlets and for those, we contacted writers in those communities and asked them to suggest poets whose work we might consider.

In the poems gathered for both editions, we noticed patterns that clearly marked the work as arising from a distinct geographical and cultural mix: the easy incorporation of the French language; the frequency of poems related to weather and physical work like farming and fishing; and the influence of poets on one another's work within and across generations. We tracked, for instance, whole traditions of poets responding to P.K. Page's glosas and to John Thompson's ghazals — delightful conversations over time, a call-and-response within the Canadian poetic tradition.

When is a form ...?

In editing thousands of poems down to 176 for the first edition and over 180 for this volume, the question very quickly arose, when is a form not a form? Many of the poems we found — and loved — seemed to occupy a kind of transitional space, similar to the liminal in ecology, where zones overlap and new developments and adaptations occur. We lingered over George Murray's book, *Glimpse: A Book of Aphorisms*, for example, but decided they were not quite epigrams. Still, fine poems, like the following by Anne Wilkinson, echoed and tantalized. But what category should we put it in?

Still life[3]

I'd love this body more
If graved in rigid wood
It could not move;
I'd cut it fresh in pine;
The little knots
Would show where muscles grew,
The hollows shadow ovals
Into eyes,
The grain be quick to point
The vein, be tendon's clue;
I'd whittle hair
A solid armoured hood
And nothing here profane,
Nor rend the wood
But bind my fluid form
To forest tree,
Be still and let its green blood
Enter me.

---

3   Dean Irvine, ed., *Heresies: The Complete Poems of Anne Wilkinson 1924–1961* (Montreal, QC: Signal Editions, an imprint of Véhicule Press, 2003), p. 60.

Back and forth we wrote notes to each other: Syllabic? Almost. Regular metre? Sort of. How about rhyme? Kind of. We kept looking.

... not a form?

In compiling this anthology we were interested not only in traditional forms, but also in what contemporary poets were doing with the traditions. It's clear from the number of variations we've found or received that Canadian poets have always experimented, using form for inspiration and in the service of a better poem. Which raised the question of how far we would watch poets bend the tradition before we called it "not form."

In the case of the sonnet, for instance, the variations seemed endless; poets called their versions "liberated," "slender," "loose," "stretched," "eclectically rhymed," "word," "anti" and "free verse" sonnets.

But early on we decided the label sonnet and fourteen lines were not enough to convince us a poem fit the form. Beyond that, however, it was impossible to lay down a one-size-fits-all rule. In the end, we accepted a poem as a sonnet if the poet retained a clear echo of, and link to, the tradition by using roughly fourteen lines along with one or more of the form's other elements (rhyme and/or metre, a semblance of argument or persuasion, a concluding couplet, and so on). What proved interesting was how cleverly some poets disguised their forms. For example, it took a tip from poet Stephanie Bolster before we recognized Diana Brebner's seven-couplet poems as sonnets.

The ghazal was also a challenge. Most of those we received (and there were many) were in the free verse mode made popular by poets like John Thompson in Canada and Adrienne Rich in the US. To distinguish these from poems simply written in couplets, we held to the widely accepted premise that, when traditional rhyme, repetition or metre are omitted, a ghazal can still be identified by what poet Aga Shahid Ali called "a formal unity," and Thompson, "a matter of tone." However, given the number of beautiful ghazals we found, we were disappointed to find so few — even for the second edition — written in the traditional form. We hope that as the tradition becomes better known, perhaps partly through this book, more poets will try it, along with other less common forms such as the madrigal and rondeau redoubled.

We were surprised to find ourselves also having to draw lines around what constitutes a formal stanza. When we began our research, we dutifully saved what soon became an avalanche of poems written in stanza form. Certainly stanza is one of the signifiers of form, but we quickly decided it is probably the most widely (and casually?) retained formal aspect in the free verse tradition. If a poem had regular stanza breaks, but no additional pattern (such as metre, rhyme or repetition), we decided not to classify it as formal.

So in the end, many poems we loved, that teased and tantalized like Anne Wilkinson's "Still Life," had to go. It was free verse, a poem deeply motivated by the formal elements of poetry, but free verse nonetheless.

When it came down to final choices for the book, once pattern, form and quality were established, the final test was oral. Often we read the poems to each other out loud and it was the ear, in the end, that decided whether we would include one poem over another.

This raised its own dilemma.

"Every revolution ..."

Particularly for the first edition, there was one large category of poems with which we wrestled for some time. We were finding powerful poems, often strongly repetitive and chant-like, but we had no name for them and no apparent pattern or form other than this strong oral quality. Several times we dropped them, then scooped them back as being too memorable to let go. Finally we ran across the term "Incantation" in Lewis Turco's *The Book of Forms*, and we had a category where these poems could be placed together. Coming from widely different sources including Anglo-Saxon, Black and Indigenous traditions, they reflect interestingly upon each other and upon the oral tradition.

Anthologists seeking to print authentic poetry from oral traditions have always faced specific difficulties. Historical Aboriginal songs, for instance, were often collected in their written form by Europeans who, even with all good intentions, understood the work in their own cultural context, and therefore missed subtleties. In addition, they often took extensive liberties by adding (European) rhyme and metre. As Daniel David Moses and Terry Goldie point out, historic work like the Inuit song in this anthology should be considered "samples of a recording process which comments on both cultures involved."[4] Written renditions of this work can never entirely replicate its original oral presentation — the gestures and rhythms, for instance, which go with the story behind the words.

Perhaps it's no coincidence that in this second edition we've included a related form we'd considered only briefly ten years before: spoken word. Spoken word has strong elements of rhythm and rhyme, yes, but a decade ago it didn't seem to us to be in the "page poem" tradition, and many spoken word artists agreed. They stressed that theirs was work meant for performance. However, here too there have been changes, including the initiation of a spoken word category of funding through the Canada Council, publication of spoken word

---

4   Daniel David Moses and Terry Goldie, eds., *An Anthology of Canadian Native Literature in English* (Toronto, ON: Oxford University Press, 1992), p. 368.

anthologies and individual books, establishment of the Calgary Spoken Word Society and Festival (the first in the world) and the Spoken Word Program at The Banff Centre (initiated and directed until 2012 by Sheri-D Wilson). Spoken word artists have been accepted into the League of Canadian Poets and there have been special editions of literary magazines focused on this form. Clearly, some spoken word poems work both on the page and in performance, though performance is the primary criterion.

For some time we also discussed the inclusion of rap and hip-hop in this second edition (rap being the music that comes out of hip-hop culture) but in the end we decided rap bears the same relation to spoken word as song lyrics to poetry, and decided against including them.

Expectations and surprises

The selection and editing process has been an intensely exciting one for us. For example, contrary to our expectations, we found that nineteenth-century Canadian poets addressed far more than the stereotypical pastoral. We were delighted at the number of poems about politics, work and women's lives from that era. Also, when we began to place poems in sections, we discovered many that refused to be boxed into one form or another. Michael Redhill's, "Haiku Monument for Washington, D.C." for example, is also a visual poem; Molly Peacock's ghazal "Of Night" is also a sonnet; Christian Bök's double acrostic, "The Nocturne of Orpheus" is also a syllabic sonnet (12 syllables per line — plus each line is exactly 33 letters) as well as an anagram of a Keats sonnet; and Phyllis Gotlieb's incantation, "Death's Head" might as easily be considered a syllabic poem (which is where we had it in the first edition).[5] There were many others, but one cross-over particularly puzzled us.

While compiling the first edition, we kept finding poems — Gwendolyn MacEwen's "The Children Are Laughing" and Annie Charlotte Dalton's "The Praying-Mantis" — that sounded to the ear like form, with irregular but clearly repeating lines and phrases. But they couldn't quite be squeezed into any of the categories we had. Back and forth they went, from roundelay (for a repeating line), to stanza, to nonce (a form created by the poet for only one poem). It was Sandy who found it: "They're fugues!" she announced one day. Following the musical cue of Robyn Sarah's poem, titled "Fugue," and in the finest (and oldest) tradition of poetry as music, we gathered those poems together as a potentially emerging form, and grouped them with another long-standing fugal form in a chapter called "Fugue and Madrigal." Since then, we've noticed this lovely circular form catching on as more Canadian poets put their hand to it.

---

5   The Keats' sonnet is "When I Have Fears That I May Cease to Be."

With space at a premium in a collection such as this, adding more recent poems meant we had to remove many that appeared in the first edition. Saying farewell to poems we admire was the single most difficult part of putting together this new edition; often, the only way we could convince one another to take a poem out was by reminding ourselves that it is still in the first edition, still available to *In Fine Form* readers. At the same time, we are excited about the many new contributions to this anthology — including the addition of two children's poems in the mix.

Overall, in making selections for both editions, we have attempted to include nuggets many readers will recognize — such as Robert Service's "The Cremation of Sam McGee" — as well as less familiar poems, like Eric Duncan's "Drought." In addition, we've sought a balance between old and new, combining, wherever possible, nineteenth- and early twentieth-century examples with more contemporary work. We faced some limitations in this because the nineteenth-century poems we found were primarily limited to couplets and tercets, stanzas, sonnets and ballads. Contemporary poets are expanding their reach to embrace a much wider and more international selection of forms, such as the glosa, sestina, haiku and ghazal.

Many readers will be surprised to find we have included poets who are considered experimental, yet who clearly follow a given form. So, for example, bp Nichol and Christian Bök nestle up against the rhyme and metre of traditionalists like Archibald Lampman and Marjorie Pickthall. Everything old becomes new, they say. We find it exciting to see form in such new shapes.

Structure

We have organized this book in a way that we hope will illuminate poetic forms for both novice and experienced readers and writers. Each chapter opens with a brief introduction to the form's origin and how it works, citing examples from some of the poems that follow to show how poets apply the tradition as well as the exciting ways they experiment with it.

Some of the changes we've made in this second edition reflect our own development and deepening understanding of forms over the past decade. Other changes are to correct some errors that snuck past us in the first edition. But most of the changes we've made are in response to feedback and/or to acknowledge current trends in poetry. We've added several new forms: spoken word (mentioned above), prose poems, doublets, found poems and *pas de deux*. We've moved several forms to new locations: triolets are now in the Rondeau Family chapter; couplets and tercets are in Stanzas; lipograms are now in their own chapter; and syllabics and sapphics are now separate sections in the "… and More" chapter. Finally, rather than only list all poets and poems in the Table of Contents, we now have, in addition to an Index of Poets, an Index of Poems by Title.

In the first edition we ordered the poems by the poet's date of birth, in part to show how, in Canada, the tendency to experiment with traditional forms has a long history. This time, we decided to order the poems according to whether they follow or vary the form — starting with poems that stay close to the rules, then with those that slightly alter them, and finishing with poems that shake things up.

A note on spelling: there is often confusion between Canadian (and British) and American usage related to the use of the word "metre" — spelled "meter" by most Americans. We've chosen to use the Canadian "metre." So it's "metre," "metres" and "metred" but switches to the "... er" spelling for the compound words "pentameter," "tetrameter," "hexameter," and so on.

By necessity in such a short space, we've had to use many technical terms, so at the end we've included a chapter, "Coming to terms," that explains the terminology of some of the key concepts used in this book and in prosody in general — line, metre, repetition and rhyme. Throughout the book we've indicated strongly stressed syllables with <u>underlines</u>, metric feet with vertical lines (|), rhymes in words with *italics*, rhyme patterns with letters (*abab*), line breaks with a single forward slash (/) and stanza breaks with a double forward slash (//).

There is also an Index of Terms and, for further reading, a Bibliography with a list of reference books, many of which we relied upon heavily.

Two of these books warrant particular mention. We are not the first Canadians to record the formal tradition. Our forefather in this endeavour is Robin Skelton, whose posthumously published *opus magnum* is *The Shapes of Our Singing: A Comprehensive Guide to Verse Forms and Metres from Around the World.* For years Robin taught poetry — and an awareness of form and metre — to students at the University of Victoria in British Columbia. His book is a compilation of established international forms, many of them little known in North America. Each form is illustrated by one of his poems. Another critical Canadian resource for us was Stephen Adams' *poetic designs: an introduction to meters, verse forms, and figures of speech,* which delves more deeply into, and beautifully explains, many elements of poetic craft.

As mentioned earlier, since the first edition of *In Fine Form* there has been a resurgence of interest in formal poetry in Canada. In addition to a traditional form or two now being standard in most literary journals, *Geist* magazine held a haiku contest in 2006 and a Jackpine sonnet contest in 2010, the *Literary Review of Canada* regularly calls for specific forms for their poetry pages, other literary journals have had special issues on forms (*Arc* in particular, on spoken word and found poetry), and writers are experimenting with a wider range of forms. For example, several poets have paired up to co-write sonnet sequences (e.g., Peter Norman and Stephen Brockwell, Catherine Owen and Joe Rosenblatt); P.K. Page and Philip Stratford created an extended renga; Kim Goldberg and others in Nanaimo collaborated on a kasen (like the renga, a

Japanese form); and M. NourbeSe Philip, Jordan Abel, Gary Thomas Morse and others are diving into erasure poetry. Other ventures into form include a book of centos (by Mary Dalton, using a form that consists entirely of phrases, lines or stanzas borrowed from other writers), a volume of free-verse ghazals (Harold Rhenisch), a book-length "exploded" sestina, which marries a very old tradition and the post-modern (Shannon Maguire), and a memoir in haibun (Terry Ann Carter). In addition, more and more poets are writing what we are beginning to think of as formal free verse — usually poems in regular stanzas that feature (much like Anne Wilkinson's poem, above) some kind of irregular end-rhyme and sound devices (assonance, consonance, internal rhyme ...) that create a distinctive, albeit unmetred, rhythm.

We have no illusions that the book you now hold represents all the formal poetry or poets writing in Canada. For space reasons we were unable to include many of the fine poems we had in hand, and we're certain there are many more we're unaware of. And, as with any anthology, this one reflects our preferences, the forms we find most intriguing.

We hope this book will continue to give readers and students insight into the way forms work and evolve, as well as offer ideas and inspiration to writers. In the end, the most successful form poems are the ones where structure is like a skeleton — hidden, yet essential. The point is not to stick to the rules no matter what, but rather, to use them as you would any poetic tool — to help create a poem that says what it must, in the best possible way, form and content supporting and strengthening each other. As poet Don McKay says in his book, *The Shell of the Tortoise*,[6] all forms and techniques are "sensors, listening devices" to enable a poet to listen more deeply.

In a field in which few things are entirely agreed upon, we also hope to generate discussion and further exploration of the fascinating world of poetic forms; but mostly we see this as a collection of Canadian poetry that will particularly please the ear as well as the heart. We hope it will bring back for all of us a (perhaps half-forgotten) pleasure in rhyme, repetition, metre and rhythm.

The Editors, May 2015

---

6   Don McKay, *The Shell of the Tortoise — Four Essays & an Assemblage* (Kentville, NS: Gaspereau Press: 2011), p. 144.

BALLAD

Folk ballads are narrative poems that originated as songs sung by wandering minstrels in Europe during the fourteenth century or earlier. As part of an oral culture, these poems tended to change as they were passed along, so often there would be several versions circulating at any given time. Regardless of the version, however, all used simple, direct language to tell stories drawn from events such as a heroic act, a lost love or the supernatural — and these features carried over to the written form.

The traditional ballad stanza is a quatrain (four lines) rhyming *abcb* with four strong stresses in the unrhymed (*ac*) lines and three in the rhymed (*b*) lines. Although he combines the quatrains into eight-line stanzas, Dennis Lee's "1838," is a good example of this tradition:

"Mackenzie had a printing press.
It's soaking in the Bay.
And who will spike the Bishop till
Mackenzie comes again?"

Another common feature of ballads is the question and answer format used by Norah Holland in "The Grey Rider": "Why ride so fast through the wind and rain, / Grey Rider of the Shee? / Lest a soul should call for me in vain / To-night, O Vanathee."

While plot is generally more important than character in a ballad, poets often insert some dialogue to give a sense of the personalities involved and make the action more immediate. Robert Service, for instance, sprinkles "The Cremation of Sam McGee" with the occasional remark from McGee: "It's the cursed cold, and it's got right hold till I'm chilled clean through to the bone."

Repetition usually plays an important role in ballads. Lee uses the refrain "Mackenzie comes again" at the end of each stanza in "1838" to mark the transition from one aspect of the story to the next. E.J. Pratt uses each reappearance of "come home" and "keep away" to add to the emotional power in "The Lee-Shore."

Over the years poets have frequently improvised on the tradition. Two variations, an *abab* rhyme scheme (as in Pratt's poem) and quatrains with four strong stresses in every line (as in Wilson H. Thomson's "The Contract Mucker") have become so common they are considered standard.

Other variations abound. Service combines ballad stanza lines to create a longer line of seven strong stresses with a couplet rhyme scheme plus an internal rhyme on the second and fourth strong stresses in every line ("It's the cursed _cold_, and it's _got_ right _hold_ …"). In other words, if you split his long lines into quatrains you'll see how Service has disguised the traditional _abcb_ rhyme scheme. Steven Price uses repetition sparingly (just three lines are repeated, and only once each). And in "Back on the Job," John G. Fisher varies the form by combining the quatrains to make two stanzas — but cutting the second one short by two lines, thus nicely emphasizing the "wreck" of the bottle's neck.

Ryan Knighton gives us a more experimental approach in "The Ballad of Echolocation." While this poem uses traditional stanzas (quatrains) and repetition (stanza 1 is the refrain), it has no regular rhyme scheme, uses a metre of two strong stresses in each short line and takes an oblique approach to storytelling. But it is those variations, especially the incantatory metre and indirect language, which give this poem its urgency.

The traditional form:

Stanzas:	An unlimited number of quatrains.
Metre:	Alternating tetrameter and trimeter lines; or all tetrameter lines.
Rhyme:	_abcb_ or _abab_
Repetition:	Usually used extensively, often in the form of a regularly repeated phrase, line or stanza.

Dennis Lee (b. 1939)

1838

The Compact sat in parliament
To legalize their fun.
And now they're hanging Sammy Lount
And Captain Anderson.
And if they catch Mackenzie
They will string him in the rain.
And England will erase us if
Mackenzie comes again.

The Bishop has a paper
That says he owns our land.
The Bishop has a Bible too
That says our souls are damned.
Mackenzie had a printing press.
It's soaking in the Bay.
And who will spike the Bishop till
Mackenzie comes again?

The British want the country
For the Empire and the view.
The Yankees want the country for
A yankee barbecue.
The Compact want the country
For their merrie green domain.
They'll all play finders-keepers till
Mackenzie comes again.

Mackenzie was a crazy man.
He wore his wig askew.
He donned three bulky overcoats
In case the bullets flew.
Mackenzie talked of fighting
While the fight went down the drain.
But who will speak for Canada?
Mackenzie, come again!

NORAH M. HOLLAND (1876–1925)

The Grey Rider

Why ride so fast through the wind and rain,
   Grey Rider of the Shee?
Lest a soul should call for me in vain
   To-night, O Vanathee.

Now, whose is the soul shall seek thine aid,
   Grey Rider of the Shee?
The soul of one that is sore afraid
   To-night, O Vanathee.

O fears he the flurry of wind and rain,
   Grey Rider of the Shee?
More deep is the dread that sears his brain
   To-night, O Vanathee.

Does he fear the tumult of clanging blows,
   Grey Rider of the Shee?
Nay, darker still is the fear he knows
   To-night, O Vanathee.

Does he fear the loss of wife or child,
   Grey Rider of the Shee?
Nay, a terror holds him that's still more wild
   To-night, O Vanathee.

O what should make him so sore afraid,
   Grey Rider of the Shee?
He fears a wraith that himself has made
   To-night, O Vanathee.

Then how shall you cleanse from fear his mind,
   Grey Rider of the Shee?
I will touch his eyes, and they shall be blind
   To-night, O Vanathee.

Yet still may he know the voice of fear,
    Grey Rider of the Shee?
I will touch his ears that he shall not hear
    To-night, O Vanathee.

Yet that wraith may linger around his bed,
    Grey Rider of the Shee?
No terror shall touch the quiet dead
    To-night, O Vanathee.

WILSON H. THOMSON (b. 1800s)

The Contract Mucker

When the dividend's set, I can say without doubt,
There is one man to thank when the cheques are sent out;
He's away down below where he can't see the sky
And he rarely complains, he's a hard working guy.
    Is the mucker.

His shovel just burns when he's working below
It's a joy just to watch how he plays that banjo,
When the car's full of muck, with four wheels off the track
He just smiles and he says: "Oh alas and alack!"
    Does the mucker.

When he's cleaned off the track, and he's got to the plate,
He will think the worst's over, but there, sure as fate,
He will find them all buckled, and bent, like a bow,
And instead of being flat, they are all in a row,
    Does the mucker.

Then the sampler comes in, and he lays down his sheet.
And he says, "you must stop cos' I'm short fourteen feet"
But who is it says to sampler "do tell"
And will answer right smartly "you go plumb to hell."
    It's the mucker.

They can say that a mucker is easily led,
That he's strong in the back, and he's weak in the head,
But that is a yarn that I cannot receive,
Because of one fact which you'll have to believe.
                    I'm a mucker.

When the sight of the bonus sheet knocks you all dead,
The sheet seems to set all the mines seeing red,
Then who is it, has the most sarcastic touch,
By informing the captain he's got far too much,
                    It's the mucker.

So upon his last shift when he's mucked his last round,
And he's up in the sky, where no shift boss is found,
When St. Peter has scanned the good book for his name,
And he says, "what are you" he can proudly proclaim,
                    "I'm a mucker."

⋆⟶

JOHN G. FISHER (b. 1800s)

Back on the Job

I sit once more at the glory hole,
  As I sat in days of yore,
And the charcoal flies in my face and eyes
  And oh! but my hands are sore.
There are blisters on my fingers
  And blisters on my thumbs,
And there are blisters every darned old place
  A blister ever comes.
My arms just feel like chunks of wood,
  I scarce can move them more,
But I sit and sing and roll my ring
  To the hum of the factory's roar.

The bottle is a sixteen ounce,
   It seems like sixteen pound,
As I drag it square upon the chair
   And roll it round and round.
I jab my tools in water
   I jab them in charcoal,
I jab them at the bottle's neck,
   But there! I've missed the hole;
And the bottle neck is a total wreck
   Because of an extra roll.

✦⟶▭

E.J. PRATT (1883–1964)

The Lee-Shore

Her heart cried out, — "Come home, come home,"
When the storm beat in at the door,
When the window showed a spatter of foam,
And her ear rang with the roar
Of the reef; and she called again, "Come home,"
To the ship in reach of the shore.

"But not to-night," flashed the signal light
From the Cape that guarded the bay,
"No, not to-night," rang the foam where the white
Hard edge of the breakers lay;
"Keep away from the crash of the storm at its height,
Keep away from the land, keep away."

"Come home," her heart cried out again,
"For the edge of the reef is white."
But she pressed her face to the window-pane,
And read the flash of the signal light;
Then her voice called out when her heart was slain,
"Keep away, my love, to-night."

✦⟶▭

ROBERT SERVICE (1874–1958)

The Cremation of Sam McGee

There are strange things done in the midnight sun
By the men who moil for gold;
The Arctic trails have their secret tales
That would make your blood run cold;
The Northern Lights have seen queer sights,
But the queerest they ever did see
Was that night on the marge of Lake Lebarge
I cremated Sam McGee.

Now Sam McGee was from Tennessee, where the cotton blooms and blows,
Why he left his home in the South to roam 'round the Pole, God only knows.
He was always cold, but the land of gold seemed to hold him like a spell;
Though he'd often say in his homely way that "he'd sooner live in hell."

On a Christmas Day we were mushing our way over the Dawson trail.
Talk of your cold! through the parka's fold it stabbed like a driven nail.
If our eyes we'd close, then the lashes froze till sometimes we couldn't see;
It wasn't much fun, but the only one to whimper was Sam McGee.

And that very night, as we lay packed tight in our robes beneath the snow,
And the dogs were fed, and the stars o'erhead were dancing heel and toe,
He turned to me, and "Cap," says he, "I'll cash in this trip, I guess;
And if I do, I'm asking that you won't refuse my last request."

Well, he seemed so low that I couldn't say no; then he says with a sort of moan:
"It's the cursed cold, and it's got right hold till I'm chilled clean through to the bone.
Yet 'tain't being dead — it's my awful dread of the icy grave that pains;
So I want you to swear that, foul or fair, you'll cremate my last remains."

A pal's last need is a thing to heed, so I swore I would not fail;
And we started on at the streak of dawn; but God! he looked ghastly pale.
He crouched on the sleigh, and he raved all day of his home in Tennessee;
And before nightfall a corpse was all that was left of Sam McGee.

There wasn't a breath in that land of death, and I hurried, horror-driven,
With a corpse half hid that I couldn't get rid, because of a promise given;
It was lashed to the sleigh, and it seemed to say: "You may tax your brawn and brains,
But you promised true, and it's up to you to cremate those last remains."

Now a promise made is a debt unpaid, and the trail has its own stern code.
In the days to come, though my lips were dumb, in my heart how I cursed that load.
In the long, long night, by the lone firelight, while the huskies, round in a ring,
Howled out their woes to the homeless snows — Oh God! how I loathed the thing.

And every day that quiet clay seemed to heavy and heavier grow;
And on I went, though the dogs were spent and the grub was getting low;
The trail was bad, and I felt half mad, but I swore I would not give in;
And I'd often sing to the hateful thing, and it hearkened with a grin.

Till I came to the marge of Lake Lebarge, and a derelict there lay;
It was jammed in the ice, but I saw in a trice it was called the "Alice May."
And I looked at it, and I thought a bit, and I looked at my frozen chum;
Then "Here," said I, with a sudden cry, "is my cre-ma-tor-eum."

Some planks I tore from the cabin floor, and I lit the boiler fire;
Some coal I found that was lying around, and I heaped the fuel higher;
The flames just soared, and the furnace roared — such a blaze you seldom see;
And I burrowed a hole in the glowing coal, and I stuffed in Sam McGee.

Then I made a hike, for I didn't like to hear him sizzle so;
And the heavens scowled, and the huskies howled, and the wind began to blow.
It was icy cold, but the hot sweat rolled down my cheeks, and I don't know why;
And the greasy smoke in an inky cloak went streaking down the sky.

I do not know how long in the snow I wrestled with grisly fear;
But the stars came out and they danced about ere again I ventured near;
I was sick with dread, but I bravely said: "I'll just take a peep inside.
I guess he's cooked, and it's time I looked"; … then the door I opened wide.

And there sat Sam, looking cool and calm, in the heart of the furnace roar;
And he wore a smile you could see a mile, and he said: "Please close that door.
It's fine in here, but I greatly fear you'll let in the cold and storm —
Since I left Plumtree, down in Tennessee, it's the first time I've been warm."

There are strange things done in the midnight sun
　　By the men who moil for gold;
The Arctic trails have their secret tales
　　That would make your blood run cold;
The Northern Lights have seen queer sights,
　　But the queerest they ever did see
Was that night on the marge of Lake Lebarge
　　I cremated Sam McGee.

‹╾══◻

STEVEN PRICE (b. 1976)

from Anatomy of Keys

XVIII .ii
That riveted iron boiler clanked
　　and gurgled dully there
while hoses gushed and sluiced the tank
　　until it held no air.
A bucket clanged. Houdini rose,
　　brandishing an axe:
it was not true he would come to rue
　　that night in Halifax.

Three stagelamps smoked and guttered lean,
　　two fanglike lid-bolts grinned;
he struck and banged the boiler's seams
　　for leakage near the hinge.
The rivets whitened knucklelike
　　as liquid sucked them shut;
but it was not he they'd come to see.
　　That crowd had come for blood.

Houdini lunked and scaled the tank,
      muscular and grim.
He gripped its rim by knee and shank,
      then let the crowd grip him.
A man can only hold his breath
      so long, he shouted down;
but it is not right you've come tonight
      half-hoping I might drown,

risking nothing more your own
      than nickels, or a laugh.
Hold your breath while I am down.
      See how long you last.
Casket-like that boiler loomed,
      its rippling waters black,
but it was no grave he'd come to brave
      that night in Halifax.

Houdini's stagehands loosed a line
      and took the axe from him;
he slithered in and floated blind
      as though within a womb
and watched the widened eye of light
      above him eyelid shut;
it was not air he latched out there.
      He latched out all he was.

That eerie belly held him warm,
      it shivered at each sound;
his blood beat like a bat up-barn,
      frantic, bashing round.
A spangled stagelight filtered in
      and lit his grey skin weak;
but he felt no fright as the locks shut tight:
      that lid was forged to leak.

At thirty seconds ladies gagged,
     at fifty-five most men;
one minute twenty an athlete sagged;
     the clock went round again.
Three swimmers choked, two divers next,
     but still that boiler sat;
at last one said, *He, he must be dead,*
     a man all thumbs and hat.

Three minutes ten. Four twenty-eight.
     No man can live so long.
A stagehand stood hefting his blade,
     the audience a throng
of throats and groans and fist-clenched thighs;
     death had seized them here;
for it's not in ease most men believe:
     true art is found in fear.

The axeblade glittered, menacing
     a bright ferocious grin,
suspended in its heft and swing
     it dragged the crowd's rage in;
yet there it hung, it hefted, hung,
     hung poised and trembled deep;
it was just this they'd feared to miss —
     when out he stepped. Free.

The curtains shook. Fine plaster fell.
     The audience had made it,
yet in that rush all somehow felt
     flushed, exhilarated,
and unaccountably depressed.
     Onstage the clock still stood.
For it was not he they'd come to see;
     that crowd had come for blood.

(*Water Torture Cell Escape*, New York, May 1907)

RYAN KNIGHTON (b. 1972)

The Ballad of Echolocation

Lighthouse the slick line
a spearing the far sky
for catching the capsize
a shipment of import.

The ocean a body
of mine is the tiding
to slacken the water
the mouth is a coastline.

The old beach a comber
of fingers the trawling
the chancing a gathering
of flesh cut the mooring.

Lighthouse the slick line
a spearing the far sky
for catching the capsize
a shipment of import.

The labour an anchor
of water the secret
the definite nation
a buoy on the last day.

The gutting a chumslop
of fish the alarming
a notion the skullcap
of ocean the longing.

Lighthouse the slick line
a spearing the far sky
for catching the capsize
a shipment of import.

The deep is the hollow
of shell pitched the captain
the whistling a not there
mayday in the once ear.

BLUES

The blues — a uniquely African-American form of folk song — evolved in the nineteenth century from the work songs of southern Black slaves who used traditional African rhythms to express feelings of grief and loss over the conditions of their lives. The music evolved using flattened third, fifth and seventh notes, known as "blue" notes. Much of our popular music, including rock and roll and jazz, has grown from this form.

The *New Grove Dictionary of Music and Musicians* points out that "since the sixteenth century 'the blue devils' has meant a condition of melancholy or depression" and the subject matter of blues music was often loss — death or love lost. The love was usually the physical kind and in this, blues poems were clearly secular and distinguished from spirituals. But no matter what the subject, the ability to express a blues feeling is key. Ralph Ellison says the blues doesn't offer a solution to felt grief or hardship, but can offer relief in the form of recognition and/or defiance.[7]

As with any oral tradition adapted to the page, blues poetry varies widely in form, but generally, following the twelve-bar sequence of the music, it is written in any number of three-line stanzas with four strong stresses per line. The rhyme scheme is usually *aaa* or (less often) *aab*.

Adam Sol's "Jeremiah's Blues on the GW Bridge" is a good example of how, in this form, the second line usually repeats or slightly varies the first, giving the singer time to find a third, rhyming line that responds to the emotion of the first two, often with a wry twist of humour. The tension this creates is reminiscent of the turn in an Italian sonnet, or the final couplet of the English one.

One of the origins of blues was a collective "call-and-response" (and later, individual "hollers"), that helped set a pace for heavy physical labour. Wayde Compton's "Jump Rope Rhyme for the 49er Daughters" applies this traditional call-and-response technique to the California gold rush days of 1849, though he varies both the number of strong stresses in his lines (between four and three) and the refrain line.

In "Conjured," R. Nathaniel Dett uses a less common blues style of four-line stanzas with two strong stresses per line — "I'm <u>con</u>jured! I'm <u>con</u>jured!" — for an eight-bar blues. George Elliott Clarke, who brought this poem to our attention, describes it as possessing a syncopated, fast-moving "ragtime" feel. Clarke's own "King Bee Blues" picks up on the theme of raunchy love ("But don't be surprised / If I sting your flower today"), and when his six-line stanzas are

---

7   In Ron Padgett, ed., *The Teachers and Writers Handbook of Poetic Forms*, p. 29.

compressed to three lines, they follow standard blues rhyme and metre. Meanwhile, Maureen Hynes's "Self-Sufficient Blues" pushes the form to its modern limits.

The traditional form:

Stanzas:	An unlimited number of tercets (sometimes quatrains).
Metre:	Accentual; tercets usually have 4 strong stresses per line, and quatrains, 2 strong stresses per line.
Rhyme:	*aaa* or *aab*
Repetition:	Line 1 is often repeated exactly or with a slight variation in line 2; this anticipates and delays the response of line 3, which often uses humour to expand the meaning of the stanza.

ADAM SOL (b. 1969)

Jeremiah's Blues on the GW Bridge

This end of the Sound is a river, this end of my mind one hair,
This end of the Sound is a river, this end of my mind one hair,
My torn tongue's tired of teaching, and I'm only halfway there.

O decrepit borough, splayed out like a skinned skunk,
O decrepit borough, splayed and rank like a skinned skunk,
This leg of your great city is lined with grime and junk.

My people breathe exhaustion, they don't fight it anymore,
Lord, my people breathe exhaustion, they don't fight it anymore,
Clouds ripe from their desires, smoke from forgotten doors.

I've got no email EZPass to speed me safe to Queens,
I've got no email EZPass to speed me safe to Queens,
I've just got words and rhythm, and the prophecies I've seen.

I've seen the passing tankers, with their loads of oil and grease,
I've seen the passing tankers, with their loads of oil and grease,
They push upriver pendulous, then descend into dis-ease.

Hey you toll booth operators, stranded like broken-soled shoes,
Hey you toll booth operators, stranded at your posts like shoes,
Go home to your plaid couches, let the diesel trucks blast through.

Let them carry their convictions upstate where they belong,
Let them carry their convictions upstate where they belong,
All they've left behind are napkins, and invoices they tallied wrong.

Here come some good policemen to pull me off the ledge,
Here come some well-trained, hard-worked, chapped lip,
              honest poor policemen, here to pull me off the ledge,
What they'll get for their good intentions is an earful of my rage.

R. Nathaniel Dett (1882–1943)

Conjured

Couldn't sleep last night!
  Just toss and pitch!
I'm conjured! I'm conjured!
  By that little witch!

My heart's all afired!
  My brain's got the itch!
I tell you I'm conjured
  By that little witch!

I'm "patchy" in feelings;
  It seems that a stitch
Has sewed me up inside out.
  Then there's a hitch

Whenever I try to think;
  Side track and switch
My thoughts do; and finally
  Dump me in the ditch.

And when I talk, my voice
  Seems all out of pitch;
When I think about her,
  My pulses, they twitch.

I'm in love or I'm crazy,
  I can't tell quite which;
But I know I've been conjured
  By that little witch!

GEORGE ELLIOTT CLARKE (b. 1960)

King Bee Blues

I'm an ol' king bee, honey,
Buzzin' from flower to flower.
I'm an ol' king bee, sweets,
Hummin' from flower to flower.
Women got good pollen;
I gets some every hour.

There's Lily in the valley
And sweet honeysuckle Rose too;
There's Lily in the valley
And sweet honeysuckle Rose too.
And there's pretty, black-eyed Susan,
Perfect as the night is blue.

You don't have to trust
A single Black word I say.
You don't have to trust
A single Black word I say.
But don't be surprised
If I sting your flower today.

⊷⟹

WAYDE COMPTON (b. 1972)

Jump Rope Rhyme of the 49er Daughters

caller   got a treasure map and a silver pick.
all   how you gonna know where to dig?

caller   map got a great big X on it.
all   how you gonna know where to dig?

caller   got 10 paces marked in black.
all   how gonna know where to dig?

caller   gonna count em off …
all   1, 2, 3, 4, 5 — gonna count em off.

caller   gonna count em off …
all   6, 7, 8, 9, 10 — gonna count em off.

caller   gonna count em off …
all   1, 2, 3, 4, 5 — gonna count em off.

caller   gonna start again …
all   6, 7, 8, 9, 10 — gonna count em off.

caller   got a treasure map with a silver spade.
all   how you gonna know where to dig?

caller   just like a pirate with a wooden leg.
all   how you gonna know where to dig?

caller   girl in the middle gotta spell her name …
all   how you gonna know where to dig?

caller   jumpin on one foot, okay?
all   jumpin on just one foot.

girl   A-l-e-x-a-n-d-r-i-a.
all   how you gonna know where to dig?

F.R. Scott (1899–1985)

Metric Blues

Mile, gallon and pound
root me in solid ground,
but metre, litre and gram!
Lhude sing goddamm!

Kill that smile
you measured mile.
The metric talon
's got you, gallon.
Frown, pound,
you're quite unsound.

Metre, litre and gram!
Lhude sing goddamm!

Oh heck
gone is the peck.
Never again
a chain.
No more search
for the tricky perch,
and the innocent yard
is barred.

Metre, litre and gram!
Lhude sing goddamm!

Yell and flinch
ell and inch.
Shudder and scram
Rood and drachm.
Poor pole
you've lost your role
and your daily bounce
ounce.
Pints and quarts?
You're torts!

Metre, litre and gram!
Lhude sing goddamm!

Furlongs, fathoms and rods
dead as the old gods.
Not so much as a stone
for an anglophone
alone.

Lhude, lhude sing
goddamm!

MAUREEN HYNES (b. 1948)

Self-Sufficient Blues

Workin girl, I wake up every day
with the wanna-stay-in-beds
Workin girl, I wake up every day
fix my house instead.

Got the self-sufficient blues, got them down fine.
Got the self-sufficient blues, just me, myself and mine.
It's the fix my own plumbing, tie my own shoes,
make my own decisions, paint my own blues.

Got my education, got my medication,
got my job down pat.
Got my education, got my medication,
got a therapist and a cat.

Got the half a head of lettuce, the salad greens go bad.
Got the full fridge, empty table, one wineglass sads.
Got the self-sufficient blues, the flying solo crime
Goin through the motions and I'm getting by just fine.

But what's missing is some kissing,
a pair of boots inside my door.
What's missing is some kissing
a little laughin' and l'amour.

Got the self-sufficient blues, got the me, myself and mine.
Got the self-sufficient blues, oh I carry on just fine.

Epigram

Epigrams are brief, witty poems defined more by tone than formal structure. The word comes from the Greek *epigramma*, meaning "to write upon." Epigrams were originally inscriptions on statues or monuments but have evolved into a literary form in their own right, usually rhymed and having two parts. The first part states the theme and the second features a turn that makes the point with a quick, impressive flourish, often using satire or humour to do so. This one, by Coleridge, provides both a definition and a good example of the form: "What is an epigram? A dwarfish whole; / Its body brevity, and wit its soul."

These small gems seem capable of anything. They will as readily praise, commemorate or compliment (e.g., Robert Hayman's "Quodlibets"), as ridicule, censor or insult (e.g., the anonymous "Bugs"). When composed as inscriptions for monuments or gravestones (regardless of whether they are, in fact, engraved in stone) epigrams like the one in this chapter by Robert Finch are known as epitaphs.

(Perhaps because they all sound so similar, the terms epigram, epitaph, and epigraph — a brief quote used to introduce a literary work — are often confused. To make matters worse, both epitaphs and epigraphs can also be epigrams.)

Epigrams are usually no more than eight lines and can stand alone as one or more stanzas, or be part of a longer poem. Although usually rhymed and metred, they can be equally effective in free verse, as shown by Margaret Atwood's sardonic "[you fit into me]" and Dionne Brand's indignant "Winter Epigram: 21."

The traditional form:

Stanzas:	Usually a maximum of 8 lines; sometimes broken into stanzas (usually couplets or quatrains).
Metre:	Often iambic pentameter, but the metric pattern (if any) is up to the poet.
Rhyme:	Often *aa* or *abab*, but the rhyme scheme is up to the poet.
Repetition:	None required.
Distinguishing feature:	A short observation with a clever twist; easy to remember.

Robert Hayman (1575–1629)

from Quodlibets

To a worthy Friend, who often objects the coldnesse of the Winter in Newfound-Land, and may serve for all those that have the like conceit.

You say that you would live in Newfound-land,
Did not this one thing your conceit withstand;
You feare the *Winters* cold, sharp, piercing ayre.
They love it best, that have once wintered there.
Winter is there, short, wholesome, constant, cleare,
Not thicke, unwholesome, snuffling, as 'tis here.

A.J.M. Smith (1902–1980)

News of the Phoenix

They say the Phoenix is dying, some say dead.
Dead without issue is what one message said,
But that has been suppressed, officially denied.

I think myself the man who sent it lied.
In any case, I'm told, he has been shot,
As a precautionary measure, whether he did or not.

ALDEN NOWLAN (1933–1983)

Aunt Jane

Aunt Jane, of whom I dreamed the nights it thundered,
was dead at ninety, buried at a hundred.
We kept her corpse a decade, hid upstairs,
where it ate porridge, slept and said its prayers.

And every night before I went to bed
they took me in to worship with the dead.
Christ Lord, if I should die before I wake,
I pray thee Lord my body take.

ROBERT FINCH (1900–1995)

from Four Epigrams

Epitaph

Here lies a man who was so bright
He beat the very flight of light,
There was no ditch he could not clear
Except the one he lies in here.

JUDITH FITZGERALD (1952–2015)

To the Boss

He taught me
To say
I need you.

RAYMOND SOUSTER (1921–2012)

Very Short Poem

"… But only God can make a tree."

(He'll never try it in Sudbury.)

⊷═◦

ANON (early pioneer)

Bugs

Each year when the vile bugs come round
To feast on my potatoes,
I let them taste the Paris green,
I give it to them gratis.

They eat it, sicken, and they die;
Death stops them in their mission:
'Tis just what every bug deserves
That eats without permission.

⊷═◦

RICHARD OUTRAM (1930–2005)

Tourist Stricken at the Uffizi

Dear God, for the rest of my life:
And how shall I tell her, my wife,
That the pallor of a Botticelli Venus
Has come, irrevocably, between us?

⊷═◦

PATRICK LANE (b. 1939)

Cowichan Valley Poem

The heron has only one leg
and he stands on both of them.

MARGARET ATWOOD (b. 1939)

[you fit into me]

you fit into me
like a hook into an eye

a fish hook
an open eye

DIONNE BRAND (b. 1953)

from Winter Epigrams

21.
so I'm the only thing you care about?
well what about the incursions into Angola,
what about the cia in Jamaica,
what about El Salvador,
what about the multi-national paramilitaries
in South Africa,
and what do you mean by "thing" anyway?

FOUND POEMS

Found poems are unique in that poets do not write them from scratch. Instead, they are discovered in other works and, one way or another, arranged into poetry.

Canada's John Robert Colombo traces the first found poem in English to Yeats, who, as editor of the *Oxford Book of Modern Verse* (1936), included a "versified" prose fragment from a Walter Pater essay.[8] In his introduction to F.R. Scott's 1967 collection of found poetry, *Trouvailles: Poems from Prose*, Louis Dudek described the form as "a piece of realistic literature, in which significance appears inherent in the object — either as extravagant absurdity or as unexpected worth." As Scott's "Pavillion Misrepresents Outlook" shows, found poetry can be an excellent platform for protest as well as for irony (saying one thing but meaning the opposite).

Colombo, Scott and Dorothy Livesay were the first Canadian poets to explore the possibilities of found poetry. The first two focused mainly on re-arranging existing texts with minimal intervention, while Livesay (and, later, others such as Michael Ondaatje and Daphne Marlatt) created what Franz Stanzel calls "documentary literature, employing historical or social documents as literature."[9] Since then, found poetry has gone in many directions and now includes everything from collage to erasure poetry. As Shane Rhodes points out, today we can "… conceptualize found poetry along an axis that ranges from non-interventionist at one extreme … to the other end where the found text is doctored, and 'poeticized,' and, perhaps, included within a larger unfound structure."

Representing one end of the spectrum, Scott's poems are examples of the non-interventionist approach, where poems are created by inserting line breaks in otherwise unchanged passages from a larger text. Brian Bartlett's "What He Chose to Record," part of a sequence of found poems, is a documentary/collage, which gathers together fragments from a variety of East Coast historical sources, including diaries, letters, newspapers and books. "The art of writing these poems," Bartlett explains, "is one of radical selection, concentration, and free rearrangement."[10]

At the other end of the spectrum, Jordan Abel's poem is an example of erasure poetry, which deletes passages from an original text — in this case, the book *Totem Poles* by anthropologist Maurice Barbeau. Abel also often leaves the

---

8   Manina Jones, "Redeeming Prose: Colombo's Found Poetry," found at www.uwo.ca/english/canadianpoetry/cpjrn/vol25/jones.htm (accessed April 8, 2015).

9   Stanzel and Rhodes quotes are from Shane Rhodes, "Reuse and Recycle: Finding Poetry in Canada," *Arc Poetry Magazine* (Winter 2013), p. 47–57.

10   Brian Bartlett, *The Watchmaker's Table* (Fredericton, NB: Goose Lane Editions, 2008), p. 131.

retained words in the same position as on the original page, giving a kind of breathlessness and pause to the new text. M. NourbeSe Philip's "Zong! #24" is another example of erasure poetry, but she combines hers with collage and documentary. For her book *Zong!*, a long poem about the 1781 deaths of 150 Africans who'd been thrown overboard from a slave ship, she "locked" herself into a legal report about the incident, much as the slaves had been "locked" on the ship.[11] She then "fractured and fragmented," and "murdered" the text, "finding" her poems "in different places on the page," and leaving large amounts of white space, "as if they need to breathe." She later began to break down words to find other words. As she says: "I use the text of the legal report almost as a painter uses paint or a sculptor stone."

Another kind of found poem, the cento, has a very long history. J.A. Cuddon, in *The Dictionary of Literary Terms and Literary Theory*, calls it a "collection of bits and pieces from various writers." He quotes an early practitioner of the form, Decimus Magnus Ausonius (circa AD 310–90), who described the cento as a poem of hexameter lines created by a complex combination of full and/or half-lines borrowed from one poet or many.

Modern centos tend to be — as poet Mary Dalton says — "collage pieces … woven together as a form of tribute," that can make, "on one level, a little anthology."[12] Any number of approaches can be used to gather and piece together the borrowed lines. Here, Maureen Hynes uses sometimes single, sometimes multiple lines from twenty-four poems by eighteen poets to create hers.[13]

The traditional form:

Stanzas: None required.

Metre: None required, though some early centos used hexameter lines.

Rhyme: None required.

Repetition: None required.

---

11 All quotes by Marlene NourbeSe Philip are from the *Notanda* (Latin, the legalese for Notes) at the end of her book, *Zong! — As told to the author by Setaey Adamu Boateng* (Middletown, CT: Wesleyan University Press, 2008).

12 from "Like the Star-Nosed Mole: John Barton in Conversation with Mary Dalton on Her Cento Variations," at www.malahatreview.ca/interviews/dalton_east_interview.html (accessed October 2015).

13 Sources for all the found poems in this chapter are provided in the "Notes to the Poems."

Distinguishing feature:	All found poems consist of borrowed words, phrases, and/or lines from one or more prose or poetry sources to create a new poem:

All found poems consist of borrowed words, phrases, and/or lines from one or more prose or poetry sources to create a new poem:
• non-interventionist approaches add line breaks to borrowed prose passages,
• erasure approaches delete words from original sources, often to challenge / reinterpret content,
• collage / documentary approaches (including centos) borrow and rearrange fragments from original source(s).

F.R. SCOTT (1899–1985)

Pavilion Misrepresents Outlook

The Canadian Indian pavilion at Expo
Misrepresents the views
Of most of this country's Indians,
Says a Catholic missionary
Who has spent 26 years among them.

"The pavilion represents the views
Of the handful of people who designed it,
But not those of the majority of Canadian Indians,"
Rev. Appolinaire Plamondon told The Gazette
Recently.

"Most Indians aren't so bitter —
They're happy with what is being done for them
By the Government and by the missionaries."

BRIAN BARTLETT (b. 1953)

from **What He Chose to Record (#1)**

The diaries of C.B. (Crawford Buntin) Lawrence,
written 1889–1918

1   a few rhymes from a life

hauled 5 hogsheads of herring   plowed down to Russells
put in cellar wall   pedelled cider and appels

hauled rockweed and sod and mixed them for potatoes
hauled load of straw from Joes   helped Joe build tables

took Mother to town   thinned turnips   went to Lodge
hauled 38 lbs of turnips to Heart & Greenlaws

mended shoes   delivered school bills   chored about barn
hauled load ceeder trees to Sir William Van Horn

put window frame in Fathers room   killed four rackoons
Crismos   went a scating in the afternoon

helped Sam MacFarlane mov hous acrost Lake
hauled 8 stakes to Chamcook for Bismark Dick

sold horse for hundred dollars   received fifteen cash
heavy Hail storm   broke four pains glass

Newton and I walked east side of Limeburner Lake
Sunday   several people called   Father veary sick

worked in Scemetary   finished harvesting grain
went to town for Doctor and brought him home again

Mr Maiders first sermon after Church sheathed
brot home 150 pounds of Bug Death

hewed sled runners   shingled shed   mixed shells
cut load logs and hauled to Bartletts mill my self

Sunday   Minnie and I went to shore   Hot weather
received inlarged Pictures of Father and Mother

repaired fence east of house and brought in last of hay
went to Red Beach to circus   took black cow away

ANNA SWANSON (b. 1974)

from The Garbage Poems

All words except titles transcribed from garbage pulled out of the swimming hole in Flatrock, Newfoundland.

For the boys cliff-jumping by the memorial stone

We, the full-throttle.
The cluster-pak of body, water, will.
We, the cold open falls, the certified fountains
of no moderation. We are this sunlight. This skin! Why?
Why not? We are the famous flavour.
We are the wonderful.
We adidas-punch our way into the water.
Are twist-happy and thick with chances.
We are not sorry. We are
the ice that will not melt,
the special extract in the root beer of not aging.
We are the sparkling under-king, the carbonated wet dream,
the premium formula good stuff. We are,
at a price you do not know,
at any price,
this.

MAUREEN HYNES (b. 1948)

Late Love Song, With an Orange: A Cento

We who are paired (1)
We had to drink spilled moon from the lake for courage (2)
scarcely talking, thoughts pass between us (3)
Nothing was speaking to me, but I offered and all was well. (4)
I married her, my face upright to the sky (5)

My glass I lift at six o'clock, my darling, (6)
my heart of mayonnaise (7)
We are in easy understanding. (8)
This summerbed is soft with ring upon ring
of wedding, the kind
that doesn't clink upon contact (9)
You can tell
I hear it, too, by the look on my face:
That inaudible thumping (10)
Now I'm a bird in the nest of your lap (11)
When you show yourself to the woman
you love, you don't know your fear — (12)
happiness is a kind of fear (13)

For the present
A body by herself cán be in love on earth (14)
the mind's
temperature   neither cold nor celibate
Ardent (15)
here, now here, closer like a mouth
opening and closing, opening and closing (16)
naked
as a heap of clothes, still whispering *undress me* (17)
body hair glistening with a thousand arts (18)
I offer a necklace of tears, orgasms, words (19)
or the soft babble of a kiss. (20)

O for a life of Kisses
Instead of painting volcanoes!   (21)
joy in my mouth like a peppered bird   (22)
This means laughter
or wings   (23)

I will be standing at the edge
of that fathomless crowd with an orange for you   (24)
and the way a woman stands
when you meet her at an unexpected corner   (25)

JORDAN ABEL (b. 1966)

from the place of scraps

"The pole transported to Toronto. *To remove this huge totem pole from the Nass, and transfer it to a museum thousands of miles away was not an easy job. Taking it down to the ground and shifting it into the water taxed the ingenuity of a railway engineer and his crew of Indians. It leaned sharply, face forwards, and had it fallen, its carvings would have been damaged. But the work was successfully carried out and after a few days the pole with two others was towed down Portland Canal, on its way south along the coast to Prince Rupert. As it floated in the water, several men could walk on it without feeling a tremor under their feet; it was so large that a few hundred pounds made no difference. When it reached Prince Rupert, it had to be cut, as it lay in the water, into three sections, for the longest railway cars are 50 feet. Nor were all difficulties overcome after the three sections had reached Toronto.*"
— Marius Barbeau, *Totem Poles*, vol. 1 (1950), 34.

                              remove
          transfer
                              shift

      face forwards
              work
                         down
                              float   in
                   feel
                         no difference
                         in the water
                              or
              Toronto.

                              . . .

his   totem

the water
his   Indians

carried
down Portland Canal

their feet

lay in the water

. . .

remove
thousands of

Indians

successfully

without feeling a tremor

M. NourbeSe Philip (b. 1947)

Zong! #24

evidence

is

sustenance

is

support

is

the law

the ship

is

the captain

is

the crew

perils

is

the trial

is

the rains

is

the seas

is

the currents

jamaica

is

tobago

is

islands

the case

is

murder

Kenyatta Mesi Nayo Yooku Ngena

is
justice

africa

is
the ground
is
negroes

evidence is
sustenance is
support is
the law is
the ship is
the captain is
the crew is
perils is
the trial is
the rains is
the seas is
currents is
jamaica is
tobago is
islands is
the case is
murder is
justice is
the ground is
africa is

negroes

was

_____

Oluyemi Esugbayi Adubifa Ogunlesi Akua

FUGUE AND MADRIGAL

Derived from the Latin *fuga*, meaning flight, the fugue is an emerging poetic form. In music, a fugue is a polyphonic (multi-voiced) composition rich in counterpoint (interweaving melodies). Originating in choral music, it usually involves three or four voices. A fugue begins with one voice introducing a brief melody called the subject. While the first voice goes on to present a counter subject, a second answers with the original melody, and so on until all are singing. The voices then take off in various directions, as if chasing one another across related keys, approaching and straying from the original subject, reinventing it as they go. The devices used to modify the subject include changing its rhythm and/or presenting it a few tones higher or lower than its previous appearance.

This is adapted to poetry through inventive uses of repetition, which can range from elaborate to relatively simple — but always unpredictable — constructions. In particular, themes are introduced in words, phrases or lines that are then irregularly repeated throughout the poem, shifting context, pace and meaning. In this, the fugue bears echoes of a pantoum and villanelle.

To our knowledge, Canadian poets have only recently set out to write in a fugual form as such. Robyn Sarah, for instance, in an interview with Canadian poet Stephen Brockwell,[14] says she "intuitively created" the form for her "Fugue," as a one-time approach to a particular subject. "Only after it was finished did I notice the pattern in which the repeating lines change their position from stanza to stanza … the pattern of repetition was indeliberate, it was dictated by ear." In private correspondence[15] she said she only later became aware of Jewish poet Paul Celan's "Todesfugue" (Death Fugue).[16] Regardless of formal intent, however, each poet here has drawn from a wide range of repetition devices to mix and match, arrange and rearrange images and ideas with an insistence that gives the poems their power as well as their unique form.

David O'Meara uses a pattern of repeated words to create his fugue — persistently repeating just two words, "nothing" and "said," to make a familiar, almost clichéd, scene poignant again.

---

14   The interview is online at www.ottawater.com/poetics/issue3 (accessed September 2015).
15   Robyn Sarah, in correspondence with the editors, February 2004.
16   "Todesfugue" can be found in *Selected Poems and Prose of Paul Celan*, translated by John Felstiner (New York, NY: Norton, 2001). US poet Dana Gioia specifically searched for a way to adapt the musical fugue to formal poetry. In *Ecstatic Occasions, Expedient Forms*, he says it took him years to write his fugue poem "Lives of the Great Composers," noting "The one example I knew of, Paul Celan's magnificent 'Todesfuge,' was too unique and lofty a model to provide any specific help, though its existence proved that the form could be approximated in verse." p. 59.

Barbara Pelman repeats both single words (sometimes in various forms) and phrases, often shifting references (see for example how she uses "perilous") to create a fugue brimming with the complex emotions of a mother watching her child move through the years from need to independence.

The rest of the poets in this chapter use recurring lines or phrases to create their fugues. Gwendolyn MacEwen, for instance, in "The Children Are Laughing," repeats phrases at the ends of consecutive lines or at the end of one line and the beginning of the next ("they believe they are princes" and "the children are laughing").

The different approaches these poets take to rhyme, stanza and metre suggest a wide range of possibilities for a fugue. Annie Charlotte Dalton writes in rhymed and metred couplets while Milton Acorn uses an irregular rhyme scheme. Acorn and MacEwen use a loose metre, while others, like Herménégilde Chiasson and Roo Borson write in free verse.

Madrigal

In music, the madrigal is a fugal form, usually sung without accompaniment. It was most popular from the fifteenth to seventeenth centuries and focused on secular rather than sacred themes. Composer Aaron Copland says it is a "typical vocal fugal [form] of the era before the advent of Bach and his contemporaries."[17]

In poetry, the madrigal dates back hundreds of years and takes several forms. Those included in this chapter, by Marilyn Bowering and Robin Skelton, follow the form that Lewis Turco, in *The New Book of Forms*, says was invented by Geoffrey Chaucer in the fourteenth century.

The traditional form:

Fugue

Stanzas:	An unlimited number of stanzas.
Metre:	None required.
Rhyme:	None required.
Repetition:	Two or more themes are introduced, each contained in a word, line or phrase that usually appears early in the poem; all are then repeated unpredictably, in part or in full and in any order, throughout the poem;

---

17   Aaron Copland, *What to Listen For in Music*, (New York, NY: Penguin Mentor, 1999) p. 142.

usually various repetition devices (see "Coming to Terms") are also employed.

Madrigal (Chaucerian)

Stanzas:

Three stanzas: the first is a tercet; the second, a quatrain; the third, a sestet.

Metre:

Iambic pentameter.

Rhyme:

Stanzas have different rhyme schemes: the tercet is AB^1B^2; the quatrain is $abAB^1$; the sestet is $abbAB^1B^2$ (capital letters stand for refrain lines, numbered capitals — e.g., B^1B^2 — indicate rhymed, but different, refrain lines).

Repetition:

The tercet provides the poem's three refrain lines; the first refrain is line 1, repeated as lines 6 and 11; the second is line 2, repeated as lines 7 and 12; the third is line 3, repeated as line 13.

David O'Meara (b. 1968)

Nothing

"Nothing," he said, "it's nothing."
Then nothing was said. Silence; nothing.

What she asked had come from nothing.
Sweet nothing, really, was all he said.

They cut their links like little wires, said
nothing about it afterward, nothing.

All over nothing.
So never to talk of what they said

until all that was ever said
was nothing, and so nothing was ever said.

BARBARA PELMAN (b. 1943)

Walk On

The first time she stood, her own feet
holding her, balance of knee and thigh,
eyes forward, her diaper sliding
perilously down, barefoot,
wearing a shirt I had embroidered in the days
she would lie still in a crib —
the first time she knew she didn't need me
to taxi her across the room,
eyes forward to where she wanted to go —
the embroidered days of breast
and sleep gone now: she balanced
need in her perilous glance, here
and here, no longer still in a crib
but standing, her own feet
marking the path embroidered
with perilous ledges, a highway
across winter, always forward
in her balance of need and knowing,
and I taxi her around
in my mind, embroider her days
with my perilous love:
cribbed and almost silent.

⊷═◑

GWENDOLYN MACEWEN (1941–1987)

The Children Are Laughing

It is Monday and the children are laughing
The children are laughing; they believe they are princes
They wear no shoes; they believe they are princes
And their filthy kingdom heaves up behind them

The filthy city heaves up behind them
They are older than I am, their feet are shoeless
They have lived a thousand years; the children are laughing
The children are laughing and their death is upon them

I have cried in the city (the children are laughing)
I have worn many colors (the children are laughing)
They are older than I am, their death is upon them
I will wear no shoes when the princes are dying

MILTON ACORN (1923–1986)

The Ballad of the Pink-Brown Fence

Against the pink-brown fence with the sprucelet
My little sister stands to be photographed;
Fire tinges from her head and the dandelions —
Tear down the pink-brown fence to make a raft

Tear down the pink-brown fence to make a raft
Where my little sister stands to be photographed
Fish poke up their noses and make rings
And memories of dandelions dance from the ripples . . .

The camera is too slow to catch the gold
of dandelions remembered around my little sister;
Stand up the old raft for a painting board
And guess the why of it — you can't recall kissing her . . .

Cut up the rotten painting for a bonfire;
The flames rush up a rattle, faint boom, and whisper;
Sparks fly gold in the night and then white;
Dandelions, and the hair of my little sister

ANNIE CHARLOTTE DALTON (1865–1938)

The Praying-Mantis

In the dark dungeons of the mind;
Strange creatures walk and breed their kind;
   The Mantis mounts the stair,
   With movements free as air.

The Praying-Mantis mounts the stair,
Her tiny arms upheld in prayer.
   In chasuble and stole,
   She stands to read my soul.

I know not what dark thing is there,
Nor why my soul must feel despair,
   Nor why she turns away
   And bids the Mantis slay.

In the deep dungeons of the mind,
Strange creatures walk and breed their kind;
   With arms upheld in prayer
   The Mantis mounts the stair.

ROBYN SARAH (b. 1949)

Fugue

Women are on their way
to the new country. The men watch
from high office windows
while the women go.
They do not get very far
in a day. You can still see them
from high office windows.

Women are on their way
to the new country. They are taking
it all with them: rugs,
pianos, children. Or they are leaving
it all behind them: cats,
plants, children.
They do not get very far in a day.

Some women travel alone
to the new country. Some
with a child, or children.
Some go in pairs or groups
or in pairs with a child
or children. Some in a group with
cats, plants, children.

They do not get very far in a day.
They must stop to bake bread on the road
to the new country, and to share
bread with other women. Children
outgrow their clothes and shed them
for smaller children. The women too
shed clothes, put on each other's

cats, plants, children, and at full moon
no one remembers the way to the new country
where there will be room for everyone and
it will be summer and children will
shed their clothes and the loaves will
rise without yeast and women will have come
so far that no one can see them, even from

high office windows.

⊷≒◎

HERMÉNÉGILDE CHIASSON (b. 1946)

And the Season Advances

(*translated by Jo-Anne Elder & Fred Cogswell*)

And the season advances
The radios are louder
The trees are taller than they were
The sky is whiter
And the season advances
The day gets shorter
The trees are whiter
The sky is more beautiful
The street is wider than it was
And you cry out to me
And I run towards you untiringly
It is ridiculous
I know
But the season advances
The day gets shorter
It is ridiculous
I know

    — Moncton, 1968

ROO BORSON (b. 1952)

One

Every Tuesday at 4 pm
he would come to me, one
of the company of the dead, familiar,
only now in Montreal, in winter;
it would be snowing wonderfully;
I would order a coffee and a sandwich;
but it had to be a Tuesday,
and at 4 pm, and Montreal,

and then, and only then,
he'd come to me.
And because I had a body,
and now he did not,
this one among the company of the dead,
whom I had known, and thought,
though without thinking, always to be present,
and because I had grown used to it,
I'd order a coffee,
anywhere on earth I'd order a sandwich,
but it had to be a Tuesday, and at 4 pm,
in Montreal, and snowing wonderfully,
and then, and only then,
he'd come to me.
I'd order the sandwich and the coffee
as if with my body his might
eat again, and drink, and see;
it would be snowing, wonderfully;
and though it could have been a Wednesday,
in Los Angeles, say, at noon, under the numbing sun,
on the street where he was raised,
where we would sometimes
go when I was young, this is how he came to me:
on Tuesdays, and at 4 pm, in Montreal,
all that winter, until finally
that winter, with its wonderful
continuously falling snow,
and with it, too, my time in Montreal
were drawing to an end, no matter how much
I'd grown used to it, he went with the snow
and did not return, whether on Tuesday,
or Wednesday, or anywhere,
for it was only there that he would come,
and then, in Montreal, on Tuesday,
just at 4 pm, while it was snowing wonderfully,
that one among the company of the dead.

⊶⟾

LEANNE SIMPSON (b. 1971)

i am graffiti

i am writing to tell you
that yes, indeed,
we have noticed
you have a new big pink eraser
we are well aware
you are trying to use it
erasing indians is a good idea
of course
the bleeding-heart liberals
and communists
can stop feeling bad
for the stealing
and raping
and murdering
and we can all move on
we can be reconciled
except, i am graffiti.
except, mistakes were made.
she painted three white Xs
on the wall of the grocery store.
one. two. three.
then they were erased.
except, i am graffiti.
except, mistakes were made.
the Xs were made out of milk
because they took our food.
one. two. three.
then we were erased.
except, i am graffiti.
except, mistakes were made.
we are the singing remnants
left over after
the bomb went off in slow motion
over a century instead of a fractionated second
it's too much to process, so we make things instead
we are the singing remnants
left over after

the costumes have been made
collected up
put in a plastic bag, full of intentions
for another time
another project.
except, i am graffiti.
and mistakes were made.

MARILYN BOWERING (b. 1949)

Madrigal, a Lullaby for Xan

She sleeps, her dreams as clear as diamond edge
that cuts the icy sky in black and white,
the stars are palest candles to her light.

The dark spills over sill and window ledge,
a river foaming bleakly through the night.
She sleeps, her dreams as clear as diamond edge
that cuts the icy sky in black and white.

The wren that sings its heart-song through the sedge,
and braves the hunter hawk in its full flight,
dreams of its mate and nest soon in its sight:
she sleeps, her dreams as clear as diamond edge
that cuts the icy sky in black and white,
the stars are palest candles to her light.

ROBIN SKELTON (1925–1997)

Night Piece

I have been dreaming half the night
of holding you beside the sea
and watching waves crash into light.

I do not know how I can write
of that heart-pounding mystery;
I have been dreaming half the night
of holding you beside the sea

and wondering if those breakers might
be telling of our times to be
when tide and moon are at their height;
I have been dreaming half the night
of holding you beside the sea
and watching waves crash into light.

GHAZAL

The ghazal originated in Persia around the seventh century. Some of this form's most famous practitioners were Hafiz in Persia (a fourteenth-century contemporary of Chaucer's, writing in Farsi) and Ghalib in India (writing in Urdu in the nineteenth century). It was introduced into Europe in 1812 with a German translation of Hafiz, and remains a vibrant form (often sung) in many languages, including Arabic, Urdu, Farsi and Hindi.

Originally, ghazals consisted of at least five but usually no more than twelve couplets (*shers*) written in what poet Agha Shahid Ali calls "a strict scheme of rhyme, refrain, and line length."[18] The spirit of the ghazal is one of great intensity and compression, somewhat like the Japanese haiku although — unlike the haiku — the ghazal relies heavily on metaphor (describing one thing in terms of another). Like traditional haiku, ghazals did not have titles.

A ghazal's lines all appear to be of the same length because originally they had the same number of syllables. The couplets were never enjambed; in fact, they were so independent of each other, their order could be changed without damaging the poem. Ali — who perhaps did most to introduce the form into English — explains in *Ravishing DisUnities* that traditionally each couplet is "autonomous, thematically and emotionally complete in itself." The form, he says, has "a formal unity based on rhyme and refrain and prosody. ... There is a contrapuntal air."

The pattern of the poem is established by the opening couplet (*matla*) where a refrain word or phrase (*radif*) ends both lines, and a rhyming word (*qafia*) immediately precedes the refrain. The second line of every succeeding couplet then ends with the refrain, immediately preceded by the rhyme. The poem uses monorhyme so the rhyme scheme is *aa ba ca*, etc. This rhyme acts as a cue to listeners who, when they hear it, traditionally join the poet in calling aloud, with much shared pleasure, the concluding refrain in each couplet. (In this way the aural power of the ghazal is similar to that of the rhyme in closed couplets, which also provides notice to listeners that something is coming to an end.) The last two lines of the traditional ghazal are a signature couplet (*mukta*), which contains the poet's name or a pseudonym.

Traditionally, poets used the ghazal to write about love — both mystical and carnal. Nadeem Parmar, who writes contemporary ghazals in Urdu, told us that the praise of women and wine in the original form was always done in

---

18 Agha Shahid Ali, *Call Me Ishmael Tonight: A Book of Ghazals*, p.19.

a "delicate and civilized manner," much like the troubadours who were writing courtly love poems to women in Europe at around the same time.

Yvonne Blomer's "Landscapes and home / Ghazal 22" is an example of a traditional ghazal. None of the couplets are enjambed and the first sets the tone and pattern for the rest of the poem. The word "home" that ends both lines of this couplet is the refrain that completes the second line of all subsequent couplets. It is preceded by a monorhyme ("takes," "makes," "claim," and so on). In the final signature couplet (*mukta*) she signs her name, "Yvonne."

Kuldip Gill takes some liberties with the tradition in "Ghazal V," where she uses the refrain "turned loose" in all but the opening line and precedes it with a loose monorhyme ("she is," "be his," "have been," "he is," "lap is," "heart is.") She also uses what we think was her pseudonym in the signature couplet when she calls out, "Awake Vasanti!" Molly Peacock makes a different leap, this time into a mix of traditions, when she writes "Of Night" in a loose iambic tetrameter, omits spaces between the couplets, repeats the refrain ("of night" or "at night") in every line, and uses a preceding monorhyme ("paws," "jaws," "laws," etc.). She calls this fourteen-line variation a "ghazal sonnet."

North American poets who first adopted the ghazal form in the twentieth century, including John Thompson in Canada and Adrienne Rich in the US, largely ignored the form's tradition, but without regular rhyme, refrain or line length, and with liberal enjambment between couplets, how did they differentiate a ghazal from any free-verse poem written in couplets? In the introduction to his book, *Stilt Jack*, Thompson answers, "the link between couplets ... is a matter of tone, nuance ... its order is clandestine. ... It is the poem of contrasts, dreams, astonishing leaps." Thompson therefore wrote what might be called free-verse ghazals. He merrily throws out virtually every aspect of the traditional form except — most importantly — a tone of drama and sadness, of leaps.

The traditional form:

Stanzas:	Usually 5 to 12 (or more) closed couplets (*shers*). The first couplet (*matla*) sets the tone and pattern for the rest of the poem but couplets stand independent of each other.
Metre:	Not metred, though each line is approximately the same length, based on the tradition of an equal number of syllables.
Rhyme:	*aa ba ca* and so on, plus an internal mono-rhyme (*qafia*) immediately before the refrain in each couplet.
Repetition:	The refrain, either a word or phrase (*radif*), ends both lines of the opening couplet, and is repeated as the end of the second line of each succeeding couplet.
Distinguishing feature:	The final signature couplet (*mukta*) may contain the poet's name or pseudonym.

YVONNE BLOMER (b. 1970)

Landscapes and home/Ghazal 22

In the dark, there, our eyes. Landscapes and home.
We traveled by boat, ship, finally a plane takes us home.

This webbing feeds memories, the recesses
Where we can name everything, makes a home.

Here is always different: Harare, Bindura.
In Canada, even, we move, try to claim a home.

The rising sun, or no sun, instead a blanket of rain
the body comes back to itself, wakes at home.

Piles of leaves or sand dunes — green battles brown.
If I blow a kiss, pressed lips snake home.

Home is hot or wet, a bird's nest:
dead-dry stalks, green leaves, a make-believe home.

Who am I? My body, this traveling thing.
Yvonne, each thread of memory aches of home.

KULDIP GILL (1934–2009)

Ghazal V

My white mare on the Punjabi plains, the stamp of her hooves
marks the borders of my land as she is turned loose.

It's the morning of her wedding. How tightly they braid her hair.
Now her doria are swinging; in hours they will be his, turned loose.

A swing hangs in the pipal tree. Baisaki: flowers yellow and gulabi.
From the roof top khoti the cucurooing doves have been turned loose.

The white stallion savours a mouth without bit and bridle.
Off with his saddle! A slap on the flanks and he is turned loose.

The doli swings as guests watch the bride leave her natal village.
Bristling with coir, the coconut in the groom's lap is turned loose.

Awake Vasanti! His imposters under gowns of virtue. On love's
wings, the phoenix by his flaming heart is turned loose.

SINA QUEYRAS (b. 1963)

Tonight the Sky Is My Begging Bowl

While I savour woodstove-scented sleep,
you move in a forest of brick and glass: sleepless.

Your eyes droop, dreaming the half-point of grades
and coffee at the end of the picket line. Sleepy.

I dress in fleece, stalk blackberries for birds,
canes flattened from a winter storm as we slept.

I embrace everything, even the slither of midnight,
but without you, time is too wide, I cannot sleep.

Clatter of dragon paw — the old year retreats, tail between
her legs. This thumping new one will not sleep.

We are simply where we are. Me, alone
in silk and fleece, you on a subway deprived of sleep.

Tonight the sky is my begging bowl: wing tip,
wood thrush I open palms, heart, enclave of sleep.

MOLLY PEACOCK (b. 1947)

Of Night

A city mouse darts from the paws of night.
A body drops from the jaws of night.
A woman denies the laws of night,
Awake and trapped in the was of night.
A young man turns in the gauze of night,
Unravelling the cause of night:
That days extend their claws at night
To re-enact old wars at night,
Though dreams can heal old sores at night
And Spring begins its thaw at night,
While worry bones are gnawed at night.
He sips her through a straw at night.
Verbs whisper in the clause of night.
A finger to her lips,
                        the pause of night.

ROB TAYLOR (b. 1983)

You Can't Lead a Horse

On a blanket beside a river, lovers
listen to the silence of water.

All Gods, even the false ones,
are born from water.

Light will dance with many partners,
but none like water.

A newborn's heartbeat
is the sound of swirling water.

God's first decision:
to name the magma *water*.

In the lake's mirror, mountains wriggle
like jellyfish diving deep in water.

The priest needs the silver basin.
His God needs only the water.

A plane crash-lands safely on the Hudson.
No one thanks the water.

A blue whale's lungs are so large
they collapse without the support of water.

The woman is drunk.
She asks the water for waiter.

Trapped in sandstone for 10,000 years, raindrops
sometimes forget they are water.

⊷═◑

JOHN THOMPSON (1938–1976)

from Stilt Jack

IX
Yeats. Yeats. Yeats. Yeats. Yeats. Yeats. Yeats.
Why wouldn't the man shut up?

The word works me like a spike harrow:
by number nine maybe I get the point.

It's all in books, save the best part; God knows
where that is: I found it once, wasn't looking.

I've written all the poems already,
why should I write this one:

I'll read Keats and eye the weather too,
smoke cigarettes, watch Captain Kangaroo.

Big stones, men's hands, the shovel
pitched properly. The wall of walls rises.

If I weren't gone already, I'd lie down right now:
have you ever heard children's voices?

Sometimes I think the stars scrape at my door, wanting in:
I'm watching the hockey game.

Likely there's an answer: I'm waiting,
watching the stones.

⊷⟹

LEIGH NASH (b. 1976)

And With Good Reason

The warlords are prepping their secret forts for battle.
A whitewashed room is empty for the next hour.

In my apartment a series of boxes are stacked
one inside the other, a drunk's bunker.

A black, three-legged dog howls at the front door.
This sign is supposed to be subtle.

The antennae on the neighbour's canvas tent scoops up
an SOS broadcast from down the coast.

A transformer turns firecracker.
A man shimmies up the drainpipe and knocks on my window.

Living on the top floor of a walk-up,
the breadbox is empty but the knife, the knife —

the apiary falls silent for the first time in memory.
A gentle rain. Tanks rumble down the golden streets.

GLOSA

Originating in the late fourteenth to early fifteenth century Spanish courts, the glosa is a delightful way for poets to exchange or build upon one another's ideas within a structured poetic tradition. And, since the publication of P.K. Page's *Hologram: A Book of Glosas*, numerous Canadian poets have taken up such conversations.

A glosa normally has four ten-line stanzas preceded by four lines quoted from another poet. This quatrain, known in Spanish as the *cabeza* or *texto*, also acts as an epigraph to the poem. The form requires that each stanza end with a line taken sequentially from the borrowed quatrain, and while there is no required metre, lines 6, 9 and 10 of each stanza are end-rhymed. (Interestingly, if a glosa were written entirely in quatrains it would have a similar repetition pattern to the rondeau redoubled described in the "Rondeau Family" chapter.)

The glosa picks up on the concept of glossing — that is, elaborating or commenting on a text (alternate names for the form are *gloss* or *glose*). In her introduction to *Hologram*, Page notes that she used the glosa "as a way of paying homage to those poets whose work I fell in love with in my formative years."

One of the glosa's challenges rests in the process of writing toward the borrowed lines so that when they appear, they seem inevitable. In expanding on these lines, the poet is working with something intrinsic to the other writer's words, something both share. This goes beyond technique; to quote Page again, it's like "a curious marriage — two sensibilities intermingling."

In her poem, "Planet Earth," Page follows the tradition described above. Edward Hirsch, in *A Poet's Glossary*, identifies another approach to the form, in which some poets feel the only restriction is that the quoted lines be repeated but not necessarily in their original order. Amber Dawn takes this approach in "Country Mice."

Poets often vary the form — for instance, by making some or all stanzas shorter than the standard 10 lines, as in Brenda Leifso's "What do you want?", or slightly altering a glossed line, as when David Reibetanz ends his poem by changing "Whoever is alone will stay alone," to "Whoever is at one will never stay alone."

A more complex variation is seen in Glenn Kletke's, "O Grandfather Dust," where he doubles the form. Working from an eight-line quotation, Kletke begins each stanza with a line taken consecutively from the first four lines and ends with one from the last four. Pamela Porter, meanwhile, halves her glosa with a two-line epigraph from Page and two five-line stanzas.

Some poets draw attention to the glossed lines with italics, while others keep the quotes in the same font as the rest of the poem and let the fact of glossing fade into the background.

The traditional form:

Stanzas:	An opening 4-line epigraph from another poet, plus 4 10-line stanzas.
Metre:	No set metre or syllable count required.
Rhyme:	Lines 6, 9 and 10 are end-rhymed.
Repetition:	Each line of the opening quatrain reappears once, in order, to close each of the other 4 stanzas (i.e., line 1 of the quatrain is also line 10 of the first stanza, and so on).

P.K. PAGE (1916–2010)

Planet Earth

It has to be spread out, the skin of this planet,
has to be ironed, the sea in its whiteness;
and the hands keep on moving,
smoothing the holy surfaces.

"In Praise of Ironing" — *Pablo Neruda*

It has to be loved the way a laundress loves her linens,
the way she moves her hands caressing the fine muslins
knowing their warp and woof,
like a lover coaxing, or a mother praising.
It has to be loved as if it were embroidered
with flowers and birds and two joined hearts upon it.
It has to be stretched and stroked.
It has to be celebrated.
O this great beloved world and all the creatures in it.
It has to be spread out, the skin of this planet.

The trees must be washed, and the grasses and mosses.
They have to be polished as if made of green brass.
The rivers and little streams with their hidden cresses
and pale-coloured pebbles
and their fool's gold
must be washed and starched or shined into brightness,
the sheets of lake water
smoothed with the hand
and the foam of the oceans pressed into neatness.
It has to be ironed, the sea in its whiteness

and pleated and goffered, the flower-blue sea
the protean, wine-dark, grey, green, sea
with its metres of satin and bolts of brocade.
And sky — such an O! overhead — night and day
must be burnished and rubbed
by hands that are loving
so the blue blazons forth
and the stars keep on shining
within and above
and the hands keep on moving.

It has to be made bright, the skin of this planet
till it shines in the sun like gold leaf.
Archangels then will attend to its metals
and polish the rods of its rain.
Seraphim will stop singing hosannas
to shower it with blessings and blisses and praises
and, newly in love,
we must draw it and paint it
our pencils and brushes and loving caresses
smoothing the holy surfaces.

SADIQA DE MEIJER (b. 1977)

Sixteen

Therefore,
Their sons grow suicidally beautiful
At the beginning of October,
And gallop terribly against each other's bodies.

"Autumn Begins in Martin's Ferry, Ohio" — *James Wright*

Already, I'm the scrawl
in the margins of hole-punched pages.
I'm slanted and gangly. See those girls
with resilient ponytails, undaunted
by crowds? They're the notes.
If I study their sure,
oval script, they might save me a seat,
but then there'd be all that revering
of quarterbacks, the rumours.
Therefore,

I keep to myself. I take books
to the creek behind the townhouses
and read under the willow,
staring at the sky after grand
paragraphs, or I walk
past the Montessori preschool
when it closes, and watch the parents
pause as their daughters
crouch over chalk portraits, while
their sons grow suicidally beautiful

intoning explosions. It's in the summers
that I sometimes imagine
surprising everyone. It must be
their absence that makes it possible.
You know, The Year Of Me; I return
in bright knee-socks, am clever
with huddles of friends. I might sustain
ambitions through the first few classes,
but things always get clouded over
at the beginning of October,

and even the perfect new pencil case
loses its lustre. Then failure's
strange amnesty, knowing
I'll be flawlessly alone on game
days, when they let us out early
and I sneak to the water,
where their cheers sound like
downpours, but far, as they
shout from the bleachers, applauding
and gallop terribly against each other's bodies.

KATE BRAID (b. 1947)

Tree Song

Naked trees extend their complicated praise
branches sway, in
        a sort of unison
not agreed upon
        each their own way

"Naked Trees" — *John Terpstra*

May I be forgiven, may I forgive
myself this endless search for someone, some
thing to explain, give me the reason we're here
and what lies after and if there's a plan
(or even better) Planner — if I could only
know for sure (just once? a deal? I'll stay
right here, you whisper in my ear, The Answer ...)
while all around me animals carry on
regardless. Plants and insects don't bother counting days
and naked trees extend their complicated praise.

Why them? How can they praise and not await
reward? Who do they praise? What? How
can they stand there, splendid, and not ask why or if
there is a goal? At least a prize
for the very best? Do they dream of after-death or fear
old age or insects or men with saws? Can it matter
that underneath the soil they're all in touch —
what one knows, all know instantly in a deciduous,
coniferous vocabulary that whispers a grace, as all around
branches sway in a sort of unison.

Perhaps I should sit and watch, listen
for a while, to the shushing of trees,
peace in one place, a salute to sky
and no complaints unless you count the crack
of the final fall and what do they see then?
Is there mortal terror? Or a welcome to the stones
they shall now lie upon, the bed from which to nourish
other trees? If we die childless are we
forgotten? Is Heaven a tonic
not agreed upon?

Some say there's nothing to be frightened of,
there's God or gods or goddesses or not, to take me "home"
or not. I'll find out soon enough, that's sure.
Perhaps this is my fascination with birds
who fly above, rest lightly on each moment,
small prayers to the beginning and end of day.
And after all, how can it matter that I get the story right
or wrong? When it comes to living — life and death —
each being sings a sort of roundelay,
each their own way.

AMBER DAWN (b. 1974)

Country Mice

crickets, monarchs, paints and sparrows
frenchman river, sweet grass sky holds still
out here everything stops
for the wind

"everything holds still for the wind" — *Leah Horlick*

We find each other
in the cosmopolitan squint, polished
concrete, smoked chrome rooms.
She's hard to peg at first
lace dress chic, Prosecco cocktail
starry in her hand. She's been
chin-upped by the west. Tested
by an incomprehensible horizon
and passed, but for her pose and bend.
For the wind

that sweeps the wide-open
motherland has left her
with a slant stance, sideways
as corn bowed to a storm.
I too am made
from orchard and axe, crop
and scythe, harvest born
humble earth miles and years
behind me. It's all rock
out here. Everything stops

making sense in the seam
of mountains and million
dollar condos, high-rise residential
more density, more gravel, more glass, more.
Where I come from elevators
are for nursing homes or sawmills.
She sees the soiled knees of my jeans
knows I kneel to a once-was prayer
late waterways, bygone wells
forgotten river. Sweet grass sky holds still

during these vigils, holds space
for choked swamp, cedar stump
tributaries split from the ocean
Vancouver's bloodstone — step forward.
My home is a backwards stamp, like hers,
parched-lawn green, forever level.
Now we find each other turned by urban obstacles.
The far-removed markers we share and seek
chokecherries, ink caps, chorus frogs, golden yarrow
crickets, monarchs, paints and sparrows

DAVID REIBETANZ (b. 1982)

Norberto Hernandez — Photographed Falling September Eleventh

A Glosa for P.K. Page

Warmed by that same summer sun.
But the dead of the near dead
are now all knucklebone
Whoever is alone will stay alone.

"Autumn" — *P.K. Page*

The picture wants to be upside down, head
first like the falling man. Air ripples
skin at that speed. Yet he was not calm water

as he jumped, nor crumbling grit blown out
by the blast. In his last choice
he spoke his mother tongue.
White shirt caressing him,
he rejected flame's touch.
Yet he too was one
warmed by that same September sun.

Puerto Rican pastry chef,
sweating, he rode
the subway, his cool patrons
in Mercedes passing him above. But
when the moment came, he went
as he was, dispossessed, shed
no corporate skin — flying
past them, his path chosen,
no end ahead
but the dead, or the near dead.

Near dead, plummeting
a free unfallen man,
the chute of his life opens.
He knows a grace of air,
spiralling against
lines of the metalled glass pantheon.
Godlike, he spins
in the mind. His hands —
unbound, become his own —
are now all knucklebone.

Freed in a lasting moment,
he falls, right leg over left,
pirouetting
towards death. What is it
he sees, eyes closed
ears open to the wind's undertone?
Beyond fear now, he rides
the light. Pouring himself into
the lens of our eye, he lives in unison:
we make his sun-drenched blue our own.
Whoever is at one will never stay alone.

⊷⇒

BRENDA LEIFSO (b. 1977)

What do you want?

want the apple on the bough in
the hand in the mouth seed
planted in the brain want
to think "apple"

from Naked Poems — *Phyllis Webb*

want back my thick tongued
child's rage, white eye light,
whole body burn, feet
drumbeat against that wall against
silence, want fruit in my belly
in my throat want the room
to speak, with my hands to sing,
to touch that eclectic finger
want to be loved before forgiven
want the apple on the bough in

the beginning. again.
and. again. want a poem
where hunger moves beyond
sound beyond naming
breast thigh stomach. want grief
burnished by plum blossoms
thrown skywards,
rain in my skin sea
in the hand in the mouth seed

caught in silk,
stored in the greenhouse until spring
or until i am wise enough
or clever enough to tell a story new
until that time, the greenhouse will stay warm
and this time, i will watch sod
born from my grandmother's hands
turning, opening, i will watch her
spread light like sundogs

planted in the brain, want
that warmth in my mouth:
mulch of fern soft fig
star fruit peeled plum
pomegranate
fingers all juice and flesh
for the bough reaching,
throat unfastened, able at last
to think "apple."

GLENN KLETKE (b. 1942)

O Grandfather Dust

And did you come there in summer, tobogganing in the slow sheets
Of earliest love; come there to work your secret name
On the frozen time of a wall; and did you come there riding
The tall and handsome horse whose name's Catastrophe.

(O grandfather dust!) thick and mousetracked, leads to rooms
Without character: boxes of boxed darkness: birdshit —
(But only the swallow nests here — the daubs of mud over doorways
Are the most live things in the house.)

"Letter to an Imaginary Friend" — *Thomas McGrath*

And did you come there in summer, tobogganing in the slow sheets
    of a child's week at the farm, the welcome of morning
    as you stepped into a world you knew nothing of? Sharp sun!
    Call of barnyard animals! Shape of a grandfather slouching
    at the edge of things: rake, fork, pail in his grasp or nothing
    at all — hands cupped to hold above prairie wind, prairie blooms
    the frail struggling life inside a rolled cigarette (Player's blue tin)
    or whirled through air — terrifying — a long poplar's stick to flick
    his two work horses to bright fields from barn's dark tombs.
(O grandfather dust!) thick and mousetracked, leads to rooms

Of earliest love; come there to work your secret name
   notched once on a poplar tree, hardly knowing what
   you were called, bringing into the world only the hunger
   to learn the calling of others: how she would open
   the torn screen door, grandmother with a heap of potato
   peels, chickens running madly towards her call, exquisite
   pandemonium as they picked and fled with flopping treasures
   to safer ground, how later in the morning you would carry to her
   (O grandmother ashes!) prairie smoke, its spidery flower a misfit
Without character: boxes of boxed darkness: birdshit —

On the frozen time of a wall; and did you come there riding
   on the slow and gentle horse of a child returning, hooves
   hardly heard through fields of blue flax on a summer afternoon?
   Silent gallop back to a gilded farm house filled with whatever
   wonders your universe once held: wood stove, piled logs, pail
   of well water (cold, so cold), tin dipper, sky dipper, Milky Way
   Farmers Weekly (German), wall of windmills, windows of geraniums
   the brilliant red cockscomb of a rooster sun going down.
   Now you look everywhere for anything to fill the dark days
(But only the swallow nests here — the daubs of mud over doorways

The tall and handsome horse whose name's Catastrophe.
   See its saddle notched with farm's felled four-footed souls:
   May and Nel (horses too), Dollie and Peg (cows), Nipper
   Yogi, beagle-shadowed Rex (first and best mongrel of the pack)
   and Sox, grey cat stolen from the city to prowl the prairie
   white elegant boots and too courtly to catch a mouse.
   Now through cracked windows fly the six-footed bees, peeling
   yellow wall a flower that spiders them, your knowledge that whole
   generations of dead workers heaped on the ground like a shot ruffled grouse
Are the most live things in the house.)

⊷⟹

PAMELA PORTER (b. 1956)

Solstice

each bright glimpse of beauty striking like a bell,
so that the whole world may toll.

"After Rain" — *P.K. Page*

This winter is all silvered moon and stars, small birds
printing runes into snow, hieroglyph of horses' hooves
frozen in the mud, rimmed in crystalled petals of ice.
Ancient, this world, these fields gone white — a cumulous sky
each bright glimpse of beauty striking like a bell,

so we may teach ourselves to be whole, and holy
as moonlit lamps of Queen Anne's lace,
so that a whiteness deeper than any of us can know
may shroud the earth to be reborn, and in us a green-belled wonder,
so that the whole world may toll.

Haiku and Other Japanese Forms

In the west, some of the best known Japanese forms include haiku, renga, tanka, senryu and haibun. Probably the best known of these is the haiku (also *haikai*, or *hokku*, meaning "starting verse").

Haiku

In Japanese, haiku consist of three unrhymed lines of 5, 7 and 5 sound beats (called *on*). The challenge in being true to Japanese forms lies in translation, for the English syllable is not an exact equivalent of the Japanese sound beat it aims to duplicate. As Japanese poet and translator Kozue Uzawa explains, the "Japanese language uses a vowel after each consonant. For instance, the word 'desk' is one syllable, but when this word is imported into Japanese, it becomes 'desuku', using more vowels. Thus the Japanese 'desuku' has three syllables, or sound beats."[19]

William Higginson, in *The Haiku Handbook*, notes that in English, about twelve syllables — not seventeen — approximates the equivalent length of sound beats of haiku in the Japanese language; accordingly, although many modern writers in English write haiku in three lines of 5, 7, and 5 syllables, others often use fewer, as here in George Swede's poem (10 syllables) and — even more minimalist — Marco Fraticelli, whose poem consists of just three words (4 syllables). At some point there is often a pause in both rhythm and grammar, usually after line 2, which divides the haiku into two parts.

Traditional haiku aim to unite nature with human nature through objective description: they use a season word *(kigo)* indicating the time of year; include a seasonal theme *(kidai)*; sketch a singular event in the present tense; convey a sense of awe or transcendence; and evoke, rather than overtly name, emotion. The form relies on clear, concrete images rather than simile or metaphor and generally makes minimal use of articles. The goal is a sudden insight or meditation. As one of its great Japanese practitioners, Yosa Buson (1716–1783) described it, haiku "use the commonplace to escape the commonplace."[20] Traditionally, they were not given titles.

Originally, all Japanese poetry including haiku was written vertically. Michael Redhill echoes this tradition, as well as the concept of visual poetry, in "Haiku Monument for Washington, D.C." which repeats a single word (vertically) five, seven and five times.

---

19 Kozue Uzawa, "English Tanka: How is it Different from English Short Verse?" in Simply Haiku: Quarterly Journal of Japanese Short Form Poetry (v.7 n.1). (Accessed online at: http://simplyhaiku.com/SHv7n1/features/Uzawa.html, December 2015.)
20 Jean Hyung Yul Chu, "Haiku," in ed. Finch and Varnes, *An Exaltation of Forms*, p. 217.

Renga

Haiku originated as the first part of a renga, a group composition in which one poet wrote a verse of 5, 7, 5 sound beats and handed it to a second poet, who added a verse of 7, 7. This was passed on to the next poet, who added a verse of 5, 7, 5 and so on, to create the renga. The haiku became a form in its own right in the hands of Japanese poet Matsuo Basho (1644–1694). Traditionally there is no limit to the length of a renga; however Basho invented a 36-verse version called the kasen.[21]

Senryu

Another Japanese form, the senryu, is structurally the same as the haiku but focuses on human nature and is more light-hearted, as in this one, by David Mc-Fadden: "Since I discovered / Takuboku my fingers / Are numb with counting." Often, however, it can be difficult to pinpoint the difference between senryu and haiku. Redhill, for instance, calls his poem a haiku, but given its focus on the human, it is arguably closer to a senryu. Poet Brian Bartlett, at the end of his haiku collection *Potato Blossom Road*, suggests the distinction to be made between the two forms: "is only thematic, tonal, and imagistic."[22]

Tanka

The five-line tanka, sometimes called *waka* (five lines of 5, 7, 5, 7, 7 sound beats) was a dominant poetic form in Japan from the seventh until about the fourteenth century, when the renga replaced it in popularity. By the nineteenth century, however, the form revived and now flourishes in Japan and many other countries. Uzawa suggests that in English, the tanka should be about 20 syllables. Traditional tanka include a break in syntax after the second or third line; its themes are primarily, though not restricted to, nature and love; and it tends to be written in long sequences. Much later, in Europe, the sonnet would follow in the tanka's footsteps to play a role in courtship.

---

21 Titles are not normally given to haiku but in the kasen, a title is taken from the opening haiku. This, and other less common versions such as the haiga, which combines haiku and visual art, are explored in Terry Ann Carter's teachers' guide to haiku, *Lighting the Global Lantern*, which also talks about how contemporary poets are stretching the tradition, taking it, for example, into the realms of slam and science fiction.

22 Brian Bartlett, *Potato Blossom Road* (Victoria, BC: Ekstasis Editions, 2013), p. 77. Higginson also discusses the considerable overlap between these two forms in chapter 15 of *The Haiku Handbook*.

Haiku sequence

The haiku sequence — several haiku on a common subject — was, like the tanka, being written long before Petrarch ever composed a sonnet sequence. Here, David McFadden combines senryu and tanka in one sequence.

Haibun

Haibun, invented in 1690 by Basho, are brief, minimalist prose pieces that end with one or more haiku. Often written as journals or travel diaries, they give a renga-like effect when written in a series. Carter says the haibun's "poetry arises in the link and shift in tone and palette between the prose and the haiku."[23] There isn't always an obvious connection between the prose and closing haiku; instead, the connection is often left to the reader to decode. Carter notes, however, that some poets feel the haiku should inform and expand — but never précis — the prose, making the connection with an emotional tone.[24] Fred Wah varies the haibun by writing both sections in what could be considered the haiku equivalent of a prose poem.

The traditional form:

Stanza:	Three lines (which also serve to open the tanka and renga, and close the haibun).
Syllable count:	• Haiku and senryu lines have a syllable count of 5, 7, 5 (or less) in English; a pause in both rhythm and grammar divides them into two parts. • Tanka lines have a syllable count of 5, 7, 5, 7, 7 (or less) in English; usually there is a break in syntax after the second or third line.
Rhyme:	Not rhymed.
Repetition:	None required.
Distinguishing feature:	Japanese forms achieve their effect through concrete images and succinct, objective description in the present tense.

---

23 from "A note about haibun" (pronounced high/boon) in Terry Ann Carter, *On the Road to Naropa: My Love Affair with Jack Kerouac: A Haibun Memoir* (Edmonton, AB: Inkling Press, 2015).

24 Private correspondence with the editors.

WINONA BAKER (b. 1924)

from Spring

in the pocket
of his woodshed coveralls
a nest of deer mice

NAOMI BETH WAKAN (b. 1931)

[untitled]

heavy frost …
in the white crocus
a sleeping bee

GEORGE BOWERING (b. 1935)

from Three Political Falltime Haiku

Yellow maple leaf
falls from branch nearest the clouds
glides off gun barrel

GEORGE ELLIOTT CLARKE (b. 1960)

Hymn for Portia White

The white, bathing moon
ogles itself in the sea,
all black and handsome.

George Swede (b. 1940)

[untitled]

Paris pond
a frog Picassos
my face

Marco Fraticelli (b. 1945)

[untitled]

spring
melting
us

Michael Redhill (b. 1966)

Haiku Monument for Washington, D.C.

RomeRomeRomeRome
RomeRomeRomeRomeRomeRome
RomeRomeRomeRome

LeRoy Gorman (b. 1949)

[untitled]

out of fall mist
      a duck

f

    e

     a

     t

     h

    e

    r

Terry Ann Carter (b. 1946)

from Maestro

French translations by Mike Montreuil

at the hospital entrance
a string
of Christmas lights
the last one
broken

à l'entrée de l'hôpital
une série
de lumières de Noël
la dernière
cassée

*

arriving at my front door
I think of what I might do
to ease
this aching heart
ice along the path

arrivant devant ma porte
je pense à ce que je dois faire
pour soulager
mon coeur blessé
glace sur l'allée

DAVID W. McFADDEN (b. 1940)

Shouting Your Name Down the Well

Beside my bedside —
Takuboku's "Poems to Eat"
Placed by dear old friends.

*

Late at night I sit
Watching the fish in the tank.
Their eyes never close.
They're like little wind-up toys.
Wonder if they know they're real.

*

Ian sees I am
Torturing myself again.
I tell him if I
Don't torture myself who will?
He says give nature a chance.

*

Everyone has a
Shitty time of it in life.
A fly in a web
Watching the spider approach —
How is it different from me?

*

Since I discovered
Takuboku my fingers
Are numb with counting.

COLIN MORTON (b. 1948)

from Hortus Urbanus / Urban Garden

Twice now this morning I am wakened by full-throated geese
Veeing over my roof. How is a poet to dream through this?
High in the wind-torn white pine a cardinal pipes his
claim to all he surveys. From chimneytop the crow replies
sharply. In cedar branches sparrows watch a blue jay splash in
the water.

Fleet light, how do you
taste? How have you left no tracks
in reaching this place?

Diana Hartog

Station 8–Hiratsuka

The Broad Plain

Another courier flies past, sandals flapping in the dust. One grows used to them, as they relay towards Edo. When from the distance a bare-chested man comes running towards me — headlong, as if robbed of his clothes and fleeing for his life — my heart continues to plod undisturbed.

Yet when footsteps pound from behind and draw close at my back — a young courier bound for Kyoto, breath coming in gasps as he scatters beads of sweat — my pace quickens: Again I'm to be overtaken!

I must learn from example.
A roadside pine.

Fred Wah (b. 1939)

Father/Mother Haibun #5

You can't drive through a rainbow I said hills to myself in the mountains glory of a late summer early fall thunder storm the Brilliant Bluffs brilliant indeed the shine rain and sunshine waves of science breaking lickety split school systems memory for the next word after colour from the other side no one could see it otherwise nature's path is home to the bluebird triangular son/event/father w/ time-space China rainbow over your youth vertical like on the prairies that rainbow stood straight up into the sky on the horizon you'd think in the winter sun ice crystals could form unbelievable

Radio on, up north an American hunter shoots a rare white moose, geese in the sky, nibbling ribbons

TERRY ANN CARTER (b. 1946)

1961

Piano lessons every Thursday afternoon at the Phila-
delphia Conservatory of Music. Flute lessons from
Mr. Janssen at the YWCA. My life is filled with classical
music. Czerny scales. Long hours of practice on our
upright piano in the sunroom. My father brings yel-
low roses to my first concert when I wear a gorgeous
butter-coloured satin dress.

> making mountains
> out of molehills —
> my first push-up bra

INCANTATION

The word incantation, defined by the *Canadian Oxford Dictionary* as "a magical formula chanted or spoken," comes from the Latin *cantare*, to sing. Although many forms of poetry use repetition, incantation relies particularly heavily on rhythmic insistence to create an intensely emotional, mesmerizing effect for magic, ritual or performance purposes. Like spoken word, incantation overtly appeals to the senses — especially the ear — and to the body's physical pleasure in repetition. (Think of how parents will soothe a baby by rocking it.)

Common incantation techniques include repetition of an initial word or phrase (anaphora), as in Thuong Vuong-Riddick's "My Beloved is Dead in Vietnam" where the initial "Dead in ..." reinforces, like a dirge, the endless numbers of dead. Renée Sarojini Saklikar's "from the archive, a continuance," about the 1985 Air India bombings also uses anaphora, in this case to reinforce the writer's/reader's impatience with the endless frustration of bureaucracy.

Incantation can be achieved in list poems (also known as catalogue poems) that cite a rhythmic accumulation of details, as in Leona Gom's "What Women Want" and Wasela Hiyate's "Wash Away Your Sorrows."

Gregory Scofield chants in his native Cree ("ôh, êkwa kâ-kimiwahk / kâ-kimiwahk") and even for those of us who cannot speak the language, the magic of pure sound adds emphasis to the power of the incantation.

Phyllis Gotlieb integrates a number of formal techniques in "Death's Head." The poem is a chant by virtue of its solid four-strong, drumbeat-like lines ("at 3 / a.m. / I run / my tongue / around / my teeth / (take in / a breath)") and its repetition of the phrases "(take in a breath)" and "(give out a breath)" until we're almost breathless for fear the next breath won't come.

The traditional form:

Stanza:

Any number of stanzas of any length.

Metre:

May or may not be metred, though the regular beat often makes it fall into a metric pattern.

Rhyme:

May or may not include rhyme.

Repetition:

The pattern and devices used for rhythmic and insistent repetition are up to the poet; this form is most poignant when spoken, chanted or performed aloud; see also the "Spoken Word" chapter.

AUA

from **Magic Words**

To Lighten Heavy Loads

    I speak with the mouth of Qeqertuanaq,
        and say:
    I will walk with leg muscles strong as the
sinews on the shin of a little caribou calf.
    I will walk with leg muscles strong as the
sinews on the shin of a little hare.
    I will take care not to walk toward the dark.
    I will walk toward the day.

THUONG VUONG-RIDDICK (b. 1940)

My Beloved is Dead in Vietnam

For Trinh Cong Son, author of The Mad Woman

Dark or blue, all beloved, all beautiful.
Numberless eyes have seen the day.
They sleep in the grave,
and the sun still rises.
— Sully Prudhomme

My beloved is
Dead in Diên Biên Phu
Dead in Lao Kay, dead in Cao Bang
Dead in Langson, dead in Mong Cai
Dead in Thai Nguyên, dead in Hanoï
Dead in Haïphong, dead in Phat Diêm
Dead in Ninh-Binh, dead in Thanh Hoa
Dead in Vinh, dead in Hatinh
Dead in Hue, dead in Danang, dead in Quang Tri
Dead in Quang Ngai, dead in Qui Nhon
Dead in Kontum, dead in Pleiku
Dead in Dalat, dead in Nha-Tranh

Dead in My Tho, dead in Tuy Hoa
Dead in Biên-Hoa, dead in Ban Me Thuot
Dead in Tayninh, dead in Anloc
Dead in Saigon, dead in Biên Hoa
Dead in Can Tho, dead in Soc Trang

Vietnam, how many times
I have wanted to call your name
I have forgotten
the human sound.

⊷⟾

MARILYN BOWERING (b. 1949)

Widow's Winter

Bless the red door open wide.
Bless the dead who play inside.

Call the waning, watchman moon,
as the baliff steps aside —

Christ, my heart's a bitter sinner,
rescue it from widow's winter.

⊷⟾

RENÉE SAROJINI SAKLIKAR (b. 1962)

from the archive, a continuance

Into this saga, there is always one continuous intervener:
June 23, 1985. There are experts and departments.

There are multiple actors. There are steps taken, untaken.
There are phenomena and failure. There is extremism.

There is Ottawa and Vancouver, Montreal and Duncan,
Norita and County Cork. There is regularly informing.

There are telexes, seen and unseen. There are policies.
There are protocols and additional measures.

There is heightened and weekends. There are the dogs.
There is the waiting. There is confusion.

There are frontline workers. There is optimal security.
There is threat fatigue. There is secrecy.

There is the conflation of several events. There is memory.
There is assessment. There is circulation.

There are eighty-two children under the age of thirteen.
There are dossiers, chronologies, rules, conclusions.

There is the basis of evidence. There is plausibility and credit.
There is interception. There is threat. There is the highest regard.

There are flotsam and jetsam. There are no records of reports.
There are reports. There are agencies and roadblocks.

Regimes and tribunals. Deficiencies and incidents.
Illustrations and charts.

Claims and contradictions.
Special procedural challenges.

There are eighty-two children —

◦⊱═◉

LEONA GOM (b. 1946)

What Women Want

not much / everything.
a bra not as sadistic as it looks,
peace on earth, not getting our periods
in rush-hour traffic, a few good friends,
remembering our postal codes,
the elimination of rape, growing old
without poverty, wearing sleeveless blouses
and unshaved armpits and not caring,
children by choice, never having to fake
orgasm or interest in hockey, work
we enjoy, size twelve thighs,
crossing off everything on the list,
that's about it / that's a beginning.

WASELA HIYATE

Wash Away Your Sorrows

    fried water
    tap water
    sweet water
    brine

    cold water
    black water
    rank water

    wine

    sea
    rain
    piss
    beer

hot water
drain water
fire water

tear

warm water
bath water
fresh water
flood

juice
sap
dew

blood

TIM BOWLING (b. 1964)

Morenz

The crowds, the cheers, the broken leg, the death.
The crowds, the tears, the open casket, the death.
The standings, the headlines, the copy-mad press.
The rushes, the goals, the sainthood in Quebec.

Ontario boy, la première étoile, Habitant captain.
O Canada in the Forum, O Canada in the Gardens.
The dekes, the grace, the wrists, the soft hands.
The masses, the headlines, the hearse, the fans.

Six Team League. The Roaring Twenties. Hat Trick.
The Stanley Cup, the records, the move, the check.
The break, the cast, the fever, the held breath.
The death, the death, the death, the death.

LEONARD COHEN (b. 1934)

Twelve O'Clock Chant

Hold me hard light, soft light hold me,
Moonlight in your mountains fold me,
Sunlight in your tall waves scald me,
Ironlight in your wires shield me,
Deathlight in your darkness wield me.

In burlap bags the bankers sew me,
In countries far the merchants sell me,
In icy caves the princes throw me,
In golden rooms the doctors geld me,
In battlefields the hunters rule me.

I will starve till prophets find me
I will bleed till angels bind me,
Still I sing till churches blind me,
Still I love till cog-wheels wind me.

Hold me hard light, soft light hold me,
Moonlight in your mountains fold me,
Sunlight in your tall waves scald me,
Ironlight in your wires shield me,
Deathlight in your darkness wield me.

His Flute, My Ears

piyis êkwa ê-tipiskâk êkwa
ôh, êkwa kâ-kimiwahk,
kâ-kimiwahk

earth smells, love medicine
seeping into my bones
and I knew
his wind voice
catching
the sleeping leaves
ôh, êkwa kâ-kimiwahk,
kâ-kimiwahk

I dreamed
him weaving spider threads
into my hair,
fingers of firefly
buzzing ears, the song
his flute
stealing clouds from my eyes

kâ-kimiwahk
I woke

numb in my bones.

piyis êkwa ê-tipiskâk êkwa
ôh, êkwa kâ-kimiwahk,
kâ-kimiwahk
At last it was night
oh, and it rained,
it rained

PHYLLIS GOTLIEB (1926–2009)

Death's Head

at 3 a.m. I run my tongue
around my teeth (take in a breath)
(give out a breath) take one more step
approaching death. my teeth are firm
and hard and white (take in a breath)
incisors bite and molars grind
(give out a breath) the body lying
next to mine is sweet and warm
I've heard that worms (take in a breath)
don't really eat (give out a breath)
the coffin meat of human kind
and if they did I wouldn't mind
that's what I heard (take in a breath)
(and just in time) I think it's all
a pack of lies. I know my flesh
will end in slime. the streets are mean
and full of thieves. the children in
the sleeping rooms (give out a breath)
walk narrowly upon my heart
the animal beneath the cloth
submerged rises to any bait
of lust or fury, love or hate
(take in a breath) my orbic skull
is eminently frangible
so delicate a shell to keep
my brains from spillage. still my breath
goes in and out and nearer death

and yet I seem to get to sleep

LIPOGRAM

The lipogram, one of the best-known techniques developed by the Oulipo[25] group, is a composition that excludes the use of one or more letters. As Ross Eckler notes in his 1997 essay on the form, the objective is to apply the constraint with such ease, the reader barely notices it.[26]

Nancy Mattson's "Her Other Language," achieves this even as she omits the letters *b*, *f*, *m*, *p* and *v* (labials, fricatives and plosives). To be spoken, these letters require the lips, or lips and teeth, to touch. Their absence from the poem, while subtle and not immediately obvious, is bleakly appropriate to her subject — a woman's inability to speak clearly after a beating.

A lipogram can also have a narrative arc, as in Christian Bök's book *Eunoia*, in which each chapter consists of poems restricted to words using only one of the five vowels. The selection here, from "Chapter 'E'" offers an irreverent view of our western culture's warrior mythology.

bp Nicol's poem uses only the letters in "turnips are." Here, there are echoes of incantation, with the repetition of "are" at the end of each line, and of the doublet (see "... and More" chapter), by juggling the letters in "turnips" until he winds up, at the end, with the only other familiar word in the poem: "spurtin."

In Brian Bartlett's "Shuffles," the constraint is whole words — yet another approach to the lipogram. The poems in each of these sequences "shuffle" the same twelve words, and in so doing, echo the quality of anagrams — in which letters or words are rearranged to produce new words or sentences, using each original only once. In structure and content (use of imagery, focus on the moment and objective description) the poems also resemble traditional haiku.[27]

---

25 Oulipo is an experimental, avant-garde group of writers who invent their own literary forms. The group was formed in 1960, when ten mathematicians and artists (some with connections to the Surrealists) came together in France. Eventually, they called themselves Ouvroir de littérature potentielle (Oulipo; roughly translated, the name in English means Workshop for Potential Literature).

26 Ross Eckler. "Lipograms and Other Constraints." Word Ways, 1997 (at http://digital-commons.butler.edu/cgi/viewcontent.cgi?article=4231&context=wordways, accessed September 2015). Thanks to Bert Almon for bringing this article to the editors' attention.

27 After the editors included Brian's poem in the haiku chapter in the first edition of *In Fine Form*, he mentioned that when he wrote them, he meant to create an entirely new form (which he called "shuffles"). Accordingly, this time around the editors decided "shuffles" and lipograms were a good fit.

The traditional form:

Stanza:	Varies, up to the poet.
Metre:	None required.
Rhyme:	None required.
Distinguishing feature:	Must have a specific constraint (e.g., omitting one or more letters of the alphabet; limiting the poem to specific words).

NANCY MATTSON (b. 1947)

Her Other Language

She has had to learn
a language that allows only
words she can say without
the thick skin lines outside
her teeth going anywhere
near each other

in this language the teeth
aching and dry, one cracked
stay a certain distance away

this is her language until
the swelling goes down
days at least

it was his hands that did this

all she can say are ice words
stone words
dust words
tongue-against-the-teeth words
dull sounds through the throat

liquids are all she can swallow
through a thick straw
that hurts when it touches

the slot in her jaw cannot shut
its corners cannot turn
towards her eyes

CHRISTIAN BÖK (b. 1966)

from "Chapter E"

Greek schemers seek egress *en ténèbres*, then enter the melee — the welter where berserk tempers seethe whenever men's mettle, then men's fettle, gets tested; there, the Greek berserkers sever men's thews, then shred men's flesh. When the rebels beset defended trenches, the defenders retrench themselves, then strengthen the embedded defences. The strengthened deterrence deters the rebels; nevertheless, these men esteem relentlessness; hence, the rebels expend themselves, then reject détente. We see them repel retrenched defencemen, then render the bested men defenceless.

NICOLE BROSSARD (b. 1943)

L.

(translated by Erin Mouré and Robert Majzels)

long-time lilac lips
liquor of light and literature
or little lizard of the Lido
louvered in my lion-lexicon of questions

long-time on lesbian lips
let loose from tears under lapis-lazuli light
I long to lick sweet lobe and loukoum
long-time I leaned into this reading
of lyric lagoon and language long ago

PAUL DUTTON (b. 1943)

so'net 3

Onset tense: no tone to set,
no sense to note — not one; no, none.
So one soon tosses on to net
tenses, notes, tones. One soon sees one
to ten senses. Soon one's not too tense:
One's not sent to see eons nest
on stone tenets set to sonnet's sense.
One senses sonnets not sent to test,
sees no noose set, no nonsense, no
set oneness. One senses entente, not
tense tones no sonnet's set to tote. So
tense not, testes, on notes to one's tot.
   Noon noses onto settee son's set on,
   one not seen to toss stone sonnet net on.

bp NICHOL (1944–1988)

Turnips Are

turnips are
inturps are
urnspit are
tinspur are
rustpin are
stunrip are
piturns are
ritpuns are
punstir are
nutrips are
suntrip are
untrips are
spinrut are
runspit are
pitnurs are
runtsip are
puntsir are
turnsip are
tipruns are
turpsin are
spurtin

Brian Bartlett (b. 1953)

Shuffles

for Rosemary and Ricky Talbot

winter blooms, turns
and throws across snow
shadows, light, leaves, a child

                winter leaves turn and
                a child blooms, throws
                snow light across shadows

across light blooms and leaves
winter throws turns,
snow shadows a child

                snow light throws blooms
                across winter: a shadow child
                turns and leaves

       *

hear the story leap
and the breath whisper
and roar through you

                story the breath
                and hear you roar
                and leap through the whisper

breath through story:
you roar the whisper and
hear the leap and —

                you hear, whisper and leap
                and roar the breath
                through the story

PALINDROME

A palindrome is commonly thought of as a word (such as the place names "Nappan" in Nova Scotia and "Kinikinik" in Alberta), phrase ("race car"), or sentence ("Able was I ere I saw Elba") that reads the same both backward and forward. The word, derived from the Greek *palindromia*, literally means a running back again.

In poetry, the concept is expanded to multiple lines (or stanzas), where the lines in the first half of the poem are repeated, in reverse order, in the second half. To our knowledge, the first palindrome published in Canada was Gudrun Wight's "The Gift Shop."[28]

When a palindrome succeeds as a poem, it does more than just reverse the order of the lines; it also provides a shift in perspective or meaning. For example, in Elizabeth Bachinsky's "ATM," what is "pink-cheeked and fussing for a nipple" in the first instance is the baby and in the second, the husband. It is the accumulation of images, seen in different ways, which gives us the full picture.

Minor changes from one stanza to the next can serve to maintain grammatical sense, as in Eve Joseph's "Halfway World" when "Prepare" becomes "prepares." But as often as not, these changes are also crucial to developing content, retaining narrative flow and shifting emphasis. In Joseph's poem, when "the children stolen" from the Pantanal become "the stolen children" in Canada, the past in one country enters the present in another. Joseph's poem pivots on an unrepeated line, "How will the dead speak?" Standing as a separate stanza, this line reinforces the ties between past and present, elsewhere and here.

A similar variation appears in Joe Denham's "The Shoreline," which is divided into two sections, "Land" and "Sea." Each section of five unrhymed couplets includes a final unrepeated line. Although they are outside the repetition pattern, those closing lines play a significant role in the poem, their insistent vowel and consonant sounds hissing in the surf like two waves, similar but not identical. The first, "... stone in the glare of the serpent-haired sun" ("Land") feels cast away, flotsam on the beach, stranded. The second, "floating in the depths of dark, saline amnion" ("Sea") is allowed to sink, something lost or fading back into its original element; and we are irrevocably drawn back to the beginning of the poem, to "the littoral space between there and here."

---

28 *Pender Island Poetry Anthology*, with a foreword by Roger Langrick, (Pender Island, BC: self-published, 1990).

The traditional form:

Stanzas:	Any number of stanzas of any length.
Metre:	No set metre or syllable count required.
Rhyme:	No rhyme scheme required.
Repetition:	The ordering of the lines in the first half of the poem is reversed in the second half.

EVE JOSEPH (b.1953)

Halfway World

In the halfway world of the Pantanal,
aquatic and terrestrial
ghosts, stars and fireflies
everywhere.
Night smelling of ripe fruit,
lilies, dirt roads.
Breathing it all in,
visitors,
the two of you
like moss green birds
exotic and endangered.
The indigenous people
gone,
the children stolen.
Prepare to listen to
the Truth and Reconciliation Commission
at home —
the stories of unmarked graves
waiting to be told.
Not knowing what's ahead.

How will the dead speak?

Not knowing what's ahead,
waiting to be told
the stories of unmarked graves
at home.
The Truth and Reconciliation Commission
prepares to listen to
the stolen children —
gone
the indigenous people,
exotic and endangered
like moss green birds.
The two of you
visitors,
breathing it all in —
lilies, dirt roads
night smelling of ripe fruit.
Everywhere
ghosts, stars and fireflies
aquatic and terrestrial
in the halfway world of the Pantanal.

⤙⟹

JOE DENHAM (b. 1975)

The Shoreline

I. Land

The littoral space between there and here
sings in the raking of wave over stone. Imagine

Hermaphroditus and Salmacis before Zeus split them:
this is the place where the harmonized voices of

sopranos and baritones become inseparable.
In the morning, clock radios air music

through twitching eyelids that open,
a trace of salt on tongues, then fall

back into the flux, dragging seaweed and sand
down with them. When they resurface, they'll turn

to stone in the glare of the serpent-haired sun.

II. Sea

Down with them. When they resurface, they'll turn
back into the flux, dragging seaweed and sand,

a trace of salt on tongues, then fall
through quivering eyelids that open ...

In the morning, clock radios air music:
sopranos and baritones become inseparable.

This is the place where the harmonized voices of
Hermaphroditus and Salmacis, before Zeus split them,

sing in the raking of wave over stone. Imagine
the littoral space between there and here

floating in the depths of dark, saline amnion.

Elizabeth Bachinsky (b. 1976)

ATM

Her husband is a gentleman and, despite all, she loves him. His image
stays in her mind even when he is away in another country. She knows
he is important and that is why she doesn't pry into his affairs,
whether at home or away. There is no changing him, and besides
he is a good father. They are comfortable. Never have to confess their truth
to anyone other than themselves. They do as they like and
she likes it that way. Spends her days in her garden, no scrutiny there.
She dislikes scrutiny, being laid bare. Her family revealed only in photographs
arranged on the mantel at home, Christmas 1981, her youngest a baby then,
pink-cheeked and fussing for a nipple. So much has changed.
Far away in a country where her husband is a giant, still
broad as a table top, he shuffles into a glass booth, inserts a card into a slit
that spits bills into his palm. He is calm. He knows what he is.
What he has split apart he knows is forgiven.

What he has split apart he knows is forgiven.
He is calm. Spits bills into his palm. He knows what he is.
Broad as a table top, he shuffles into a glass booth, inserts a card into a slit
far away in a country where he is a giant, yet still
pink-cheeked and fussing for a nipple. So much has changed,
arranged on the mantle at home. Christmas 1981, his youngest a baby then.
His wife dislikes scrutiny, being laid bare. Her family revealed only in photographs.
She likes it that way. Spends her days in her garden, no scrutiny there
from anyone other than themselves. They do as they like and
he is a good father. They are comfortable. Never have to confess their truth
whether at home or away. There is no changing her, and besides
he is *important* and that is why she doesn't pry. Though his affairs
stay in her mind even when he is away, in another country, she knows
her husband is a gentleman. Despite all, she loves him. His image.

PATRICIA YOUNG (b. 1954)

Menorca #1

My husband and son are up to their necks
in the Mediterranean. First

something about me. I am not wind-driven
but the smell of ancient clay

is lodged in my brain. Any moment now
Odysseus et al. could sail around the corner

rape and plunder on their minds.
So many steps, the girls coming up said

as we were going down. Last week
squid carapaces washed up on shore:

stink of blue ink rimming the bay.
No one knows what to do

with a landscape like this
except bow down to the madness of God.

Within the hour the sun will slide
behind sandstone cliffs riddled with caves

in which Moors once hid from invading
Christians and Christians once murdered

the next army of unholy conquerors.
Unholy conquerors! Armies of

Christians murdering other Christians
then hiding from invading Moors

behind sandstone cliffs riddled with caves.
Within the hour the sun will slide

down. When the madness of God bows
to a landscape like this

no one knows what to do.
A stink of blue ink rims the bay.

Squid carapaces wash up on shore.
Last week, as we were going down,

the girls coming up said, *So many steps*
rape and plunder far from their minds.

Could Odysseus et al. sail around the corner
any moment now? Lodged in my brain

is the smell of ancient clay.
I am *not* wind-driven but something about me

is Mediterranean. Look —
my husband and son ... up to their necks.

PAMELA GALLOWAY (b. 1953)

Remembering. Autumn.

Let the leaves scatter the path,
pale lemon tears,
small stains
separate and precise.

Let them layer,
layer, wide-palmed,
rusted. Leaves
fallen from an empty sky
washed in grey
denial.

Leaves pile
against a tree, against
a fence,
deep as memory.

Deep as memory, against
a fence, against
a tree leaves pile.

Denial
washed in grey
fallen from an empty sky
rusted leaves
layer, wide-palmed
let them layer

separate and precise
small stains,
pale lemon tears

let the leaves scatter the path.

ARLEEN PARÉ (b. 1946)

More

vision doubles
the lake's surface calmed
trees displaying roots into roots
their upside-down selves

tree selves downside-up
in the water where their roots
touch their roots   a surfeit of calm
redoubles the lake

PANTOUM

The pantoum, derived from the Malay pantun, has any number of metred four-line stanzas rhyming *abab*, but its most alluring feature is an intricate pattern of line repetition.[29] It was first used in France by Ernest Fouinet, and was popularized there by Victor Hugo and Charles Baudelaire in the 1800s.

Each line of a pantoum is used twice — lines 2 and 4 of the first stanza become lines 1 and 3 of the second, and so on until the last stanza. The final quatrain consists entirely of repeated lines: the first and third are the preceding stanza's lines 2 and 4; the second and fourth are the opening stanza's lines 3 and 1 in that order. So the poem eventually circles back to its beginning, but with a deepened understanding.

Sticking closely to the formal tradition, in "Doug Hill," Alexandra Oliver writes in iambic pentameter and uses the *abab* rhyme scheme. Laura Ritland forgoes the metre and — with the exception of the single word "Zundert" — keeps to an *aaaa* rhyme scheme using assonance, or near rhyme (m*e* / stor*ies*, famil*y* — perc*eive*, etc.).

One optional feature of the pantoum is to follow the original Malay pantun form and develop different themes in the first and second couplets of each quatrain. This allows the interwoven couplets to reflect on each other, adding complexity — as when Peter Garner, in "Lucy, *Lucie*," alternates lines in French and English.

The effect of the pantoum's somersaulting lines can be delicate and hypnotic, as in Kirsten Emmott's "Labour Pantoum," or obsessive, as in Anita Lahey's "Post-War Procession." Lahey's poem also shows the effect enjambed lines can have in this form — as when "... your head / inside the helmet ..." in stanza 3 shifts emphasis to "... this endless trudge / inside the helmet ..." in stanza 4. Poets can also make important yet subtle shifts in meaning by playing with syntax, so for example Kayla Czaga's, "the discourse on language, insisting it need not be beautiful" in stanza 1 becomes "language needs to be beautiful? Their insistent discourse" in stanza 2.

Another popular variation is to make small changes in the repeated lines. Maxianne Berger, in "Empty Chairs," subtly alters words (and genders) to develop the sense of her poem. For instance, "She really misses her boyfriend" at

---

29   The pantun began as improvisational oral poetry, but by the fifteenth century it had become part of Malayan written literature as a single quatrain with an *abab* rhyme scheme and from eight to twelve syllables per line. Robin Skelton, in *The Shapes of Our Singing*, says the first half makes "a statement which proves to be a metaphor for the statement made in the second, or which is the basis for an elaboration." p. 235.

the beginning becomes, at the end, "he" who "really wishes he had a boyfriend." Frequently, she rhymes a variation with the word it replaces (e.g., "misses" and "wishes" in the above), or makes a slight change to a word to come up with another (e.g., "debating" in line four loses its *eb* to become "dating" in line seven).

The traditional form:

Stanzas: Any number of quatrains; may end in a couplet.

Metre: Can be iambic tetrameter or iambic pentameter.

Rhyme: *abab*

Repetition: Lines 2 and 4 of each quatrain are repeated as lines 1 and 3 of the next, until the last stanza.

Final stanza: all are repeated lines; in addition to maintaining the above pattern, lines 2 and 4 are the same as lines 3 and 1 of the first quatrain, so the poem ends as it begins.

A four-stanza pantoum, for example, would use eight lines in the following pattern:
1st: 1 2 3 4   **2nd**: 2 5 4 6   **3rd**: 5 7 6 8   **4th**: 7 3 8 1
(variation to 4th quatrain: 7 1 8 3)
If the above example closed with a couplet instead of a quatrain, it would end: **4th**: 3 1

Alexandra Oliver (b. 1970)

Doug Hill

I want the sun to swallow up Doug Hill,
said the tenth-grade student (through her tears).
He said he loved me, but he never will;
I can't go on like this for sixty years.

Said the tenth-grade student, through her tears,
he said he needed time and he would call.
I can't go on like this for sixty years.
I can't go on. I can't go on at all.

He said he needed time and he would call.
He brushed the leaves from off his pants and rose.
I can't go on. I can't go on at all,
I thought, and reached in darkness for my clothes.

He brushed the leaves from off his pants and rose
the next day. Back at school, they looked at me,
I thought. I reached in darkness for my clothes,
feeling bare and horrible and free.

The next day, back at school. They looked at me,
but all I saw was him, though he was gone,
feeling bare and horrible and free.
I am the one the tigers fell upon.

And all I see is him, though he is gone.
I see him in the locker doors, the sky.
I am the one the tigers fell upon.
I want the bell to ring. I want to die.

I see him in the locker doors, the sky;
he said he loved me, but he never will.
I want the bell to ring. I want to die.
I want the sun to swallow up Doug Hill.

LAURA RITLAND (b. 1990)

Vincent, in the Dream of Zundert

In my illness, I dreamed I saw our house again in Zundert
going on under an endless afternoon sun without me.
Each path, each field, the magpies in the acacia in the cemetery,
and Mother, there, like a colour I find sometimes in stories

that go on under an endless afternoon sun without me.
How simply we lived then, dear Theo. We had bread, family,
and Mother. There is a colour I find sometimes in stories
that reminds me there was a time before I began to perceive

how simply we lived then. Dear Theo, we had bread, family,
and I believed in the eternity of those ageless acacia trees.
That reminds me: there was a time before I began to perceive
how these shadows now thicken my memories.

And I believed the eternity of those ageless acacia trees
could be painted — as if paint were all we'd ever need.
Oh, how these shadows now thicken my memories,
dear Theo. If I were well again and if those leaves

could be painted, as if paint were all we'd ever need,
we'd be more than two lines leaning over in grief.
Dear Theo, if I were well again and if those leaves
would be what they seemed to be in my sleep,

we'd be more than two lines leaning over in grief.
Each path, each field, the magpies in the acacia in the cemetery
would be what they seemed to be, as in my sleep,
in my illness, when I dreamed I saw our house again in Zundert.

PETER GARNER (b. 1965)

Lucy, *Lucie*

In 1974, Donald Johanson discovered a near-complete female hominid skeleton near Hadar, Ethiopia. On trouvera, un jour lointain, sur une autre route montagneuse, les restes d'une femme qui aura perdu le contrôle de son véhicule.

three million years later, they found her
tire marks leading to the edge of a gully
sur un coteau, une côte et un os pelvien se trouvent
en bas, une nouvelle Grand Prix, renversée

des traces de pneus mènent au bord du ravin
la fumée monte, se mêle avec la brume
below, a grand new prize is overturned
a wheel, spinning slowly, seeks the road

rising into the mist, smoke mingles
the radio plays a Beatles song
lentement, une roue tourne, cherchant la route
sans nom: on l'appellera « Lucie »

la radio chante une chanson des Beatles
elle marche maintenant la tête haute
she has no name — let's call her "Lucy"
she had no past, but she will have a future

walking now with head held high
on a hillside, a rib, a pelvic bone lay there
elle n'avait pas de passé, mais elle aura un futur
dans trois millions d'années, ils la trouveront

KIRSTEN EMMOTT (b. 1947)

Labour Pantoum

are we there yet? are we there yet?
this is what it seems like
riding in the back seat of the car
that someone else is driving endlessly

this is what it seems like
sitting long hours by the labour bed
that someone else is driving endlessly
that her labour is bringing to inevitable birth

sitting long hours by the labour bed
with my hand on her brow or her swelling belly
that her labour is bringing to inevitable birth
while I, unimportant, look out the window

with my hand on her brow or her swelling belly
the trees and sky slide past
while I, unimportant, look out the window
and I daydream while it all goes by

the trees and sky slide past
as she lies back and rests, eyes closed
and I daydream while it all goes by
then she tenses and pants with a contraction

as she lies back and rests, eyes closed
we are silent in quiet expectation
then she tenses and pants with a contraction
we will be with her for as long as it takes

we are silent in quiet expectation
the night is long, day will soon break
we will be with her for as long as it takes
the city will turn pink with sunrise

the night is long, day will soon break
many babies are born at this hour
the city will turn pink with sunrise
the baby will turn pink with her first breath

many babies are born at this hour
eventually the baby will get to her destination
the baby will turn pink with her first breath
she will travel hopefully, having arrived

eventually the baby will get to her destination
like pulling into your driveway after days on the road
she will travel hopefully, having arrived
this is what it seems like

like pulling into your driveway after days on the road
days spent asking from the back seat —
this is what it seems like —
are we there yet? are we there yet?

MARLENE COOKSHAW (b. 1953)

In the Spring of No Letters

Do I think of you often, my husband wants to know.
I lie and say no or lie and say yes.
I do not think of you, exactly.
My body has words with your ghost sometimes.

I lie and say no, or lie and say yes.
We are never upright when the truth is spoken.
My body has words with your ghost sometimes.
We speak in tongues, a lingual exchange.

We are never upright when the truth is spoken.
I am used up by what the body cannot parse.
We speak in tongues, a lingual exchange
I understand and do not at the same time.

I am used up by what the body cannot parse.
The sauna stove next door's alight again.
I understand this and do not at the same time.
Is time the issue? How many times, he asks.

Next door the sauna stove's alight again.
I know, for instance, from the smoke that it is evening.
Is time the issue? How many times he asks,
as if day were a pie: proportional, divisible, dessert.

For instance, from the smoke, I know it's evening.
I'm baking yams. The dog's content.
And day's a pie: proportional, divisible, dessert.
The smoke rises like a finer form of blossom.

I'm baking yams. The dog's content.
I do not think of you exactly.
The smoke rises like a finer form of blossom.
Do I think of you? My husband wants to know.

ANITA LAHEY (b. 1972)

Post-War Procession

— *after* "Infantry, near Nijmegan, Holland, 1946"
Alex Colville, oil on canvas

Envy the barrel's ability to contain nothing.
You stink of blood, a blown-open field, severed
limbs. The march in was less pungent. Puddles, open
wounds along the ditch. Your rifle cools your neck.

You stink of blood, a blown-open field. Severed,
still following orders, boots, the men in front,
wounds along the ditch. Your rifle, your neck,
yellow leak of sky. Bodies reek in your head.

Still following orders. The boots of men in front
reflect your own: polished, tightly tied.
That yellow leak of sky. Bodies reek. Your head
inside the helmet; gripping your skull.

Reflect. Your own polished, tightly tied
meltdown. Mud. This endless trudge
inside the helmet gripping your skull.
The march continues. On the other side:

meltdown, mud, this endless trudge —
hands unfolding letters you barely wrote.
The march continues on the other side.
The horizon claws you back with white fingers

unfolding. Letters you barely wrote,
wishing your work was done. Forget glory being alive.
The horizon claws you back; its white fingers
draw out your every accomplishment, ghastly

wish. Your work is done. Forget glory: being alive
is the long walk you knew it would be.
Draw out your every ghastly accomplishment.
Envy the barrel's ability. Contain nothing.

⊷══◑

Kayla Czaga

Song

Outside my window, seagulls and crows continue
the discourse on language, insisting it need not be beautiful
to be song. If song accompanies their shallow black
and white bickering over garbage at 5 A.M., do I still believe

language needs to be beautiful? Their insistent discourse
pecks holes in the morning. Here I am still trying
to believe, at 5 A.M. despite the bickering over garbage
because faith describes perfectly how my mother is dying.

Here I am still trying to peck holes in the morning;
song is just the word I use for wanting
faith to describe how perfectly my mother is dying
thousands of miles away, in a small town I rarely visit.

Song is just another word I want to use.
Illness is just another word. Mother is just a word
thousands of miles away, in a small town I rarely visit.
The winter light pours slowly through my window.

Illness is just a word. Mother is just a word
with someone in it. Can I sing without words?
The slow winter light pours through my window.
Long after I've stopped making sense, I'm just a sound

with someone in it. Can I sing without words
and still be song, accompanying the crows, shallow and black,
making sense with just sounds? Long after I've stopped
seagulls and crows continue outside my window.

MAXIANNE BERGER (b. 1949)

Empty Chairs

She really misses her boyfriend
some mornings sitting alone
with coffee in her dark kitchen
debating what she might've done.

The same mornings he sits alone
and wonders why he's so depressed
dating; what he might've done
also to get a pick-up for sex.

She wonders why she's so depressed
without this man — her mind astir
also at what he'd pick up from sex —
face to face with his empty chair.

Without any man in mind, stirring
his coffee in the dark kitchen
he faces a faceless empty chair,
    really wishes he had a boyfriend.

PAS DE DEUX

The pas de deux was formally recognized and named as a poetic form by poet Rachel Rose in 2004. In the "Notes" at the end of her book *Song and Spectacle*, she describes it as "... a pair of poems that analyze and debate a subject. It allows for opposing and contradictory points of view, and supports a multiplicity of voices. In art, this form would be a collage; in science, a symposium; in tragedy, a Greek chorus; in philosophy, a dialectic; and in dance, a pas de deux."

This is a form based more on content than structure. Rose consistently uses couplets for her pas de deux, while a much earlier example of something very like what she has done is a pair of poems written in ballad stanza form by Duncan Campbell Scott. "The Sea by the Wood" and "The Wood by the Sea" bookend his 1905 collection, *New World Lyrics and Ballads*. In both cases, the poems present two perspectives, ironically each longing for what the other has.

Both Rose and Scott use the form to explore "the other" through the eyes of "us" and "them." In Rose's poems, it's Canadians' and Americans' assumptions about each other. In Scott's, it's the sea viewing the wood / the wood viewing the sea. In both cases, the result is a more complete picture than either poem could achieve on its own.

Daryl Hine's "Woods," strikes us as an intriguing variation of the form. Instead of two separate poems, Hine gives us differing perspectives in two rhymed and metred stanzas that could also be considered a variation on the sonnet. As well, rather than identifying his narrators, he uses unspecified voices, one disparaging, the other appreciative of a common subject/experience (the woods where they live).

The traditional form:

Stanzas:
Not required but available examples indicate poets choose the same stanza form for both poems (or parts of one poem).

Metre:
None required.

Rhyme:
None required.

Repetition:
The same subject matter must be addressed, but from different perspectives, in both poems (or parts of one poem).

RACHEL ROSE (b. 1970)

What We Heard About the Americans

We heard there was much to admire about the Americans.
Historically.

Their cuisine is buffet, all you can
overeat.

We heard they hire whisperers, buy guides for
idiots.

Foster special needs kittens. Are visited by
aliens.

We heard the Americans are our
brethren.

That they keep ten percent of black men
imprisoned.

Are stockpiling weapons for
Armageddon.

Believe that all good dogs go to
heaven.

God bless the Americans. God bless their inalienable
freedoms.

Bless Guantanamo. Americans sure know how to have
fun.

Even their deaths are more important than our
own.

Happiness is cosmetic
dentistry.

The global dream is the American
dream.

Liberty is a statue holding a soft ice
cream.

What We Heard About the Canadians

We heard they were not American.
Not British and not quite French.

They were not born in Hong Kong
did not emigrate from Russia with a single pair of shoes.

They were not all russet-haired orphans
who greeted the apple blossom dawn with open arms,

crying *Avonlea*! They were not immodest,
did not want God to save the Queen.

Their leaders were not corrupt.
They were not all Mounties on proud horseback

with hot tasers. *Fuck me* was not considered impolite
in their living rooms.

There was no great Canadian hush of things not to be talked about.
Not all of them ignored genocide.

Not all of them sang a "cold
and broken Hallelujuah" as the bells broke crystal ice

across parc Lafontaine. They were not rich and also
not poor. Not overachievers. Neither believers nor unbelievers.

C'était pas toute l'histoire, and they would not
be caught clubbing seals on TV, red bloom

on white coat, melting eyes. They did not mine asbestos
in Quebec, make love in skidoos,

sleep in showshoes. Never danced hatless
under dancing Northern lights. They were polite.

DUNCAN CAMPBELL SCOTT (1862–1947)

The Sea by the Wood

I dwell in the sea that is wild and deep,
But afar in a shadow still,
I can see the trees that gather and sleep
In the wood upon the hill.

The deeps are green as an emerald's face,
The caves are crystal calm,
But I wish the sea were a little trace
Of moisture in God's palm.

The waves are weary of hiding pearls,
Are aweary of smothering gold,
They would all be air that sweeps and swirls
In the branches manifold.

They are weary of laving the seaman's eyes
With their passion prayer unsaid,
They are weary of sobs and the sudden sighs
And movements of the dead.

All the sea is haunted with human lips
Ashen and sere and grey,
You can hear the sails of the sunken ships
Stir and shiver and sway,

In the weary solitude;
If mine were the will of God, the main
Should melt away in the rustling wood
Like a mist that follows the rain.

But I dwell in the sea that is wild and deep
And afar in the shadow still,
I can see the trees that gather and sleep
In the wood upon the hill.

The Wood by the Sea

I dwell in the wood that is dark and kind
But afar off tolls the main,
Afar, far off I hear the wind,
And the roving of the rain.

The shade is dark as a palmer's hood,
The air with balm is bland:
But I wish the trees that breathe in the wood
Were ashes in God's hand.

The pines are weary of holding nests,
Are aweary of casting shade;
Wearily smoulder the resin crests
In the pungent gloom of the glade.

Weary are all the birds of sleep,
The nests are weary of wings,
The whole wood yearns to the swaying deep,
The mother of restful things.

The wood is very old and still,
So still when the dead cones fall,
Near in the vale or away on the hill,
You can hear them one and all,

And their falling wearies me;
If mine were the will of God — O, then
The wood should tramp to the sounding sea,
Like a marching army of men!

But I dwell in the wood that is dark and kind,
Afar off tolls the main;
Afar, far off I hear the wind
And the roving of the rain.

SUSAN OLDING (b. 1958)

What We Thought About The Chinese Mothers

We tried not to think. We tried to pretend
they didn't exist. We thought about paint chips —

we picked colours for the nursery,
we thought about cribs and baby monitors.

The bellies of pregnant women bothered us,
so we ignored them. We shopped for socks,

sleepers and bottles, suitable gifts
to bring the *ayis* — make-up, we were told,

take them eyeliner and lipstick — but that
advice seemed suspect, since even the best

brands bore the label *Made in China*. We
packed our suitcases, renewed our passports,

filled out forms and got our shots. Some of us
studied Mandarin, but most decided

not to. We didn't want to know the details —
how they spoke about their shame or fear.

We knew they were oppressed by law;
that made their choice impersonal

and we preferred to let it seem
that way. We refused

to plant imagination
in their windswept rice fields, could not bear

the thought of giving birth to sorrow.
An inkwash ponytail or the play of pearls on skin

might prompt the question — *will my daughter look
like that?* But mostly we thought of ourselves.

What the Chinese Mothers Seemed to Think About Us

They tried to pretend we didn't exist.
Showed or feigned ignorance when told

about the orphanages hulking just outside
their cities' walls. They defended the one-child

policy, said it made their country strong
and those who gave birth over-quota should

be punished. They thought we were fat, too big
and too big-nosed, unbeautiful — though rich.

They thought we meant their children harm,
thought we'd treat them as slaves and never tell them

about their Chinese past. They thought we were
fools for taking trash that someone else had wisely left

to die. They thought we were saints. They thought
the babies were lucky, they thought we

were lucky. Time was short. They did their best
to teach us how to dress the infants,

their fingers fumbling with buttons and socks
to cover the skin we'd left bare. They served

us meals, cleaned our rooms, assembled the cots
the babies slept in. If their eyes grew damp

at the thought of so many children leaving
their shores, their faces were smooth as folded linen.

DARYL HINE (1936–2012)

Woods

We live in an insubstantial wood
Under slumberous, umbrageous trees,
Among menacing, misunderstood,
Pliant, plaintive properties
Standing stupid where they stood
For witless, wicked centuries
That could not wander if they would.

These woods are wise and wild and dense
As otherworldly solitude,
Exemplars of a perfect tense
And petrified experience,
Like ideas that extrude
Through consensual innocence
A curious beatitude.

PROSE POEM

"A passage read as though addressed to the reason is prose; read as though addressed to the imagination, it might be poetry."
—Jorge Luis Borges[30]

Typically, poetry has been distinguished from prose in terms of its structure. Unlike prose, poetry features a deliberate series of lines identified by line breaks; in addition, formal poetry often has a regular pattern of rhyme, repetition metre and/or rhythm. In terms of content, John Newlove explains the distinction this way: "Poetry is the shortest distance between two points; prose, the longest."[31] And George McWhirter suggests prose is story, while poems — prose or otherwise — are cameos, quick glances at a moment that take us somewhere unexpected.[32] But as early as the mid-1800s, poets in France, from Charles Baudelaire to Francis Ponge, had begun to abandon one of the oldest structural elements of poetry — the deliberate line break — to create a hybrid genre known as the prose poem.

When we began looking into including prose poetry for this edition, it seemed few poets agreed on precisely what distinguishes it from prose. Often, it came down to "it just feels like poetry to me." A quick search of the internet took us to more conflicting opinions.[33] After sitting down with poet Zöe Landale and talking through the various views on this form, we identified some key ways in which prose and poetry overlap in one piece of writing.

As *The New Princeton Handbook of Poetic Terms* says about the prose poem: "Its principal characteristics are those that would insure unity even in brevity and poetic quality even without the line breaks of free verse: high patterning, rhythmic and figural repetition, sustained intensity, and compactness."

A prose poem keeps its claim to poetry by virtue of its use of heightened language — e.g., simile, metaphor, alliteration, vivid imagery. It is distinguished by its language, by its ability to compress and distill emotion, and by a particular energy that's more focused than prose; it takes you somewhere unexpected with the particular suddenness of poetry.

---

30 from "Author's Foreword" in *Jorge Luis Borges: Selected Poems 1923–1967*, ed. Norman Thomas diGiovanni, (London: The Penguin Press, 1972), p. xiii.

31 Quoted from "John Newlove's 'Ottawa Poems'" by rob mclennan in Ottawa Poetry Newsletter, June 19, 2006, at http://ottawapoetry.blogspot.ca/2006/06/john-newloves-ottawa-poems.html (accessed October 2015).

32 Private correspondence with the editors.

33 See, for example, the section "Learn More: What Is One?" of The Prose-Poem Project, Spring 2013, www.prose-poems.com/definition.html (accessed October 2015).

Yet like prose, this form relies on sentences in paragraph form. Poet Patricia Young warns, however, that "it's easy to become prosaic when working in sentences."[34]

Even when it has a narrative arc, the prose poem often leans on a single moment, as Gwendolyn MacEwen does in "Barker Fairley and the Blizzard." Whether the incident happened exactly this way or not, this snapshot of an encounter in the midst of a dramatic storm ("people held onto each other's waists,") and the surprise at what Fairley is thinking in the mist of such chaos, as well as his conclusions, surprise and delight us.

Likewise, in "Horses," Glen Downie uses a serious tone which — once we get the joke of exactly what kind of horses these are — makes the description all the sweeter. "One is sometimes found mounting the other, but woodenly," gives increased pleasure to a reader now "in" on the metaphor. The poem ends with the nostalgic image of the single saw "horse," now "fit only for the child cowboy." John Terpstra's "Habitat" has less of a narrative arc, but shares an intensity of language.

Meanwhile, Lorna Crozier's "Glossography of G" is a crossover poem, with elements of a list (the persistent repetition of "Let") and a lipogram (subjects primarily restricted to words or phrases that start with "g").

The traditional form:

Stanzas:	Rather than stanzas, there are one or more paragraphs; like prose, there are no deliberate line breaks.
Metre:	Like prose, not metred, but like poetry, features rhythmical language.
Rhyme:	No end rhyme (as there are no line breaks) but, as in poetry, internal rhyme and repeated sounds (assonance, consonance, alliteration) are important.
Repetition:	Not required, but as in poetry and prose, may be an important device.
Distinguishing feature:	Must feature elements of both prose and poetry.

---

34 From "The Prose Poem: Favours of the Moon and Other Moon Shine: An Interview with Eve Joseph and Patricia Young," *The New Quarterly* (No. 135, Summer 2015), p. 7.

Gwendolyn MacEwen (1941–1987)

Barker Fairley and the Blizzard

It was freezing and wet and everybody was being blown all over the street and taking shelter wherever they could, when Barker emerged from the swirling cloud of the blizzard, walking slowly and thoughtfully, his cap at a superb angle. It was a few years ago, so he couldn't have been much more than ninety. *Gwendolyn*, he said, as the gale pushed me sideways and I crashed into a wall, *I've been thinking about suffering. Does the artist have to suffer, do you think? Yes*, I said. *Definitely. The older I get the more I suffer so it must be necessary. And furthermore it is packed with meaning.* Barker looked at me quietly as several people held onto each other's waists with the man in front attached to a telephone pole, to avoid being blown away. *I don't think so, I really don't think so*, he said, as two women and a man were washed into the gutter. *We're here to bring joy; we weren't meant to suffer at all.* And he leaned into the exquisite storm and was gone.

-><==o

Glen Downie (b. 1953)

Horses

Feet in the grass but never eating, what else could they be but skeletal? They lack the spirit to gallop and will not pull, yet sleep standing up and have strength to bear all manner of burdens between them. The screams of the saw and banging of hammers cannot startle them, blinkered to all but each other. In tandem, the very models of forbearance, a working team, yoked in rigid marriage, able to endure all labour, all confinement so long as it be shared. In a crowded shed, one is sometimes found mounting the other, but woodenly — neither shows pleasure, and like mules, they are sadly infertile. Should one break its back or a leg, its life of service ends. The mate inevitably pines away, useless in singularity: one wooden horse with nothing inside, a creature bereft, fit only for the child cowboy.

-><==o

CHRISTINE WIESENTHAL (b. 1963)

blues

If these tests fail, depend only on an expert. You will save money, time and worry by calling a reliable service organization for a man who knows your appliance thoroughly.

— Home Laundry Guide

what is this weakness that washes over me as I sort through *the blues*
always make me think of the sight of his denim clad hips sauntering
along in slim cut *jeans* jeans old jeans good jeans his jeans my jeans a
combination *I like to fantasize about* pants a couple pair crumpled in a
heap tangled legs pockets peeled inside out in haste *slip in* four socks
and some lightly scented soap *like ABC* things get out of hand though
and the agitator starts churning my gut to slush sucks me into his spin
and puts me through the wringer till I find myself all washed up and
hung up and strung out on a long thin line or two *flap flap flapping* on
about a load of *nothing at all* can console me now *as Dinah Washington
sings* I'm seeing red and feeling blue/holding my breath waiting for you
sucker just can't wait to see him again *can you* maybe get in the last lick
this time breezing along out of the blue give him a smack on the cheek a
smart wet one too

JOHN TERPSTRA (b. 1953)

Habitat

Trees inhabit the world between geography and population, between earth and animal. A tree, on the one hand, may provide that fixed point on a shifting landscape, a signpost, the welcome outcrop of brown and green without which your destination over the hill, across the fields (to grandma's house?) might not be found. But at the same time the flurry of leaves outside your window and that steady accumulation of rings flaunts a visible, increasing history: trees participate.

Trees are the stakes that hold down this dark tarp of soil and civilization.

Or, they are superfluous, ornamental, added on to the twin requirements of place, people.

It is the open otherworldliness of the individual tree upon the landscape that encourages us to see it as being, at once, so necessary, and so simply gratuitous.

LORNA CROZIER (b. 1948)

Glossography of G

Let there be geraniums, gerbils, gutters, galoshes, gizmos, gramophones and goo. Let there be Girl Scouts strumming green guitars in graperies in Grenada. Let there be gimcrackery among the grackles. Let da Vinci paint another *La Gioconda*; let gingivitis be cured by gingerbread; let the Gorgon repopulate the garden with garter snakes and glass. Let there be god, god, god, all good and gladsome and Glaswegian, enough of them to pay attention, a glut of glorious and gosh. Let there be more Van Goghs, gnus and gnocchi; fewer gnats, germs, girdles, graves and glee clubs. Let gonorrhea go the way of the glyptodont; let give-and-give take over take. In spite of grime and grim and gruel, in spite of gone, gone, gone, which you and everything you love will be too soon, with gratitude and gusto let genesis begin with *g*.

Patricia Young (b. 1954)

Sisyphean

They don't come anymore, the man and his small son, but for two years they
came every Sunday, hand in hand, down the slippery steps to the beach wrapped
around the bay. The man wore garden gloves and carried an industrial-strength
garbage bag. His son wore gloves too. No matter the season or weather they'd
scour the beach for washed-up trash, the boy running ahead of his father: *Look
at this! And this!* The ocean's wonderous belly spitting up more and more
booze bottles, lampshades, condoms, bits of synthetic rope. And sometimes
the man knelt to examine a hairbrush or telephone receiver before dropping
it into the bag. In those moments what did he say to the boy? Did he explain the
Sisyphean task set before them? That plastic breaks down slowly, over thousands
of years? That mermaid tears never dissolve? Holding a mug of tea between my
hands, I'd stand at the window and wonder: was the man saying *food chain,
chemical pollutant, death of the sea*? Or was he avoiding the eye of the one to
whom he'd so carelessly given life: *What you got there, Bub — doll's head, BB
gun, baby's bootie?*

Diana Hartog

Entry

The silence of the desert is too strong for the walls of the ranch house. The
feeble bleats of the radio are overpowered at night by the presence of the high
white dune to the west, by the whispers of the tamarisk around a hidden, needle-
strewn grave.

And even in here I can feel the stars through the ceiling; feel their glitter
at the roof of my skull as each new spark of thought is snuffed; overwhelmed by
an intelligence which thinks not in words but in Bears, Scorpions, Giants with
fine diamond-edged swords. And sapphire-set Dippers — bent at the handle to
scoop the mercury of memory, or whatever it is, off the top of our heads, that
gods drink.

Rondeau Family

Poems in the rondeau family are distinguished by their use of refrains and just two rhymes. Those included in this chapter are the rondeau, roundel, rondeau redoubled, rondel, triolet and roundelay.

Rondeau

The term rondeau originally referred to all French fixed forms that included refrains of any sort. Over the years the term roundel has sometimes been used as a synonym for the rondeau and the rondel, which can get a bit confusing — but in fact, while these forms have similarities, each also has its own distinct features.

By the fifteenth century the rondeau had emerged as a form in its own right. A poem with three stanzas of five, four and six lines, it has just two rhymes and one, unrhymed, refrain. The refrain is the first part of line 1, repeated at the end of stanzas 2 and 3. The other lines can be either syllabic or accentual-syllabic. They usually have eight or ten syllables each, rhyming *aabba* in the first and third stanzas and *aab* in the second. John McCrae's "In Flanders Fields" is one of the best known rondeaux.

Roundel

English poet Charles Swinburne developed the roundel as a variation of the rondeau. His version, too, is divided into three stanzas, but these are shorter — four, three and four lines. He uses the first part of line 1 as a refrain, but departs from the French form by repeating it at the end of stanzas 1 and 3 only. The other differences are that, throughout, he laces the two rhymes (e.g., *aba bab aba*) and requires no set metre or syllable count. Colin Morton closely follows the form, with a refrain of "In this empty room," but compresses the eleven lines into two stanzas.

Rondeau Redoubled

There is yet another variation of the rondeau, the rondeau redoubled (also called rondeau redoublé), which has six stanzas — five quatrains and a closing quintet. (The quatrains resemble a glosa in that the first quatrain provides the last line for each of the next four.) Like the rondeau, this poem ends as it begins, i.e., with the first half of the initial quatrain's opening line. The stanzas alternate between two rhyme schemes, *abab* and *baba*, and normally all lines except the last have a common metre or syllable count. Margaret Avison, in "Rondeau Redoublé," shortens the form to five stanzas — four quatrains and a quintet.

Rondel

The rondel is a thirteen- or fourteen-line poem, usually divided into three stanzas — two quatrains and either a quintet or a sestet. The first two lines of stanza 1 reappear as refrains at the end of stanzas 2 and 3 (the final line is optional). While the form requires no set metre or syllable count, often poets keep all lines to either eight or ten syllables. Émile Nelligan's "Roundel to my Pipe" is actually a thirteen-line rondel of eight-syllable lines and a somewhat varied rhyme scheme. Nelligan's poem (in this translation) keeps to the usual pattern, *abba*, in the first four lines, but varies the next eight lines, using *baab* instead of *abab abba*.

Triolet

An early version of the rondel, the triolet dates back to the 1300s. This French fixed form made a brief appearance in English in the sixteenth century, but didn't take hold until the late 1800s. Shorter than the rondel, it features two refrains and two rhymes in just eight lines. Because the two refrains take up five of the poem's eight lines, this form poses a particular challenge — how to avoid tedium. In English, the triolet is usually written as a single, self-contained stanza, but its brevity invites possibilities for a sequence, as in Christopher Wiseman's "Triolets for Ken." To help avoid monotony, poets often dispense with the rhyme scheme, use free verse rather than metred lines, change internal punctuation to vary the meaning of a refrain line, and/or — as in Elise Partridge's "Vuillard Interior" — change words or phrases in the refrains.

Roundelay

More flexible is the roundelay, which requires only the use of a refrain. Poets often vary the refrain or use additional repetition devices to intensify a poem's effect. For example, Mark Abley's refrain appears at the start and end of each stanza, and he changes the final word from one stanza to the next: day becomes night becomes hour, underscoring how relentlessly the trees are chopped down.

The traditional form:

Rondeau

Stanzas:	Three stanzas: the first is a quintet; the second, a quatrain; and the third, a sestet.
Metre:	Usually 8 or 10 syllables in each line, except for the shortened refrain lines.
Rhyme:	*aabba / aab*R / *aabba*R (R stands for the refrain, which repeats the first part of line 1.)

| Repetition: | The refrain is the first phrase of line 1, repeated as the last line in both the quatrain and the sestet; the refrain is outside the rhyme scheme. |

Roundel

Stanzas:	Three stanzas: the first is a quatrain; the second, a tercet; and the third, a quatrain.
Metre:	No set metre or syllable count required.
Rhyme:	*aba*R / *bab* / *aba*R (R stands for the refrain.)
Repetition:	The refrain is the first part of line 1, which is repeated as lines 4 and 11 (R may rhyme with line 2, but this is optional).

Rondeau redoubled

Stanzas:	Six stanzas; the first five are quatrains and the sixth is a quintet.
Metre:	All lines, except for the final shortened refrain, have a common metre or syllable count (the pattern is up to the poet).
Rhyme:	$A^1B^1A^2B^2$ / $babA^1$ / $abaB^1$ / $babA^2$ / $abaB^2$ / $babaR$ (capitals stand for refrain lines and R stands for the repeated half line; numbered capitals, e.g., A^1A^2 represent rhymed, but different refrain lines).
Repetition:	Five refrains, each repeated once; the first quatrain provides the fourth line for each of the next four stanzas; the first part of line 1 is line 5 of the last stanza (and is thus outside the *ab* rhyme scheme).

Rondel

Stanzas:	Three stanzas; the first two are quatrains and the third can be either a quintet or sestet.
Metre:	No set metre or syllable count required, though often the lines are 8 or 10 syllables each.
Rhyme:	*ABba / abAB / abbaA(B)* (Capitals stand for refrain lines.)
Repetition:	Two refrains: the first is line 1, repeated as lines 7 and 13; the second is line 2, repeated as lines 8 and 14 (line 14 is optional).

Triolet

Stanzas:	One octet.
Metre:	Lines are usually iambic trimeter or iambic tetrameter.
Rhyme:	*ABaAabAB* (Capitals stand for refrains.)
Repetition:	The first refrain appears three times as lines 1, 4, 7; the second appears twice as lines 2 and 8, so the pattern becomes: 12315612.

Roundelay

The only requirement is the use of a regularly repeated line or stanza.

JOHN McCRAE (1872–1918)

In Flanders Fields

In Flanders fields the poppies blow
Between the crosses, row on row,
  That mark our place; and in the sky
  The larks, still bravely singing, fly
Scarce heard amid the guns below.

We are the Dead. Short days ago
We lived, felt dawn, saw sunset glow,
  Loved and were loved, and now we lie
    In Flanders fields.

Take up our quarrel with the foe:
To you from failing hands we throw
  The torch; be yours to hold it high.
  If ye break faith with us who die
We shall not sleep, though poppies grow
    In Flanders fields.

COLIN MORTON (b. 1948)

from Three Small Rooms

In this empty room we gather
The reports of all the blind men
Without asking how or whether
In this empty room
These tales of snake or tree or fan
Can be reconciled together.

We mix guesses, lies and half-lies, then
From the ludicrous palaver
Try to sort out truth from lie again
And start the conjuring over
In this empty room.

MARGARET AVISON (1918–2007)

Rondeau Redoublé

Along the endless avenue stand poles.
Divorced from origin, their end's obscure.
There are doors lined up all along these walls.
Some open by the clock, and some immure

No sick child gazing out, but furniture
For dentists, typists, or those crooked halls
To empty lofts lost countrymen endure.
Along the endless avenue stand poles.

Under the negro sun the full tide rolls.
Crowds straggle gradually. There are fewer
By 3 p.m. (with these a pigeon strolls).
Divorced from origin, their end's obscure.

Dark brings the estuary, no vein pure
Enough to bleed freely. Horizon's holes
Fill slowly. Lights. Night's for the amateur.
There are doors lined up all along these walls.

Neons blaze lonelier. The foghorn bawls.
Taxis are knowledgeable now, and sure.
The wary one eyes EXIT. It appals.
(Some open by the clock and some immure
Along the endless avenue).

→→○

ÉMILE NELLIGAN (1879–1941)

Roundel to my Pipe

(translated by P.F. Widdows)

Feet on the fender by firelight,
With glass in hand, good pipe, content,
Let's keep our friendly precedent
And dream alone, this winter night.

Since heaven has grown so virulent,
(As though my troubles were too slight!)
Feet on the fender by firelight,
With glass in hand, let's dream, content.

Soon death, by my presentiment,
Will drag me from this hellish site
To good old Lucifer's; all right!
We'll smoke in that establishment,

Feet on the fender, by firelight.

CHRISTOPHER WISEMAN (b. 1936)

Triolets for Ken

> *The recollection of happiness is no longer happiness.*
> *The recollection of pain is still pain.*
> — from the film *The Secret of Nandy*

1.
Three times a year the nightmare comes again.
Time heals a lot but this appalls me yet —
The plunge off a cliff, terrified, alone.
Three times a year the nightmare comes again.
Down, down, grey sea, sharp rocks, but then no pain
As half way down I wake, caught in some net.
Three times a year this nightmare comes again.
Time heals, they say, but this appalls me yet.

2.
There is no happy music, Schubert said.
We were told before we sang — the cliff, the fall,
His body broken. The oldest of us dead.
There is no happy music, Schubert said,
Though we choirboys went into the church and tried.
Smashed on rocks. The violence filled us all.
There is no happy music, Schubert said.
We heard before we sang. The cliff. The fall.

3.

He collected seabirds' eggs and wanted more.
He little thought he'd wreck my dreams today
As he clambered Bempton cliffs, feeling so sure,
Collecting seabirds' eggs and wanting more.
Shrieking gulls, rocks falling, the sea's huge roar,
His screams — his last song — drowned in that *forte*.
He wanted seabirds' eggs, and wanted more,
And never thought he'd wreck my dreams today.

1945

⊷⟹

ELISE PARTRIDGE (1958–2015)

Vuillard Interior

Against brown walls, the servant bends
over the coverlet she mends —
brown hair, brown flocking, a dun hand
under the lamp, the servant bends
over the coverlet she mends
draped across her broad brown skirts;
knotting, nodding, the servant blends
into the coverlet she mends.

⊷⟹

LESLIE TIMMINS (b. 1955)

Triolet for Afghanistan

> *my country*
> *is a fractured mirror*
> *a continuous fire*
> *a burning garden*
>   — Asadulla Habib

At Kag Khana four boys flee
the peacemakers' war, the Pashtun lord.
Sandflies tear their cheeks, scars seed
at Kag Khana. Four boys flee
across mountains bereft of the grace of trees
that will cast them back
to Kag Khana four shadows to be
peacemakers, lords of war?

MARK ABLEY (b. 1955)

Down

These are the trees chopped down, chopped in a day.
The mahogany stretches from here to St. Eustache.
Teak sprawls even farther in the opposite direction.
Oaks are jostling ginkgos, figs rub up against maples,
date palms disturb the highways; the birchbark is white trash.
These are the trees chopped down, chopped in a day.

These are the trees chopped down, chopped in the night.
I never thought so many walnut logs could fit on the back
of a truck. Now nothing surprises me: not the littered olives,
not the stink of eucalyptus, not even the crumpled
mountains of bamboo. Something lived in a snarl of sumac.
These are the trees chopped down, chopped in the night.

These are the trees chopped down, chopped by the hour.
Tomorrow they'll emerge as plywood, pulp or fire.
A lifetime ago last week they sheltered rainbows in a canopy
or tangled against snow, subarctic bonsai:
willow, larch, arbutus, the chainsawed fruits of desire.
These are the trees chopped down, chopped by the hour.

JANE MUNRO (b. 1943)

In the slow spin of stars, a dancer turns

He wears a tall hat. His arms stretch —
one out, one up. His robes flow.

In the slow spin of stars, a woman sings.
Her voice floats on her breath.
She opens her mouth and words emerge.

In the slow spin of stars, a boat glides.
It rides the currents.
It is made of glass. It carries the sun.

In the slow spin of stars, a yellow dog
lies on the pavement, her nose in her groin.
She is a bitch, a cur. She has tits and pups.

In the slow spin of stars, a tree grows.
Its branches curl up and are wrapped
by two vines. It's a pillar of greenery.

In the slow spin of stars, crystals form
All the elemental glyphs.
Alphabets.

SESTINA

The sestina was invented in medieval Provence by the troubadour Arnaut Daniel.[35] *In The Making of a Poem,* editors Mark Strand and Eavan Boland note that the troubadours often competed with one another to create "the wittiest, most elaborate, most difficult styles" and that the sestina "was the form for a master troubadour." It consists of six unrhymed stanzas of six lines each, followed by a concluding three-line envoy, and features an intriguing pattern of word repetition.

The delight and challenge of the sestina is that the end words of each line in stanza 1 must be repeated in a particular order as the end words in the following stanzas. The envoy contains all six of the repeated words, two in each line, again in a particular order. There was probably once a magical significance to this order, but if so, it appears to have been lost. Daniel Tammet, however, in *Thinking in Numbers,* identifies an intriguing connection to gambling: "A die, as everyone knows, has six faces. The throw of a pair of dice creates a range of outcomes amounting to thirty-six, which is the total number of lines in the poem's six stanzas." He also points out that Marcia Birking and Anne C. Coon, in *Discovering Patterns in Mathematics and Poetry,* "compare the rotation of words in a sestina to the shifting digits in a cyclic number."[36] Perhaps, then, the sestina's magic is rooted in the mysteries of math.

The Comte de Gramont was responsible for the revival of the sestina in France in the nineteenth century. The *New Princeton Encyclopedia of Poetry and Poetics* cites his description of this form as "a reverie in which the same ideas, the same objects, occur to the mind in a succession of different aspects, which nonetheless resemble one another, fluid and changing shape like the clouds in the sky." The invitation to the poet is to keep the clouds moving — to divert the reader from the pervasive presence of the final six words.

---

35   Ron Padget, in *The Teachers & Writers Handbook of Poetic Forms* comments that, "The troubadours were travelling French poet-musicians, some of them noblemen or crusader-knights, who flourished from the end of the eleventh century through the thirteenth century. The female counterparts of the troubadors were called trobairitiz." p. 175.

36   Temmet explains that "Cyclic numbers are related to primes. Division using certain prime numbers (such as 7, 17, 19 and 23) produces decimal sequences (the cyclic numbers) that repeat forever. For example, dividing one by seven (1/7) gives the decimal expansion 1.142857142857142857 … where the six digits 142857 — the smallest cyclic number — continue around and around in a never-ending ring dance." Daniel Temmet, *Thinking in Numbers: On Life, Love, Meaning, and Math* (New York, NY: Little, Brown and Company, 2013) p. 183–186.

This can be done whether adhering to the form or varying it. In "Sestina: Whiskey Canyon" Tanis MacDonald stays true to the sestina pattern, varying only the envoy. She often enjambs lines to give the repetitions a different emphasis or meaning when they reappear ("Dredge the bottom / of her hard-drinking heart" and "She spends beauty's bottom / dollar"). Marilyn Dumont, on the other hand, distracts us from the persistence of the six words by varying the form with a refrain element. This extra repetition in "Fiddle bids us," where the entire last line of one stanza is also the first line of the next, is reminiscent of the repetition in a crown of sonnets (see "Sonnet" chapter).

Sue Wheeler, in "In Juarez," varies the form by using translations and close forms of the Mexican word "Cucaracha," ("cockroaches," "brooches," "roaches," "reaches" and "breaches"). Variety (and diversion) can also be found in her use of inclusive words such as "olive," "alive," and "live." In "Ritual," Sue Chenette introduces yet another variation with what she calls "a disguised sestina." Instead of end words, she uses end categories: tree or tree part, earth, water, creature, body part, and grassy plant.[37] So, for example, the "tree or tree part" becomes "sapling," "maple's crown," "shoots," "leaves," "roots" and "tree."

Poets can also create their own pattern for repeating the end words. Al Purdy, in "Sestina on a Train," simply used the last word of line 6 in one stanza as the last word of line 1 in the next, then kept the remaining end words in the same order, rather than continuing with the traditional sestina pattern.

The sestina is well suited to writing about obsession. Bruce Meyer uses this feverish quality in "The Lovers' Sestina," where the very short lines and incessantly repeating words emphasize the obsessions of a lover. The weaving in and out, back and forth of the six words can create, as in Purdy's sestina, a net in which the reader is caught and from which s/he may run — only to discover, by the time the envoy snaps the net shut, there is no escape.

The traditional form:

Stanza:	Six sestets with a concluding three-line envoy.
Metre:	None required.
Rhyme:	None required.
Repetition:	The concluding words of each line in stanza 1 are repeated in a set pattern in the following stanzas: If the numbers 1, 2, 3, 4, 5, 6 represent the end words in stanza 1, then the pattern for the end words in each

---

37 In correspondence with the editors.

of the next five stanzas (when compared with stanza 1) is: stanza 2: 6-1-5-2-4-3; stanza 3: 3-6-4-1-2-5; stanza 4: 5-3-2-6-1-4; stanza 5: 4-5-1-3-6-2; stanza 6: 2-4-6-5-3-1.

Another way to see the pattern is to compare each stanza with the one preceding it (i.e., stanza 2 with stanza 1, stanza 3 with stanza 2, and so on):

> In this case, if the pattern in stanza 1 is: 1, 2, 3, 4, 5, 6 (where the numbers represent the end words in each line) then, in each of stanzas 2 through 6, the pattern will always be: 6, 1, 5, 2, 4, 3.

> (In other words, as a friend of the editors explained in private correspondence, the pattern is that the line-ending words of one stanza work inward in a 6, 5, 4 and 1, 2, 3 progression from the previous stanza.)

In the envoy, the pattern is 2-5 / 4-3 / 6-1 (where 2, 4, and 6 are used mid-line and 5, 3, 1 are used at line ends) — so the poem finishes with the same word that ends its opening line.

TANIS MACDONALD (b. 1962)

Sestina: Whiskey Canyon

She's fifty, sits tall in the saddle, and owns up
square to the blood vessels she's broken. Her strange
florid beauty. Rosacea breaks like a wave, charm
blooms in truth particles, each spinning atop
another in the fabric of her face. Dredge the bottom
of her hard-drinking heart; you can't dress her down.

Last of the bloody-minded women, she rides down
the crooked canyon every Thursday to stock up
on lipstick and bourbon. She spends beauty's bottom
dollar on fat tubes of hot colours — "Stranger's
Kiss" and "Scarlet Truth" — before she twists the top
off a fifth of JD: her fatal sour-mash charm.

Twice-divorced, she knows third time's a charm
in love and hanging; she has let herself down
off the long rope and climbed over the top
to unknot the noose. But truth, like blood, flies up.
It will spot and stain each word of an estranged
confession. She calls me when she hits rock bottom.

Truth is, last time I rode with her to the bottom
of the gulch she showed her rattlesnake charm.
A diamond-dusted beauty peeled away strange
and hissing into the sage and she jumped down
from her roan and picked the writhing snake up.
She grinned and offered it, but I stayed safe atop

my pinto while she laughed at me. Back at the top
of the arroyo, we danced the Black Bottom
and she drank me under the table and back up
into her bed. Me, I haven't an atom of charm
and the beauty of waking up thirsty and face down
beside her is a truth coloured no less strange

than the diamond skin shifting on that strange
undulating back. On her cabin porch by the cliff top,
six glasses line the rail. It's a whiskey sundown.
Drink up, darling; it'll sweeten you. The bottom
line is, every time, that her true poison is her charm.
Beauty endures but in a bastard life, any way is up.

Because her beauty's low-down, they call her strange
but if the truth calls for a smile, she'll come out on top.
Let's call it a sure-thing copper-bottomed bet: her charm.

BRUCE MEYER (b. 1957)

The Lovers' Sestina

Am I
this song
celebrating you,
each drawn
breath praising
the world?

The world
that I
know, praising
with song,
is drawn
loving you.

Are you
the world
completely drawn,
all I
am, song
for praising?

This praising
that you
call song
is world
enough. I
am drawn,

slowly drawn
to praising
what I
love: you,
the world,
becoming song,
simple song

simply drawn,
a world
where praising
canticles you,
declaring I

am alive, a song of you
drawn from praising
all I know of the world.

MARILYN DUMONT (b. 1955)

Fiddle bids us

The first high call of the fiddle bids us dance
Baits with its first pluck and saw of the bow
Reels us, feet flick-fins to its lure and line
Steady second fiddle stoking the fire below
our red river jig and step-dance will witness
that we long kissed this earth with our feet

that we long kissed this earth with our feet
before the surveyors executed their dance
of lines and stakes at the corners to witness
the Dominion's decree to leave just fiddle and bow
and no quarter sections to bury our relatives below
because we resisted the government's line

because we resisted the government's line
we will now dance and speak with our feet
our provisional council will guide us from below
their suffering and sacrifice renewed our dance
our single-minded celebration of the fiddle and bow
will continue for generations to be our witness

will continue for generations to be our witness
when politics and greed try to twist our lines
we'll begin to jig to fiddle and bow
when the fiddler arrives we'll vote with our feet
we, the improvident ones proclaim our dance
to the ministers and lords who tried to set us below

to the ministers and lords who tried to set us below
our well documented petitions will be our witness
when Imperial powers elect to perform their dance
the "greasy rebels" and "unhung felons"[38] will not fall in line
because the Metis forever more will vote with their feet
now that the Dominion has left us with fiddle and bow

now that the Dominion has left us with fiddle and bow
who will call the dance, but our ancestors below
who have directed us to vote with our feet
Drops of Brandy and the Reel of Eight will witness
How we generated our own steps and lines
Without permission from the National dance

Dance bow   Line below   Witness feet

⇥

SUE WHEELER (b. 1942)

In Juarez

This is the girl's first nightclub, in Juarez.
Kids can get in anywhere in border
towns, the trinketed streets and make-you-sick water.
Wide-hat musicians blare "La Cucaracha."
The father buys the girl a Shirley Temple and aims
his gin-soaked toothpick at an olive.

---

38 Joseph Howard, *Strange Empire: Louis Riel and the Métis People* (Toronto, ON: James, Lewis & Samuel, 1952), p. 41.

This afternoon they passed alleys alive
with rats and the souvenirs of Juarez,
hands slapping tortillas and hands held out for alms,
the gold cloth, a saint's knuckle stitched in its border
where anyone can kiss it, cockroaches,
bandits, and do the local people drink the water?

Fault of the Pope. That's what her
father says. The band cranks it up for the live
floor show, sequins and shimmying brooches.
The marquee said "Bestest dancers de Juarez!"
a fraction the price of shows across the border,
and look! — one is the girl's double, there, by the potted palms.

Rhinestones river her look-alike arms.
Her hairdo is the very same ducktail, slicked with water.
Same smile, eyes, colour. (Everyone is brown this side the border.)
If the girl learned Spanish could she live
here? Would she fit right in, in Juarez,
ignoring for the moment the roaches?

She stares and wonders. The music reaches
its climax — maracas, a windmill of arms.
The father, who looks a little like the hero Benito Juarez,
holds his hand up to call the waiter.
The twin's bare back cha-chas toward the rest of her life.
In childish Spanish, the father gives his order.

A dried-up riverbed patrols the border.
Rifles and chainlink, uncountable breaches.
Are there, then, a number of possible lives?
Holes in the expected, like magic charms?
Whisha-whish go the dusty palms. *Answers are water.*
The girl sips the night-sugar taste of Juarez.

Dinner arrives on the arms of the waiter.
The father reaches for his *cabrito*, specialty of Juarez.
Life, whispers the sweating glass at the drink's sweet border.

⊶⊐◝

FRED COGSWELL (1917–2004)

The Edge

The old fear of the dark has not returned
For fifty years. It perished the last year
Of my boyhood one evening when I
Heard — hunting for moths at the woodland edge —
A swishing noise from just behind my head
And fled through moonlit fields with panic speed.

I could not outrun it. Despite my speed
The thing I heard grew louder till I turned
Suddenly and my straw hat fell off my head.
I realized then the fearful sound my ear
Had caught was merely that hat's broad-brimmed edge
On my shoulders. The monster? It was I.

And then beneath the moon's sardonic eye
I homeward sauntered at a decent speed,
Knowing at last where the nerve-prickling edge
Of my terror lay. It was I who'd turned
The dark into a nightmare land of fear
And the real *loup-garou* was in my head.

With fear of darkness went the very head
And heart of my intimate delight. I
No longer found the quest for moths a dear
And sharp enjoyment as I bade God-speed
To the relief that came when horrors turned
Out to be moth wings at the wood's dark edge.

Perhaps I simplify, but still the edge
Where fear and hope meet — whether in the head
Or not — is the one space on which are turned
Most masterworks, though dread for sanity
Impels us with worldly wisdom's speed
To change heaven and hell for a safer sphere.

Today I mourn the conquest of my fear
Even as my life slips closer to the ledge
From which one day this routine self will speed
I know not where. I wish that to my head
That wild boy's madness had again returned
To conjure phantoms in the night's dark eye.

As boy, I turned my head from hope and fear.
Now, safe too long, I cannot find the edge
Where the wolf-eyes gleam and frail moth wings speed.

-⋅≍⊃

SUE CHENETTE (b. 1942)

Ritual

All summer I've watered your maple sapling,
spindly bole in a new-mounded collar of earth.
I plant puddled footprints at the river's edge,
squat to fill a bucket, scatter minnows
with my small commotion, then, arm out for balance,
tramp up the bank through brush and waist-high grasses.

In the sunny back and forth a stem of purple loosestrife
might catch my thought ... or the maple's crown
bent toward the river. Grasses mat under my feet.
At the tree's base I tilt the bucket and watch soil
darken, each time a wider ring. Dog-walkers
pass on the path, mallards on the slow current.

Seven years since you died. You walked by this river
in your good times, when you visited, scanned the weeds
for muskrats. Once you saw a great blue heron.
Even when darkness branched in you, pushed shoots
into each thought, you were eased seeing an oak in a field,
clouds of birds settled with beating wings.

Belatedly I've chosen a memorial, this tree, muscled
into spring ground by a city crew. *Soak it,*
they said, *enough so water stands in the dirt saucer.*
I hadn't counted on that — weekly ritual of reeds
and river, lift or droop of leaves.
Once, the current I stirred drew a crayfish

from under its rock. I remembered my brother saw a beetle
and knew it was you, visiting, with an iridescent green back.
I couldn't accept such solace, your death like twisted roots
still buried in me, closed off, tears sealed up
with questions that spiral and cling like bindweed.
I didn't ask them, as I crossed the hard ground

between river and maple in fresh-dug sod.
But I've felt an ease in my physical self,
something soothed in hours among wild phlox
and alder brush that left fine scratches on my knees
while my arm grew stronger with the sloshing pail,
a ring of grass greened round your tree.

I think you'd like the fall colors across the river —
and that crayfish that scutters in the rocks and mud —
here, where, pail in hand, I've worn a grassy path.

AL PURDY (1918–2000)

Sestina on a Train

I've always been going somewhere — Vancouver
or old age or somewhere ever sinceI can remember:
and this woman leaning over me, this madwoman
while I was sleeping, whispering, "Do you take drugs?"
And the sight of her yellow-white teeth biting
the dark open wide and white eyes like marbles

children play with but no children play with marbles
like those — saying, "Do you take drugs?" And Vancouver
must be somewhere near this midnight I can't remember
where tho only the sister holding the madwoman,
fighting her: me saying stupidly, "No, no drugs."
She wanting to talk and sitting there biting

at something I couldn't see what the hell she was biting,
only her white eyes like aching terrible marbles
and mouth crying out, "I don't want to go to Vancouver!
Don't let them take me!" She didn't remember
the sad scared children, children of the madwoman
herself, recognized only me the stranger, asking what drugs

I took and wouldn't stop asking that. What such drugs
do besides closing those eyes and keeping those teeth from biting
that tongue into rags and soothing a forehead damp as marble's
cold stone couldn't be altogether bad eh? All the way to Vancouver
where I was going and thought I could remember
having lived once I comforted the madwoman

while the sister minded her frightened children: madwoman,
courtesan, mother, wife, in that order. Such drugs
as I know of don't cause this snapping and biting
at shadows or eyes like glaring lacustral marbles
and mouth crying, "Don't let them take me to Vancouver!"
And leaning her head on my shoulder's scared calm . . . I remember

now the promise I made and do not wish to remember
going somewhere and falling asleep on the train and the madwoman
shakes me softly awake again and, "Yes, I do take drugs,"
I say to her and myself: "I get high on hemp and peyote biting
at scraps of existence I've lost all the smoky limitless marbles
I found in my life once lost long before Vancouver —"

I've forgotten that child, his frantic scratching and biting
for something he wanted and lost — but it wasn't marbles.
I remember the Mountie waiting, then the conductor's "Vancouver next! Vancouver!"

⋆⇒

SONNET

"Rhetorically it's a genius little nugget. You build, build, turn, pirouette, and you're out!" — Sina Queyras[39]

Jorge Luis Borges has said, "there is something mysterious about the sonnet,"[40] and perhaps there is no more logical explanation for this form's power and longevity.

The sonnet was created early in the thirteenth century by Giacomo da Lentino, a notary in the court of Emperor Frederick II in Sicily. Based on a Sicilian folk song, the name derives from the Italian, *sonetto*, for "little sound" or "little song." The Italian sonnet was revolutionary in its time, written in the popular local language (Italian rather than Latin) and intended for individual silent reading rather than public performance. In his book, *The Birth of the Modern Mind: Self, Consciousness, and the Invention of the Sonnet*, Paul Oppenheimer concludes that the sonnet was the first lyric form of "self-consciousness."[41] In a sonnet, writers — and readers — were, for the first time in European poetry, encouraged to think for themselves.

There was another bonus. Until this time in Europe, under the code of courtly love, the dominant style of poetry was derived from the French troubadours. Strictly for the upper classes, it consisted of lyrics that allowed a man (but rarely a woman) to praise, but not to persuade, a lover. The sonnet offered a solution to both exclusions. Here was a poem of only fourteen lines that was both persuasive and emotionally charged, that could easily be slipped into a waiting hand. Not only were women among the earliest writers of sonnets, but the form encouraged both women and men of all stations to communicate directly without having to know Latin. The power of the new form for both thinking and feeling, for exploring any subject matter — love, politics, religion ... — presented a threat to the powers-that-be.

By the late sixteenth century, most poets in Europe were writing sonnets; as Marilyn Hacker says in *An Exaltation of Forms*, "they were the rap music of the day," and poets have never stopped exploring their potential.[42] Poet Phillis Levin nicely sums up the sonnet's essence when she calls it "a chamber of

39 Sina Queyras, "To Sonnet, To Son-net, TusconNet" (March 9, 2010), www.poetryfoundation.org/harriet/2010/03/page/3/ (accessed September 2015).

40 Jorge Luis Borges, in Edward Hirsch, *How to Read a Poem And Fall in Love with Poetry* (San Diego, New York, London: Harvest, 1999), p. 311.

41 Paul Oppenheimer, *The Birth of the Modern Mind*, Preface, p. vii.

42 Annie Finch and Kathrine Varnes, eds., *An Exaltation of Forms*, p. 300

sudden change."[43] Both the Italian and English sonnets achieve this essence by following a particular structure.

Italian (Petrarchan)

The Italian sonnet, developed by Dante and especially Petrarch (therefore often called Petrarchan), features an opening eight-line stanza (octave) that presents and develops a situation. This is followed by a closing six-line stanza (sestet) that offers a response to the octave — often a resolution to a dilemma. This shift in content occurs at the end of the octave or beginning of the sestet and is known as the turn (volta), which may or may not be represented by a blank line. It uses five rhymes and is most often (in English) in iambic pentameter. In the first eight lines the rhyme scheme is *abbaabba*; in the last six, it is some variation of *cdecde*. (In English, the *abba* pattern is called envelope rhyme; in Italian, *rima baciata* or "kissing rhyme.")

There has been some debate around the mysterious popularity of the Italian form in particular. Some argue that it has to do with its mathematical beauty and proportion, and that da Lentino deliberately chose the eight- and six-line divisions to correspond to the Pythagorean-Platonic theory of numbers and the "harmonic" proportion of certain numbers including Pythagoras' Golden Mean.[44] In this, the form perhaps echoes some of the mystery of the order of the sestina.

English (Shakespearean)

Sir Thomas Wyatt introduced the sonnet to England and the Earl of Surrey modified the rhyme scheme, increasing the number of rhyming words from five to seven to better suit the rhyming possibilities of the English language. The traditional English (or Shakespearean, after its most famous practitioner) sonnet is written in iambic pentameter. It has three, four-line stanzas rhyming *abab cdcd efef* and a concluding couplet rhyming *gg*. Generally, the first twelve lines present a situation (often exploring a theme from three different perspectives) and a turn leading into a couplet that comments on or offers a summation of the opening stanzas.

As befits a radical form, the sonnet has numerous significant variations including:

* *Miltonic*, named after poet John Milton
* *Spenserian*, developed by the Elizabethan, Edmund Spenser

---

43 Phillis Levin, *The Penguin Book of the Sonnet: 900 Years of a Classic Tradition in English*, p. xxxvii.
44 Ibid., p. xli–xliii.

- *Jackpine*, invented by Milton Acorn
- *curtal*, developed by Gerard Manley Hopkins
- *crown of sonnets*
- *sonnet redoubled*, a longer version of the crown
- *terza rima sonnet*

Canadians have played a part in this rich tradition, from following closely in the established form, as Alexandra Oliver does in "Meeting the Tormentors in Safeway," to creating variations, as when W.H. New, in "Acoustics," uses seven rhymed couplets that echo each other both in sound and sense ("Listen: when the summer sun began / "Lesson one: December will begin") to Milton Acorn's Jackpine sonnet, which "… has a basic form, yes, but grows to any shape that suits the light, suits the winds, suits itself."[45]

Diana Brebner's "The Golden Lotus" is an English sonnet presented or (as Stephanie Bolster suggests in *Arc* 51) "disguised" as couplets. John Reibetanz' "Head and Torso of the Minotaur" is a paired sonnet written in blank verse (unrhymed iambic pentameter) that opens and closes with the same line. Herménégilde Chiasson's bilingual "Apollo at Aberdeen" is an Italian sonnet written in alexandrine lines of six strong stresses each, the English adaptation of the traditional twelve-syllable metre in French verse. Milton Acorn and Ken Babstock return to the Miltonic tradition of political commentary, loosely applying the essence of a traditional form to contemporary issues.

Mary Dalton draws on the *Dictionary of Newfoundland English* to write an unrhymed sonnet, "Flirrup," in Newfoundland's unique folk vernacular. As Stephen Burt and David Mikics point out in *The Art of the Sonnet*,[46] Dalton's division of the poem into indoor and outdoor, present and future, actual and imagined, correspond to the traditional Italian sonnet's division into octave and sestet. Sandy Shreve's crown of sonnets retains the traditional repetition pattern but uses a terza rima stanza and rhyme scheme and accentual metre, rather than accentual-syllabic.

---

45 Milton Acorn, *Jackpine Sonnets* (Toronto, ON: Steel Rail Educational Publishing, 1977), found online at: http://www.geist.com/contests/jackpine-sonnet-contest/jackpine-sonnet-campaign/ (accessed October 2015).
46 Stephen Burt and David Mikics, eds., *The Art of the Sonnet*.

The traditional form:

Italian (Petrarchan)

Stanza:	Two stanzas, an octave and a sestet.
Metre:	Iambic pentameter.
Rhyme:	*abbaabba cdecde* (the *cdecde* pattern can be varied).
Repetition:	None required.
Distinguishing feature:	A turn or resolution (volta), often marked by a blank space, separates the octave and the sestet.

Miltonic (variation of the Italian)
As the Italian (above) but delays or omits the volta

English (Shakespearian)

Stanza:	Three quatrains and a concluding couplet.
Metre:	Iambic pentameter.
Rhyme:	*abab cdcd efef gg*
Repetition:	None required.
Distinguishing feature:	Ends with a closing (often epigrammatic) couplet.

Spencerian (variation of the English)
As the English (above) but with an *abab bcbc cdcd ee* rhyme scheme.

Terza rima (variation of the English)
As the English (above) but with an *aba bcb cdc ded ee* rhyme scheme.

Jackpine

Stanza:	Varies, but usually anywhere from 12 to 20 lines; stanza lengths, up to the poet.
Metre:	Can vary, but ideally between 7 and 13 syllables.

Rhyme:	The pattern is up to the poet.
Repetition:	None required.
Distinguishing feature:	Flexible application of traditional formal elements, but must include some of them.

Curtal

Stanza:	One eleven-line stanza, the last line being a short line, or two stanzas of 6 and 4 lines with a final short line.
Metre:	Can vary.
Rhyme:	*abcabc dbcd c*
Repetition:	None required.
Distinguishing feature:	A truncated sonnet.

Crown of Sonnets (also called corona, chained or linked)
Stanza, metre and rhyme: The same as the Italian, (above).

Repetition:	Seven sonnets, the last line of each one repeated as the first line of the next; the first line of the first sonnet is repeated as the last line of the last one.
Distinguishing feature:	Seven sonnets featuring a specific repetition pattern (above).

Sonnet Redoubled

As the crown of sonnets (above) but fifteen poems, the final sonnet consisting of the repeated lines of the previous poems, in the same order of appearance.

ALEXANDRA OLIVER (b. 1970)

Meeting the Tormentors in Safeway

They all had names like Jennifer or Lynne
or Katherine; they all had bone-blonde hair,
that wet, flat cut with bangs. They pulled your chair
from underneath you, shoved their small fists in
your face. Too soon, you knew it would begin,
those minkish teeth like shrapnel in the air,
the Bacchic taunts, the Herculean dare,
their soccer cleats against your porcine shin,
that laugh, which sounded like a hundred birds
escaping from a gunshot through the reeds —
and now you have to face it all again:
the joyful freckled faces lost for words
in supermarkets, as those red hands squeeze
your own. *It's been so long!* They say. Amen.

HERMÉNÉGILDE CHIASSON (b. 1946)

Apollo at Aberdeen

(translated by Jo-Anne Elder & Fred Cogswell)

quelqu'un m'a dit que tu n'écris plus qu'en anglais
I wonder if you do write about the same things
using new words to say the same old and sad meanings
les mots on pris d'autres tournures qu'en français

je suis trop lin sans doute pour me défaire l'oreille
credit cards sing they come and go but you will scream
in your own way even if their music fills your dream
j'entends ta voix intraduisible demain la veille

je me revois le jour où j'ai appris à lire
la lumière défonçait l'espace de ma prison
how far we came along yet I can hardly hear

prison is the same word in both languages you say
je sais mais maintenant je parle de la maison
de quoi parlerons-nous quand vous me visiterez

KENNETH LESLIE (1892–1974)

from By Stubborn Stars

1

The silver herring throbbed thick in my seine,
silver of life, life's silver sheen of glory;
my hands, cut with the cold, hurt with the pain
of hauling the net, pulled the heavy dory,
heavy with life, low in the water, deep
plunged to the gunwale's lips in the stress of rowing,
the pulse of rowing that puts the world to sleep,
world within world endlessly ebbing, flowing.
At length you stood on the landing and you cried,
with quick low cries you timed me stroke on stroke
as I steadily won my way with the fulling tide
and crossed the threshold where the last wave broke
and coasted over the step of water and threw
straight through the air my mooring line to you.

DIANA BREBNER (1956–2001)

from The Golden Lotus

"The pears fatten like little buddhas."
— Sylvia Plath, *The Manor Garden*

1. The Golden Lotus

We are always surprised that pears survive
so far north. Driving north, we watch the day

shrink in trees. It's behind us. We arrive.
Will it always be difficult to say:

I love you: caught at the cabin door, latch
unhooked? Yes, there are pears on the tree. And

a dead mouse in the sink. Bright fish to catch,
like kisses, in a lonely heaven. Hand

in hand. First things first. We go down the grass
stairway to the water. This is the blue

I would die for, the colour of tenderness,
and your forgiveness. Fish jump: silver, new.

In blue lakes, the golden lotus appears.
We sink our teeth into the yellow pears.

⟶══◎

JOHN REIBETANZ (b. 1944)

Head and Torso of the Minotaur

1. Theseus at the Heart of the Labyrinth

The monster and the sacrifice are one,
the weapon anchored in the skull that bred it.
The first secret the hero has unearthed
disturbs him least — the torso of a woman
charging under the maned, snorting head.
His eye reads all as bestial, takes for proof
ripe breasts made monstrous by the drying blood.
The second will drive dream to sacrifice;
yet, only when their ship ties up at Naxos
does he take in what flickered by too quickly
as he plunged the horn into the skull's fountain.
Beyond the end of Ariadne's silk,
the snout's black nostrils, the jowl's slobbered fur:
eyes — human, hers, and anchored in them, his.

2. Ukrainian Miner Rescued from Underground Explosion

Only the eyes say human, the trunk and arms
speechless with animality, immured
in their caked hide, the head a clay melon
sprouting furry leafage. The eyes' thick lids
speak a familiar language of exhaustion;
and we can read the panic flaring from
the bloodshot whites, their anguish at the snarl
that has escaped from the ranged teeth where lips
once smiled, because our greed created this
slide into bestiality. Our will
to power carved his subterranean lair
and drove him down the scale of evolution
into a rubble-filled labyrinth where
the monster and the sacrifice are one.

YVONNE BLOMER (b. 1970)

In the box from the World Wildlife Fund

there is the last Polar Bear.
In the belly of the box, the bear's
hollow high-strung heart
rhythmed in plush down,
a stroke of a black frown
for what melts and what is dead.

The boy's blonde-shod head hangs
off his bed. He sleeps and snores,
his toes curl his fingers slacken straight.

The boy, his skin white under the lantern
of Ursa's light.

W.H. NEW (b. 1938)

Acoustics

Listen: when the summer sun began
      Lesson one: December will begin.
warming earth and air and every bud,
      worms will eat, and errant winds forbid
all creation dressed in sudden wonder;
      eloquence. Predestined sullen winter;
high up in the cherry orchards, white
      who appreciates its icy white
blossom sets, day approaches noon,
      blast, its adze-grey reaches? No-one.
crickets leap, chirp, chatter, and repeat:
      Cracked lips, sharp shattering retreat.
listen to the summer take its easing.
      Lesson two: remember echo's season.

MARY DALTON

"Flirrup"

Fairy squalls on the water.
I'm marooned at the window,
Waiting for the fog man,
Sewing the old black veil.
The Walls of Troy on the floor.
There's Dickey just gone up
The road in a red shirt. He's
Sure not the fog man —
Traipsing along with the swagger
Of a swiler in the spring fat.
Not a feather out of him.
Now he'd be the one to have in
For a feed of fresh flippers,
A taste of my fine figgy cake.

MILTON ACORN (1923–1986)

Pigs

Truck's painted red, sun yellow, pigs quite pink
From sunburn — I wouldn't be surprised:
It being precious little they get
Of wind and sun. Now here's this jolly trip.
Never mind . . . They don't feel burnt yet
And never will — the way things are set.

So far they've been well kept by the man;
Confined, but otherwise done much good by
Nourishing meals, delivered right on time.
Now comes this surprise . . . A world to scan
While they zip through it. There's another sky
Higher and brighter than above their pen.

Filling their eyes with nearness and distance;
Two of them stand up, almost like men —
Balancing by forelegs on top of the cab;
Like the Cabot Brothers, gazing wide ahead.
It's for this they were bred, born, doctored, fed.

⊶⇒

Ken Babstock (b. 1970)

from SIGINT

And it is evening already, so swollen.
Suppose one rips up the blue, one takes
away the quiet, the pealing

in the ears, and is ashamed of something.
No, but … There … I have just thrown
the feeling into your mouth. Now you tell it.

Perhaps you truly don't own it but it's
in your mouth now so take it
for a walk

past radomes, damask, reel-to-reel,
the analysts of Virginia under
whatever vector this year's probe is re-entering on.

May 3, 1989, at 08:20, not far from Tyumen. Altitude unknown at time of incident.

⊷⇨

Sandy Shreve (b. 1950)

Whisper Songs

"… there is a phenomenon called the "whisper song" in which the bird sings almost inaudibly, as though in the back of its throat, so quietly that one must be very close in order to hear it."
— John A. Livingston (Rogue Primate)

1.
An ordinary draft disturbs the curtain,
lets morning whisper in, a brief surprise —
sunlight wavers, then goes out again,

a candle snuffed, another shuttered eye
and day descends weighted with regret.
More cloud, more cold; rain turns to flurries

turn to rain — even the weather forgets
what it's supposed to do. Voices scramble
into the room, the news a breakfast of threats

I wish I could ignore. Listen to the babble
and destruction pouring in, the gossip and thunder,
the conviction. I'd rather sweet nothings — fragile

vows, nonsense words, the lust of love-birds,
the hustle of buds bursting the seams of winter.

2.
The hustle of buds bursting the seams of winter,
a dream away — these days reluctant stubs
of their summer selves. Chimney-smoke lingers,

the air sweet-scented with indifference. A mob
flaps at the feeder, another squabble in the chill
drags on. (What whisper songs?) Seeds like crumbs

from the table of unlikely gods are trampled and spill,
attracting mice — and mice find all the flaws
in our foundation. We poison them. A little

life is taken just because it crawled
to us for shelter — and we are not ashamed,
refill the feeder because we want to be awed

by finches and chickadees, their antics, the untamed
feasting outside our window, unafraid.

3.
Feasting outside our window, unafraid
though a merlin lives nearby, sparrows festoon
the bamboo, preen their muted plumage and wait

their turn the way we wait for change. In the woods
sap begins to run, a sure sign. Spring thaw
always starts with a trickle. It dawdles, then pools

in our hearts, hope tiptoeing in to sprawl
on the couch — an old friend who never left.
When the cold snap comes hope fades as fast as the hawk

snatches food. Somehow I never expect
a varied thrush in its talons. From the brambles, a clamour
in the key of grief, a slight shudder when the breath-

less wind settles. Hidden in Douglas firs
a flicker clings to the bark and starts to hammer.

4.
A flicker clings to the bark and starts to hammer
in a language we think we understand. The tempo
insists we listen again, dares us to measure

the space between each beat, imagine echoes
that live there. Out of the shadows, a coyote appears,
a grey hesitation. She holds something in her yellow

stare, poised on the periphery where need meets fear
and contemplates. The flicker changes his tune
to laughter — the song, a haunted mockery piercing

the air, mocking the coyote's indecision
or mocking mine. Then the coyote, in one smooth leap,
leaps over thorns into the afternoon.

Above the garden long since gone to seed,
overcast hours drift on, seamlessly.

5.
Overcast hours drift on, seamlessly
shifting tenses. A wayward breath is intent
on shaking loose the silver gleam we see

in the drop that clings to a leaf — the not yet
and the irrepressible now. The wait for a wish
almost granted; the song in a whispered moment

almost heard. Perhaps I've grown deaf to riffs
floating over my head, euphonious hymns
from a world beyond my eager reach, my stiff

wings. Far off, two bald eagles hem
a ragged cloud, then ride thermals — feather
and wind, adrift and dreaming, carry them

into the infinite. When they return they offer
no answer, only an elegant will to endure.

6.
No answer. Only an elegant will to endure
where anything can happen (and soon). We know
too much and too little to rely on gestures

toward faith we keep making. (A prayer said, *sotto
voce*, against aggression; then after it happens,
the vigil, a crowd gathered in darkness, holding

hands and candles.) A wing-beat before sundown,
the feral world around me seems to retreat
in the last light, a quiet so intimate even

rooks rephrase their accusations, their bleak
prophecies — though the roost is in the crosshairs
of survey crews and planners. Who will speak

up for troublesome crows, when all across
the city, rush hour idles at the crossroads …

7.
City rush hour idles at the crossroads,
a grey hesitation filled with echoes, imagined
and real, incantations from restless shadows

where a coyote stands in the rain. As night beckons
to fragile, *sotto voce* vows, a delicate
light wavers around neglected questions

in the irrepressible now. In the not yet,
an eagle and hawk drift toward spring thaw
while unlikely gods pause to contemplate

the reluctant heart — how it can still be awed
watching sparrows feast, undeterred.
Bursting through seams of indifference, today at dawn

a whispered song was sung (and almost heard) when
an ordinary draft disturbed the curtain.

⊶⟹

Spoken Word

In virtually every culture, poetry began as an oral form, often accompanied by an instrument such as the drum or lyre. Long before the invention of paper or the printing press, poets preserved and passed on local stories, news, genealogy, survival tips, spiritual, religious and healing practices, and information about proper interactions with nature. They spoke, sang or chanted them, using metre, rhyme, repetition, music and gesture as memory aides.

In a recent essay, Sheri-D Wilson points out the breadth of spoken word's oral tradition, from "the Griots, the Bards, the Seanchai, /the First Nations, the Azmari, / the Minstrels, Skalds, Scops, Rhapsodists, and the Ashiks, / the Balladeers, Troubadours, and the Taliesins. // From Aristotle and the Greeks, … continuing through the Beats.[47]

Only after the invention of the printing press did poetry begin to appear in written form. But even as reading on the page became more prevalent, poetry continued to be performed aloud, and some poetic forms such as ballad, blues, incantation and madrigal continue to rely particularly heavily on sound for their full impact. In recent decades, however, there has been a growing spoken word movement, which again emphasizes poetry's roots in oral performance.

With this re-emergence of the oral tradition there has also come some overlap in terminology. Spoken word is probably the best overall term to include sound, performance, dub and slam. All are tuned more or less directly to music — to the rise and fall of the voice, to what dub poet Lillian Allen calls the "emotional embodiment" of the poet's intention.[48] As Wilson says, spoken word is written — and read — "through the eye of the orator," as if it were a theatre script.[49] Poets also often stress that the form is not separate from its social activist content. Perhaps it's appropriate that this new/old comer to form is a shape-shifter, difficult to define. Music, dance, audio poetry (created for recording), video poetry and especially the electronic arts, have all been a part of what Hilary Peach calls this "hybrid" form, "born in the intertidal zone between text and sound."[50] It's interesting that one of the most popular and classic of English forms, the sonnet, also came out of a spirit of resistance and a return to the popular voice.

Many contemporary poetic (as well as musical) forms also emerged directly from the African oral tradition that arrived in the Caribbean and North America

---

47 Sheri-D Wilson, "A Lyric Essay: Spoken Word Variations," in *Arc Poetry Magazine* (Fall 2015), p. 116–117.
48 In private conversation with the editors.
49 In private conversation with the editors.
50 In private correspondence with the editors.

with enslaved peoples in the nineteenth century. In her essay, "Black Voice — Context and Subtext," Allen says African oral forms crystallized in New York City around 1918 with the Harlem Renaissance movement that asserted — in the face of white racism and stereotypes of "the Negro" — there was, in fact, a rich Black culture of the arts. But it wasn't until the 1970s that this culture exploded, largely out of the impoverished South Bronx area of New York. Here again, spoken word has a strong element of protest and an appeal for social justice.[51]

Sound

Traditionally an emphasis on regular rhythm and rhyme was one of the marks of incantation (see Incantation chapter). But in the 1970s, four poets — Paul Dutton, Rafael Barreto-Rivera, Steve McCaffery and bp Nichol, calling themselves The Four Horsemen — introduced a more dramatic form of sound and performance to Canadian poetry. Dutton says sound poetry "is *not* simply poetry where the sounds of the words matter more than their meaning, which is a feature of all kinds of poems. It is, in its strictest definition, poetry that doesn't use words at all, but sounds."[52] Nonetheless, The Four Horsemen's work often incorporated some words. Performance poet bill bissett (who Wilson calls "the grandfather of Canadian spoken word") says, "in th crib uv kours we ar all dewing sound poetree."[53] Dutton holds that the roots of sound poetry lie in the nonsense lyrics of folk songs, speaking in tongues (glossolalia), Scottish and Inu mouth music and Indian solkatu (orally rendered drum rhythms), but that the current movement of sound poetry emerged again out of France and Germany in the 1950s, then spread across Europe, Russia and North America.

Dub

Dub emerged directly from a musical tradition that included musicians like Bob Marley calling for social justice ("Get up, stand up: stand up for your rights!").[54] Lillian Allen, who established the Dub Poets Collective in Toronto, describes dub as having, in addition to the "regular and traditional attributes of 'poetry', recognizable image, evocative language, metaphor, simile, assonance, etc." Dub poetry is specifically performance based, "playing with different aspects of

---

51   Lillian Allen quotations are from "Black Voice — Context and Subtext," The Anne Szu-
      migalski Memorial Lecture, *Prairie Fire* (Winter 2014-15, Vol. 35, No. 4).
52   Paul Dutton, in Sheri-D Wilson, ed., *The Spoken Word Workbook: inspiration from poets who
      teach* (Calgary, Banff: The Calgary Spoken Word Society and The Banff Centre Press.
53   bill bissett, in *The Spoken Word Workbook*, Ibid., p. 13.
54   Bob Marley and Pete Tosh, "Get up, stand up."

'sounding' for effect." This is clear when you read Allen's poem, "Nellie Belly Swelly," a powerful indictment of the rape of a thirteen-year-old that stands out on the page but is even more powerful in performance.

Slam

Out of these oral forms evolved the poetry slam, a competition in which poets read or recite their work and are judged by the audience. The first slams took place in the 1980s in the US, and they have become a regular feature in several Canadian cities including Halifax, Montreal, Toronto, Calgary and Vancouver.

The traditional form:

Stanza: Any number of lines or stanzas of any length.

Metre: Usually has a strong, regular beat.

Rhyme: Usually has a strong rhyming element.

Repetition: The pattern and devices used for rhythmic and insistent repetition are up to the poet; this form is most poignant when spoken, chanted or performed aloud.

Distinguishing feature: Uses silence and space to create a particularly dramatic effect in performance.

The challenge of presenting spoken word on the page is obvious: it's an oral form meant to be heard in performance. Below, in addition to a few examples of spoken-word poems as they appear on the page, are several we found on You-Tube by Canadian spoken word artists (listed alphabetically and including some of the earliest), in performance. These, and many more, can be found online:

- bissett, bill: "time"
- Davina, Dia: "U-Haul"
- Evanson, Tanya: [untitled] at Calgary Spoken Word 2013
- Fannon: "Elevator Conundrum"
- French, Ian: "Outdated"
- Joseph, Clifton: "Slo Mo"
- Karasick, Adeena: "Messy Necessity"
- Kellough, Kaie: "Alphabet"
- Kidd, Cat: "the Lottery"
- Koyczan, Shane: "Troll"
- L'Hirondelle, Cheryl: [untitled] at Calgary Spoken Word 2008 Event #10
- Peach, Hilary: "Hey Short Britches"
- The Four Horsemen: [sound poetry]
- Young, D'Bi: "anitafrika: We women are warriors"

LILLIAN ALLEN (b. 1951)

Listen to this poem at www.lillianallen.ca *on audio free download.*

Nellie Belly Swelly

Nellie was thirteen
don't care 'bout no fellow
growing in the garden
among the wild flowers

she Mumma she dig & she plant
nurtures her sod
tends her rose bush
in the garden pod

lust leap the garden fence
pluck the rose bud
bruk it ina the stem

oh no please no
was no self defence
oh no please no
without pretence
offered no defence
to a little little girl
called Nellie

Nellie couldn't understand
Mr. Thompson's hood
so harsh, so wrong
in such an offensive

Nellie plead, Nellie beg
Nellie plead, Nellie beg
but Mr. Thompson's hood
went right through her legs

knowing eyes blamed her

Nellie disappeared from sight
news spread wide
as the months went by
psst psst psst Nellie belly swelly
Nellie belly swelly Nellie belly swelly
children skipped to Nellie's shame

Nellie returned from the night
gave up her dolls
and the rose bush died
Nellie Momma cried Nellie Momma cried
little Nellie no more child again

No sentence was passed
on this menacing ass
who plundered Nellie's childhood

In her little tiny heart
Nellie understood war

She mustered an army within her
strengthened her defence
and mined the garden fence

No band made a roll
skies didn't part
for this new dawn
in fact, nothing heralded it
when this feminist was born

ANDREA THOMPSON (b. 1967)

Listen to this poem at www.andreathompson.ca

One

Holographic ambassadors
microcosmic metaphors
prismatic reflections
of the essence at the core

one
we are — all
nothing less
nothing more.

Cataclysmic, the division
unnatural disaster of racism
like a nuclear explosion
our one heart, split apart
anger, an understandable outcome.

But when anger replaces reason
we start the cycle all over again.

Vengeance is dance that has no end
instead turns in, confusion begins
implosion of thought when logic is lost.

Psycho-logical police state
guns and violence
follow like a blood stain.

Hate can't heal a community
dig a little deeper G
your soul, not your skin,
holds the key that you need
to unlock the door to
your spiritual identity.

Take a tip from the prophets
Buddha, Krishna, Jesus, Mohammed
each came to teach us
the purpose of this earth trip
is learning how to love —

absolutely everybody.

Embrace the sacred irony
find the space in your heart that is moved
by the music of humans in unity.

Place faith in the path
of tolerance and patience

tame the temptation
to judge one another

replace looking outward
with looking in the mirror.

As a woman of colour
I know — in the future
everyone will look like me
but this isn't about genetic history.

This poem comes from a well spring way down deep
from the drum of the universal heart beat
from the sum of our energy in harmony
through the tongue of a sea-dwelling Pisces

who dreams of a utopia
writes poems about unity
to counter the hypocrisy
of hate in our community
disguised as self-esteem.

We need to pick up the pace
embrace the fact that we now live in a time and space of integration
a merging of the world's population
through advances in travel and communication
we have begun to leave in the dust
the notion that being home means
only seeing faces that look like us.

We need to learn to trust
the global village that is waiting to embrace us —

where we build inclusive communities
make space for the human race

every colour
every faith

all fruit from the same root
all saplings from the same seed.

Celebrating our spectrum of ethnicity
elevating the common in community
participating in the healing
of our wounded human family

One we are — all
a microcosm of the whole

One
we are — all
nothing less
nothing more.

⟶◦

SHERI-D WILSON

Listen to this poem at www.sheridwilson.com

Drones

Home/ home/ home sweet home
What happens when the drones come home?
Home/ home/ home sweet home
What happens with the drones at home?

I guard the deep ID of my inner id
amid invisible lines on a neon grid
buzzing overhead, severing the sky
aerial robots with the bloodshot eye
of Sauron, of so long, of no long good-byes
of another apple-less piece of Miss American pie

and they say one drone's a spy — 5,000 feet high
while another one kills without questioning, why/why/why —
cause the pilot's remote, and widgets don't hear the cries
of children at school hit by Hellfire flies,
of a hostile hi-tech missile.
And in a warzone of droning-drone-drones
is a classroom which is filled with firing tears
instead of shooting stars and spinning spheres
and wishes, tingling with tadpoles and fishes,
and rhizome dreams
while back at home in a Vegas strip mall
are hi-tech fan boys who don't hear the screams
as they perform video game drone-strikes
slurping coke, eating chips and searching for viral memes

Bazinga!
The drones that walk — and talk and talk and talk
drone on about peace, but there is no cease-fire,
as they target practice, with so-called surveillance apparatus
artificial intelligence with security clearance status, sniper
and they're calling it a covert smart/ smart/ smart drone,
like downloading an endangered animal ringtone
on your disposable smart phone — for free

it's a totalitarian parody — *ignis fatuus* homeland security
will-o-the-wisp, fatality after fatality after fatality

Home/ home/ home sweet home
What happens when the drones come home?
Home/ home/ home sweet home
What happens with the drones at home?

A sales rep drone circles for another Pass
and I hope I'm not being paranoid about the asteroid
but really, there's no way home,
as I speak in a superflux of this recceing drone
with 20-20 vision — and facial recognition
of our bones and our chromosomes
which hovers above, scanning and gauging us, dystopian
draconian, and any privacy policy's a fallacy —
as mechanisms replace organisms
and our behavior pattern's reduced to predictable algorithms
credit ratings, purchase records, and filter bubbles
phobias, hang-ups and emotional troubles
are all known by the mighty surveillance drone
and the drone drones, as if to say
We know what you want to buy
by the glint in your eye
don't worry you don't have to be home
we'll deliver your package from Amazon
tomorrow by air drone

And I reply, who's the user now?
as I replace the word *it* with *thou*,
and God forbid we can't just disallow
a potential cash cow — overhead is over-overhead
like licking an apocalyptic moon
but I say, another word for drone is parasite
as Fahrenheit 9/11, reports a newfangled gun
and the old peeping Tom is now carrying a bomb
for social media and the pentagon
who conveniently call drones UAVs and RPAs
next they'll name them "flying cabarets"
while Orwell staggers in a scopophiliac haze
don't say the D–word—drone/ drone/ drone

don't say the D–word—drone/ drone/ drone
drones kill the birds and the bees
as they become voyeurs in all of the trees, paparazzi in parentheses
they collide with airplanes and screw with disease,
as they shrink in size, they'll be micro-Mordor-articles
small as gnats, like tiny flying God particles
and then they'll become more and more difficult to detect
as humans will find it harder to trust and connect

Drones Circle for one last pass,
as off-the-grid living, writes its epitaph
along with airspace, and Merlin's staff
the sea fortress and the holy grail
and …
all that's left is dead nightingale
or find someone to love
and look them in the eye
and see their soul
celestial and whole
and know we are home, sometimes,
sometimes, we find our way home

⊷≡⊃

STANZAS

A stanza is a group of lines arranged in a pattern which is determined by the number of lines, the number of feet in each line, the metre and the rhyme scheme. As can be seen in other chapters, they are an important organizing principle for most fixed forms, but they also constitute intriguing forms in and of themselves. Beyond this, however, there are myriad patterns to choose from — and invent.

The word stanza means "room" or "apartment" in Italian. Much as you move from room to room in your own home, you move through a stanzaic poem: racing up the stairs or sauntering along the hallway; opening or closing doors; stopping suddenly, caught short by something previously unnoticed or out of place; or turning back, the familiar reminding you, perhaps, of something you meant to do. The pace, music and emotion of the tour depend upon how the poet selects and employs a stanza's central elements (rhyme and metre, phrase and sentence, line and stanza break, refrain and repetition) to develop and enhance meaning. The white spaces between stanzas are thus part of the tour, creating pauses, a resting place.

Other words for stanza are *strophe* from the Greek for "turning," and *stave*, which is a musical term.

The most common stanza patterns are:
- *monostitch* (one line — rarely on its own; normally part of mixed stanza poems)
- *couplet* (2 lines)
- *tercet* or *triplet* (3 lines)
- *quatrain* (4 lines)
- *quintet* or *quintain* (5 lines)
- *sestet* (6 lines)
- *septet* (7 lines)
- *octet* (8 lines)
- *mixed* (a poem with stanzas of varied lengths)

Couplets and Tercets

While couplets and tercets can stand alone as verse units, they are just as often found either within longer stanzas or as key elements of other forms such as the epigram, ghazal and English sonnet (couplets) or the haiku, villanelle and terzanelle (tercets). Whether on their own or in combination with other forms, however, couplets and tercets have their own specific traits.

Couplets

The simple couplet — two consecutive rhyming lines — has been one of the most widely used English poetic forms since it was introduced by Geoffrey Chaucer in *The Legend of Good Women* and *The Canterbury Tales*. The couplet's power comes from its compression and intensity; as such, it demands a creative use of rhyme and a good ear to keep it from falling into a monotonous rhythm.

The three most common couplet forms are closed, heroic and open, all of which rhyme *aa*. In a closed couplet both sense and syntax are complete within the two lines, and this is often marked by punctuation that shows either a stop or pause. For example, Jay Macpherson's "The Third Eye" begins with a closed couplet: "Of three | eyes, I | would still | give two | for one. / The third | eye clouds: | its light | is near | ly gone." The heroic couplet is closed and written in iambic pentameter, as in the Macpherson quote.

An open couplet carries its sense forward to the next line or lines, as in these lines from Barker Fairley's "Bach Fugue" ("Please be at pains to fix it in the head, // Or else you'll miss the beauty. Now the next, / So different and so subtly interflexed,").

Consistent with its long lineage, the couplet embraces many variations, one of which is the short couplet, written in lines with four strong stresses, as illustrated by Sir Charles G.D. Roberts' "The Skater" ("My glad feet shod with the glittering steel"). Peter Culley oscillates between tetrameter and longer lines, ending with a trimeter line, to capture the unpredictable movements of the birds in "Junco Partner."

Tercets

A tercet is a three-line verse unit that either stands alone or makes up part of a larger stanza. It can be rhymed or unrhymed, but when all three lines rhyme (*aaa*) it is called a triplet. An enclosed tercet rhymes *aba*, as in most of Phyllis Webb's "The Second Hand."

A tercet is easily as versatile as a couplet, perhaps more so because the third line gives added room to develop content and use rhyme and metre to advantage. In Ann Wilkinson's "Tigers Know From Birth," for instance, in an otherwise predominantly pentameter pattern, the third line is abbreviated to three strong stresses, releasing the energy and emotion of the preceding longer lines with an oomph we feel bodily as we read.

This succinct form offers numerous rhyme and metre combinations. Throughout Webb's poem, the insistent recurrence of internal rhyme ("of the tick, the tock, the icy draught / of a clock's arms …") and end rhyme ("not," "knot," "not," "caught") reinforces a sense of "the pressing stress of time."

Terza rima was invented by Dante as the engine that pulled his *Divine Comedy* into the depths of hell and up again toward heaven (with obvious reference to the Christian Trinity). Its series of linked rhymes (*aba bcb cdc* etc.) create a pattern that steadily pulls the reader through the poem. The form usually ends with either a single line or a couplet, and in English, is usually written in iambic pentameter. Sharon Thesen's "The Broken Cup," however, relies primarily on the unifying effect of rhyme rather than metre. When written in fourteen lines, terza rima can be a variation of the sonnet (called, fittingly, the terza rima sonnet — see Sonnet chapter).

The traditional form:

Couplets

Stanza:	Two lines each, no set number.
Metre:	Heroic couplets are in iambic pentameter; short couplets are in iambic tetrameter; otherwise the pattern is optional.
Rhyme:	*aa*
Repetition:	None required.
Distinguishing feature:	Closed couplets are complete in sense and syntax; open couplets use enjambment.

Tercets/Triplets

Stanza:	Three lines each; no set number.
Metre:	Lines are usually metred but no set pattern required.
Rhyme:	Tercets can be rhymed or unrhymed, enclosed tercets rhyme *aba*, triplets rhyme *aaa*.
Repetition:	None required.

Terza rima

Stanza:	Three lines each; no set number.
Metre:	Lines are usually metred but no set pattern required.

Rhyme: *aba, bcb, cdc,* etc.

Repetition: None required.

Distinguishing feature: Final stanza can be a single line or a couplet; in either case, the line(s) rhyme with the middle line of the preceding stanza.

JAY MACPHERSON (1931–2010)

The Third Eye

Of three eyes, I would still give two for one.
The third eye clouds: its light is nearly gone.
The two saw green, saw sky, saw people pass:
The third eye saw through order like a glass
To concentrate, refine and rarify
And make a Cosmos of miscellany.
Sight, world and all to save alive that one
Fading so fast! Ah love, its light is done.

BARKER FAIRLEY (1887–1986)

Bach Fugue

This is the first of the themes, the lecturer said,
Please be at pains to fix it in the head,

Or else you'll miss the beauty. Now the next,
So different and so subtly interflexed,

And now the third (I forget if there were ten;
To tell the truth, I had forgotten then).

And remember to listen across as well as along,
It's a Bach fugue you'll hear and not a song.

The voice stopped short. And then there was a pause
With screwing of faces remembering rules and laws.

I remembered nothing. The fingers touched the keys,
And I travelled across and along with a swimmer's ease.

Sir Charles G.D. Roberts (1860–1944)

The Skater

My glad feet shod with the glittering steel
I was the god of the wingèd heel.

The hills in the far white sky were lost;
The world lay still in the wide white frost;

And the woods hung hushed in their long white dream
By the ghostly, glimmering, ice-blue stream.

Here was a pathway, smooth like glass,
Where I and the wandering wind might pass

To the far-off palaces, drifted deep,
Where Winter's retinue rests in sleep.

I followed the lure, I fled like a bird,
Till the startled hollows awoke and heard

A spinning whisper, a sibilant twang,
As the stroke of the steel on the tense ice rang;

And the wandering wind was left behind
As faster, faster I followed my mind;

Till the blood sang high in my eager brain,
And the joy of my flight was almost pain.

Then I stayed the rush of my eager speed
And silently went as a drifting seed, —

Slowly, furtively, till my eyes
Grew big with the awe of a dim surmise,

And the hair of my neck began to creep
At hearing the wilderness talk in sleep.

Shapes in the fir-gloom drifted near.
In the deep of my heart I heard my fear.

And I turned and fled, like a soul pursued,
From the white, inviolate solitude.

ERIC ORMSBY (b. 1941)

Jaham Sings of the Fear of the Moon

The moon is thin with fear,
the delicate moon is thinner than despair.

The fear of the moon is the fear of the hare
curved in its burrow when the fox is near.

The fear of the moon is the fear of the fog
(The fog is afraid of the fox and the dog

and the moon is afraid of all three.)
The moon is a thorn in midnight's tree.

The moon is thin as the edge of a cry,
as fine as the side of a word.

The thin moon hides in the dark of my eye.
Night-hidden I heard

its thinness crackle like the stalks of fall
before the hail comes and the first stars fall.

Night-hidden I heard its thin feet run
away from the golden horror of the sun.

PETER CULLEY (1958–2015)

Junco Partner

Two juncos, giddy & drunk with display
on their last available hookup day
flew interlocking spirals down toward the ground
& with short hard strokes then pivoted up & around
to some pre-arranged & lofty space.
They did this in the dusty face
of burnt out topsoil where the
little forest leaned hard against a bare
woodboard fence not everyone could see.
By the fifth repetition their spiral was sweet —
if they'da been ravens they could've locked their feet —
until at the last moment, a foot off the yard,
they part as if pushed, not pivoting but hard
down again shift for two-point brakings in the dust.
After shaking off the landing, the bird just
missed the fence then turned toward it, lowered its head
and ran under, fast, toward the shed.
The other bird followed *bam!* both gone
they footchased each other onto the lawn
for quite a few feet before turning south
toward the old trees behind the house,
a place where they wouldn't be harassed —
an odd, rolling gait, but *fast.*

ANNE WILKINSON (1910–1961)

Tigers Know From Birth

My bones predict the striking hour of thunder
And water as I huddle under
      The tree the lightning renders

I'm hung with seaweed, winding in its caul
The nightmare of a carp whose blood runs cold,
      A crab who apes my crawl

My lens is grafted from a jungle eye
To focus on the substance of a shadow's
      Shadow on the sky

My forest filtered drum is pitched to hear
The serpent split the grass before the swish
      Is feather in my ear

I've learned from land and sea of every death
Save one, the easy rest, the little catnap
      Tigers know from birth

PHYLLIS WEBB (b. 1927)

The Second Hand

Here, Love, whether we love or not
involves the clock and its ignorant hands
tying our hearts in a lover's knot;

now, whether we flower or not
requires a reluctance in the hour;
yet we cannot move, in the present caught

in the embrace of to be or not;
dear, shall we move our hands together,
or must we bear the onslaught

of the tick, the tock, the icy draught
of a clock's arms swinging themselves together —
or now shall we kiss where once we laughed?

all time is sadness but the heart is not
unmoved in the minute of the dancing measure,
for if in the pressing stress of time

the dancer stays, or act is mime,
hands must break by being caught
as the clock covers its face with an evil weather.

⊷⇒

MARIANNE BLUGER (b. 1945)

In Oak

Where will you drift, Sadie,
now that you lie
in the velvet boat

with your shot-silk dress,
the jade at your throat
and those ferret eyes shut —

where will you float,
now you have had to let go —
you who would always row?

SHARON THESEN (b. 1946)

The Broken Cup

Bits of prosody fall near what remains of me
that drifts on the sofa in a trance
made of loves, lazy rivers, unmended crockery.

I feel so broken now by a too-long dance.
Shot exhausted horses fall behind the stadium
and shards of mirror lance

What could have been a fatal wound, fatal tedium
or a spiritual lesson to have learned
endlessly postponed like closure & delirium.

One wants clear endings, beginnings to burn
big holes through old obdurate patterns, one wants
love to "triumph" as it were but not to earn

A thousand bardos, a daily headache, an ounce
of comfrey for a cure when I am acting up
& slink around ashamed of getting trounced

At life & coping, nearly. Like certain music
refuses transcendence (that strange vulgarity),
and how I threw the broken cup

Away because I know to hope for clarity
where things are broken is just to lie.

Quatrains and more

The quatrain, rhymed or unrhymed, is probably the most common stanza form in the world, used in forms from ballad to pantoum. The widely used ballad stanza alternates four and three strongly stressed lines, traditionally rhyming *abcb*. It is also often used within longer poems such as the Italian sonnet, where the eight initial lines are actually two quatrains, usually rhyming.

Richard Outram's "Barbed Wire" is in heroic quatrains using iambic pentameter and an *abab* rhyme scheme. Perhaps to emphasize the sense of history and looking back in the poem, he also uses an older technique of capitalizing the beginning of each line. In "Keine Lazarovitch," Irving Layton takes more liberties with the form, using irregular rhyme and metre.

The aural pleasures of rhyme and metre are often emphasized in the quatrain for a light-hearted effect. Its regular pattern and beat can give intense pleasure to children (and adults!) who delight in rhythm. The solid four-beat line and perfect end rhyme ("pie," "die," "sky," "pie") in Dennis Lee's "Alligator Pie" create verses to which it's hard not to stamp your feet.

Pauline Johnson writes "The Train Dogs" in a metred quintain (with a pattern of 3, 3, 4, 4, 3 strong stresses), while Bliss Carman's "Low Tide on Grand Pré" is a Spanish quintilla, a form that has five-line stanzas with eight syllables per line, which in English tend to fall into four iambs.

Charles Bruce in "Eastern Shore" and David Zieroth in "Hollow" write in heroic sestets, which traditionally are in iambic pentameter with an *abbacc* or *ababcc* rhyme scheme, although Zieroth varies the metric pattern.

Over the centuries, various stanzas have been named, often to acknowledge an important poem, a popular pattern, or a particularly skilled poet. Eric Duncan's Spenserian stanza, "Drought," is one of the more common forms. Named after Edmund Spenser who developed the pattern for "The Faerie Queene," the form consists of nine lines rhyming *ababbcbcc*. The first eight lines are in iambic pentameter and the ninth, with two more syllables, is an alexandrine (an iambic hexameter line, as in Duncan's: "For I | have none | to spare | – I think | of months | to come"). This is widely considered one of the most challenging, yet versatile of the stanza forms. For instance, the rhyme scheme offers various options for organizing content, of which *abab|bcbc|c* or *aba|bb|cbc|c* are just two possibilities.

Archibald Lampman's "The City of the End of Things" and Marjorie Pickthall's "Ebb Tide" show how seemingly small differences in metre and rhythm can work with content to create poems that sound and feel entirely different. Both poets use an *abab* rhyme scheme. Lampman's metre, however, rarely veers from iambic tetrameter ("Of mid|night streams | unknown | to us") while Pickthall's lines of primarily 4, 3, 4, and 2 strong stresses rely on the frequent combination of two- and three-syllable feet, as in "And <u>hark</u> | for the <u>surge</u> | and the <u>strong</u> | <u>thun</u>der." And while Lampman's long stanzas are organized according to major shifts in narrative content, Pickthall's are all quatrains based on the metre and rhyme pattern. The overall effect, in Pickthall's poem, is a softer, slower pace and a deeply elegiac tone; in Lampman's, it's a relentless urgency that emphasizes the dystopian vision.

Madeline Bassnett uses the merest scaffold of stanza in "Cell Sequencing" to create a nonce, or one-time form that blends unrhymed and only roughly metred mixed stanzas with aspects of the fugue, repeating images ("water," "sand," "drift," "digestive tube," rippling" and so on). In a sort of crown effect, she also repeats the last words of each stanza as the first words of the next. And hidden in the poem is solid scientific information about this thing called "cell sequencing," so that the actual shrinking shape of the poem reflects what a cell does.

The traditional form:

Stanzas:	Usually two to nine lines.
Metre:	Lines are usually metred.
Rhyme:	Lines are usually end-rhymed.
Repetition:	None required.
Named Patterns:	Among the poems in this chapter, five are examples of stanza patterns that have acquired their own names over the years. There are numerous others, which are described in most handbooks, including the resources listed in the bibliography at the end of this book. The patterns included in this chapter are:

• *Heroic quatrain*: a four-line iambic pentameter stanza rhyming *abab* or *aabb* (Richard Outram's "Barbed Wire").
• *Heroic sestet* (also called Shakespearean, and Venus & Adonis): a six-line iambic pentameter stanza rhyming *abbacc* or *ababcc* (Charles Bruce's "Eastern Shore").
• *Long metre*: tetrameter quatrains rhyming *abab* or *aabb* (Charles Lampman's "The City of the End of Things" embeds this metre and rhyme scheme in longer stanzas).

• *Spanish quintilla*: five lines of eight syllables each or in iambic tetrameter, rhyming *ababb*; may also rhyme *ababa, abbab, abaab, aabab,* or *aabba* (Bliss Carman's "Low Tide at Grand Pré").

• *Spenserian stanzas*: nine-line stanzas rhyming *ababb-cbcc*, the first eight in iambic pentameter and the ninth an alexandrine (Eric Duncan's "Drought").

Other traditional stanza patterns include:

•*Ballad stanza*: alternating tetrameter and trimeter lines rhyming *abcb* or *abab* (see Ballad chapter).

•*Ottava rima* (Italian in origin): an eight-line iambic pentameter stanza rhyming *ababbcc*.

•*Rhyme royal*: a seven-line iambic pentameter stanza rhyming *ababbcc*. "Royal" because it was used by James I of Scotland, who borrowed it from Chaucer.

RICHARD OUTRAM (1930–2005)

Barbed Wire

Consists of two tight-twisted, separate strands
Conjoined as one: and not unlike, in fact,
Our own familiar silver wedding bands,
Though these are loosely woven, inexact,

With wide interstices, so that each makes
A circle of ellipses. Tightly caught
At random intervals, two little snakes
Of wire are crimped into a snaggled knot,

That four short ends, sharp bevel-cut, present
Unsheathed, ingenious fangs. And when in place,
Stretched taut, or strewn in loose coils, may prevent
The passage through some designated space

Of beast, or man. You got used to the stench;
The mud was worse than being under fire,
My father said. A detail left the trench
At night, to get the dead back from the wire,

And no one volunteered. They stood, to view
Our brief exchange of rings and vows, for both
Our fathers had survived that war: and knew
Of death, and bright entanglement, and troth.

IRVING LAYTON (1912–2006)

Keine Lazarovitch 1870–1959

When I saw my mother's head on the cold pillow,
Her white waterfalling hair in the cheeks' hollows,
I thought, quietly circling my grief, of how
She had loved God but cursed extravagantly his creatures.

For her final mouth was not water but a curse,
A small black hole, a black rent in the universe,
Which damned the green earth, stars and trees in its stillness
And the inescapable lousiness of growing old.

And I record she was comfortless, vituperative,
Ignorant, glad, and much else besides; I believe
She endlessly praised her black eyebrows, their thick weave,
Till plagiarizing Death leaned down and took them for his mould.

And spoiled a dignity I shall not again find,
And the fury of her stubborn limited mind.
Now none will shake her amber beads and call God blind,
Or wear them upon a breast so radiantly.

O fierce she was, mean and unaccommodating;
But I think now of the toss of her gold earrings,
Their proud carnal assertion, and her youngest sings
While all the rivers of her red veins move into the sea.

Earle Birney (1904–1995)

From the Hazel Bough

I met a lady
  on a lazy street
hazel eyes
  and little plush feet

her legs swam by
  like lovely trout
eyes were trees
  where boys leant out

hands in the dark and
  a river side
round breasts rising
  with the finger's tide

she was plump as a finch
  and live as a salmon
gay as silk and
  proud as a Brahmin

we winked when we met
  and laughed when we parted
never took time
  to be brokenhearted

but no man sees
  where the trout lie now
or what leans out
  from the hazel bough

DENNIS LEE (b. 1939)

Alligator Pie

Alligator pie, alligator pie,
If I don't get some I think I'm gonna die.
Give away the green grass, give away the sky,
But don't give away my alligator pie.

Alligator stew, alligator stew,
If I don't get some I don't know what I'll do.
Give away my furry hat, give away my shoe,
But don't give away my alligator stew.

Alligator soup, alligator soup,
If I don't get some I think I'm gonna droop.
Give away my hockey-stick, give away my hoop,
But don't give away my alligator soup.

BLISS CARMAN (1861–1929)

Vagabond Song

There is something in the autumn that is native to my blood —
Touch of manner, hint of mood;
And my heart is like a rhyme,
With the yellow and the purple and the crimson keeping time.

The scarlet of the maples can shake me like a cry
Of bugles going by.
And my lonely spirit thrills
To see the frosty asters like a smoke upon the hills.

There is something in October sets the gypsy blood astir;
We must rise and follow her,
When from every hill of flame
She calls and calls each vagabond by name.

MARJORIE PICKTHALL (1883–1922)

Ebb Tide

The Sailor's Grave at Clo-oose, V.I.

Out of the winds' and the waves' riot,
Out of the loud foam,
He has put in to a great quiet
And a still home.

Here he may lie at ease and wonder
Why the old ship waits,
And hark for the surge and the strong thunder
Of the full Straits,

And look for the fishing fleet at morning,
Shadows like lost souls,
Slide through the fog where the seal's warning
Betrays the shoals,

And watch for the deep-sea liner climbing
Out of the bright West,
With a salmon-sky and her wake shining
Like a tern's breast, —

And never know he is done for ever
With the old sea's pride,
Borne from the fight and the full endeavour
On an ebb tide.

PAULINE JOHNSON (1862–1913)

The Train Dogs

Out of the night and the north;
  Savage of breed and of bone,
Shaggy and swift comes the yelping band,
Freighters of fur from the voiceless land
  That sleeps in the Arctic zone.

Laden with skins from the north,
  Beaver and bear and raccoon,
Marten and mink from the polar belts,
Otter and ermine and sable pelts —
  The spoils of the hunter's moon.

Out of the night and the north,
  Sinewy, fearless and fleet,
Urging the pack through the pathless snow,
The Indian driver, calling low,
  Follows with moccasined feet.

Ships of the night and the north,
  Freighters on prairies and plains,
Carrying cargoes from field and flood
They scent the trail through their wild red blood;
  The wolfish blood in their veins.

Bliss Carman (1861–1929)

Low Tide on Grand Pré

The sun goes down, and over all
These barren reaches by the tide
Such unelusive glories fall,
I almost dream they yet will bide
Until the coming of the tide.

And yet I know that not for us,
By an ecstasy of dream
He lingers to keep luminous
A little while the grievous stream,
Which frets, uncomforted of dream —

A grievous stream, that to and fro
Athrough the fields of Acadie
Goes wandering, as if to know
Why one beloved face should be
So long from home and Acadie.

Was it a year or lives ago
We took the grasses in our hands,
And caught the summer flying low
Over the waving meadow lands,
And held it there between our hands?

The while the river at our feet —
A drowsy inland meadow stream —
At set of sun the after-heat
Made running gold, and in the gleam
We freed our birch upon the stream.

There down along the elms at dusk
We lifted dripping blade to drift,
Through twilight scented fine like musk,
Where night and gloom awhile uplift,
Nor sunder soul and soul adrift.

And that we took into our hands
Spirit of life or subtler thing —
Breathed on us there, and loosed the bands
Of death, and taught us, whispering,
The secret of some wonder-thing.

Then all your face grew light, and seemed
To hold the shadow of the sun;
The evening faltered, and I deemed
That time was ripe, and years had done
Their wheeling underneath the sun.

So all desire and all regret,
And fear and memory, were naught;
One to remember or forget
The keen delight our hands had caught;
Morrow and yesterday were naught.

The night has fallen, and the tide ...
Now and again comes drifting home,
Across these aching barrens wide,
A sigh like driven wind or foam:
In grief the flood is bursting home.

⊷⇛

Charles Bruce (1906–1968)

Eastern Shore

He stands and walks as if his knees were tensed
To a pitching dory. When he looks far off
You think of trawl-kegs rolling in the trough
Of swaying waves. He wears a cap against
The sun on water, but his face is brown
As an old mainsail, from the eyebrows down.

He has grown old as something used and known
Grows old with custom; each small fading scar
Engrained by use and wear in plank and spar,
In weathered wood and iron, and flesh and bone.
But youth lurks in the squinting eyes, and in
The laughter wrinkles in the tanbark skin.

You know his story when you see him climb
The lookout hill. You know that age can be
A hill for looking; and the swaying sea
A lifetime marching with the waves of time.
Listen — the ceaseless cadence, deep and slow.
Tomorrow. Now. And years and years ago.

DAVID ZIEROTH (b. 1946)

Hollow

Suddenly I am hollowed out, at the lip
of weeping, panic in my throat, because
   the season changes, and into the pause
   between the shifting moments slips
a blankness unprepared for, and someone's
leaving, and all my plans come undone.

Nor does it help that the dark
falls early, clouds blocking light
   so even a pleasant walk cannot ignite
   inside me the necessary spark
of hopefulness that gives a shape to each hour
that fights off what comes to devour

the little I've now become: alone
to make the day, routine not yet kicked in.
   I kick the sidewalk trash while within
   whirls my own lean cyclone
sucking from me what once I was: one whose joy
at living and arriving was not so easy to destroy.

P.K. PAGE (1916–2010)

Water and Marble

And shall I tell him that the thought of him
turns me to water
and when his name is spoken pale still sky
trembles and breaks and moves like blowing water
that winter thaws its frozen drifts in water
all matter blurs, unsteady, seen through water
and I, in him, dislimn, water in water?

As true: the thought of him
has made me marble
and when his name is spoken blowing sky
settles and freezes in a dome of marble
and winter seals its floury drifts in marble
all matter double-locks as dense as marble
and I, in other's eyes, am cut from marble.

ERIC DUNCAN (1858–1944)

Drought

August returns, but not with plenty crowned;
    Thin, dwarfed, and light of head is all the grain.
The meagre hay was, ere its blossom, browned;
    The root crops withered, all for want of rain.
The cows for aftergrass do seek in vain,
    And through the boundless woods afar they roam.
They anger me; but when driven home again
    Their sad eyes plead for hay, and I am dumb,
For I have none to spare — I think of months to come.

ARCHIBALD LAMPMAN (1861–1899)

The City of the End of Things

Beside the pounding cataracts
Of midnight streams unknown to us
'Tis builded in the leafless tracts
And valleys huge of Tartarus.
Lurid and lofty and vast it seems;
It hath no rounded name that rings,
But I have heard it called in dreams
The City of the End of Things.

Its roofs and iron towers have grown
None knoweth how high within the night,
But in its murky streets far down
A flaming terrible and bright
Shakes all the stalking shadows there,
Across the walls, across the floors,
And shifts upon the upper air
From out a thousand furnace doors;
And all the while an awful sound
Keeps roaring on continually,
And crashes in the ceaseless round
Of a gigantic harmony.
Through its grim depths re-echoing
And all its wearing height of walls,
With measured roar and iron ring,
The inhuman music lifts and falls.
Where no thing rests and no man is,
And only fire and night hold sway;
The beat, the thunder and the hiss
Cease not, and change not, night nor day.

And moving at unheard commands,
The abysses and vast fires between,
Flit figures that with clanking hands
Obey a hideous routine;
They are not flesh, they are not bone,
They see not with the human eye,
And from their iron lips is blown
A dreadful and monotonous cry;
And whoso of our mortal race
Should find that city unaware,
Lean Death would smite him face to face,
And blanch him with its venomed air:
Or caught by the terrific spell,
Each thread of memory snapt and cut,
His soul would shrivel and its shell
Go rattling like an empty nut.

It was not always so, but once,
In days that no man thinks upon,
Fair voices echoed from its stones,
The light above it leaped and shone:
Once there were multitudes of men,
That built that city in their pride,
Until its might was made, and then
They withered age by age and died.
But now of that prodigious race,
Three only in an iron tower,
Set like carved idols face to face,
Remain the masters of its power;
And at the city gate a fourth,
Gigantic and with dreadful eyes,
Sits looking toward the lightless north,
Beyond the reach of memories;
Fast rooted to the lurid floor,
A bulk that never moves a jot,
In his pale body dwells no more,
Or mind, or soul, — an idiot!

But sometime in the end those three
Shall perish and their hands be still,
And with the master's touch shall flee
Their incommunicable skill.
A stillness absolute as death
Along the slacking wheels shall lie,
And, flagging at a single breath,
The fires shall moulder out and die.
The roar shall vanish at its height,
And over that tremendous town
The silence of eternal night
Shall gather close and settle down.
All its grim grandeur, tower and hall,
Shall be abandoned utterly,
And into rust and dust shall fall
From century to century;
Nor ever living thing shall grow,
Or trunk of tree, or blade of grass;
No drop shall fall, no wind shall blow,
Nor sound of any foot shall pass:
Alone of its accursèd state,
One thing the hand of Time shall spare,
For the grim Idiot at the gate
Is deathless and eternal there.

MADELINE BASSNETT (b. 1966)

Cell Sequencing

However we might understand the cell:
a numbered sequence; a loop of ribbon; the drift of water
on sand. A cherubim, all fire and eyes and wings.
Translucent, an amoeba: digestive tube exposed, rippling
flagella. It rises to our bodies' shores to shed
and die, divide and multiply. However we understand —
and perhaps it is not much at all — it is what we are.

We are what it is: all wings and fire. Exposed and numbered,
a looping sequence shedding our shores. A ribbon of digestive
tube and dying bodies, rippling. The cell understands,
however we multiply and divide. It is not much at all —
translucent flagella, the drift of cherubim — sand on water.
Rising, all eyes: however we might understand.

However we might understand our bodies: perhaps they
are all we are: dying and shedding, a numbered drift of loops,
a ribbon of cell. Translucent we rise on the shores. It is not much.
Sequenced flagella dividing and multiplying, all eyes
and water — amoebas of fire: cherubim.

The amoeba, perhaps. Exposed loop numbered. It drifts and rises,
the cell translucent. We are not what it is. Wings and eyes multiplying,
bodies dying on shores of sand. A ribbon of fire
shedding cherubim. The cell dividing.

Divide translucent bodies, ribboned and looped.
The amoeba drifts, the cell sheds wings and eyes, fire and sand,
a cherubim, perhaps.

A cherubim divides and loops, a fiery cell,
a winged amoeba. Drift and shed.

Drift and shed, a cell, a cherubim.

A cell.

⤙⇒

VILLANELLE

Mark Strand and Eavan Boland, in the *Making of a Poem*, say the villanelle probably originated in Italy as a round sung while harvesting crops. But it made its first appearance as a poetic form in France in the sixteenth century. What began as a loose form for pastoral themes requiring only the use of a refrain, gradually became a more structured form embracing a wide variety of subjects. By the seventeenth century the villanelle had evolved into a poem that turned on two rhymes and two refrains in an unlimited number of tercets plus a closing quatrain.

The English version, which came into fashion in the nineteenth century, limited the villanelle to six stanzas. Lines 1 and 3 of the first tercet alternate as line 3 in the others, and together form the closing couplet in the quatrain. The form's challenge lies in creating an interesting poem that develops, rather than merely repeats, its content. Add to this the limited *aba* rhyme scheme over nineteen lines, and the poet also faces the difficulty of making the poem sing, rather than grate on the ear.

The villanelle's restrictions, like those of so many set forms, can become strengths. Eli Mandel takes advantage of the incessant repetition to steadily deepen the sweetly mournful metaphor of the circling carousel in "City Park Merry-Go-Round." David O'Meara's "Ever" shows how enjambment can both vary the emphasis of the repeated lines and help soften the recurring rhymes ("we'll see // Delphi," and "maybe // shade-trees") — in this case, making the promises both concrete and ephemeral.

As with the triolet (see "Rondeau Family" chapter), contemporary poets often vary or dispense with the villanelle's rhyme and metre to keep the form from calling too much attention to itself. They also often play with the repeated lines — as when Molly Peacock, in "Little Miracle," not only alters the refrain line, but adds to it the final phrase "we're here," (from the non-refrain line in stanza 1) to close the poem. O'Meara takes variation in another direction, giving his poem a strong dramatic impact by restricting lines 1 and 3 to two syllables each.

Terzanelle

An American variation of the villanelle is the terzanelle. Lines 1 and 3 of a terzanelle's first stanza are repeated only once, either as lines 3 and 4 or 2 and 4 of the final quatrain. The second line of each tercet becomes the third line of the next one, all the way through to the quatrain, creating a terza rima rhyme scheme (i.e., *aba*, *bcb*, *cdc*, etc.). The first example here is David Waltner-Toews' "Woods," which begins with an echo of Robert Frost's famous line, but moves in an entirely different direction. Sandy Shreve varies the form by elaborating on the theme of a line in its second appearance, as when "The estranged friends who get over it" becomes "The estranged friend who calls first and the one who gladly answers."

The traditional form:

Villanelle

Stanzas:	Six stanzas; the first five are tercets and the sixth is a quatrain.
Metre:	Usually all lines have a common metre or syllable count (the pattern is up to the poet).
Rhyme:	*aba* for the first five stanzas; *abaa* for the last stanza.
Repetition:	Lines 1 and 3 of the opening tercet alternate as line 3 of the subsequent tercets and together provide lines 3 and 4 of the quatrain (below, superscript R1 and R2 stand for the different refrain lines, the letters *a* and *b* represent the rhyme scheme):

$$a^{R1}ba^{R2} \quad aba^{R1} \quad aba^{R2} \quad aba^{R1} \quad aba^{R2} \quad aba^{R1}a^{R2}$$

Terzanelle

Stanzas:	Six stanzas; the first five are tercets and the sixth is a quatrain.
Metre:	Usually all lines have a common metre or syllable count (the pattern is up to the poet).
Rhyme:	*aba bcb cdc, ded efe fafa* (or *ffaa*)
Repetition:	This form has seven different refrains, rather than just the two of a villanelle:

• lines 1 and 3 of the opening tercet are repeated as lines 3 and 4 (or 2 and 4) of the final quatrain;
• line 2 of each tercet is repeated only once, as line 3 of the following tercet;
• line 2 of the last tercet may be repeated as either line 2 or 3 of the quatrain.
Below, the numbered Rs stand for the various refrain lines:

$$a^{R1}b^{R2}a^{R3} \quad bc^{R4}b^{R2} \quad cd^{R5}c^{R4} \quad de^{R6}d^{R5} \quad ef^{R7}e^{R6}$$
$$ff^{R7}a^{R1}a^{R3}(\text{or } fa^{R1}f^{R7}a^{R3})$$

ELI MANDEL (1922–1992)

City Park Merry-Go-Round

Freedom is seldom what you now believe.
Mostly you circle round and round the park:
Night follows day, these horses never leave.

Like children, love whatever you conceive,
See then your world as lights whirled in the dark.
Freedom is seldom what you now believe.

Your world moves up and down or seems to weave
And still you pass you pass the same ringed mark.
Night follows day, these horses never leave.

You thought your past was here, you might retrieve
That wild illusion whirling in the dark.
Freedom is seldom what you now believe.

Sick on that circle you begin to grieve.
You wish the ride would end you could escape the park.
Night follows day, these horses never leave.

Mostly you circle round and round the park.
You'd give your life now to be free to leave.
Freedom is seldom what you now believe.
Night follows day, these horses never leave.

CATHERINE OWEN (b. 1971)

Villanelle

As if in a dream, we were already there
The woods of Calais, the park at Béziers
And after, the autumn you stroked from my hair.

Though it was still summer, the sun burning fair
Then the star-less night sky, its darkness so clear.
When, as if in a dream, we were already there

The woods of Printemps, the park of Hiver
Where you held me as though we had little to fear
Then, gentle, the autumn you drew from my hair.

After the hour that our flesh was held bare,
We were both now as far, we were both just as near
As if in a dream we were already there

In the woods of Alsace, the park at Beaucaire,
You speaking the words I'd long wanted to hear
While the autumn you stopped to caress from my hair

Spun down to the pavement, blew wild in the square
As we left the freed woods, the park without care
Where, as if in a dream, we were already there
And, always, the autumn, your hands in my hair.

BRUCE MEYER (b. 1957)

The Ferry to South Baymouth

My daughter's eyes are blue as Georgian Bay
and sparkle with the glint of tiny stars
that define each wave on a summer's day;

for among the vacationers who have run away
with all their necessities packed in cars,
my daughter's eyes are blue as Georgian Bay.

This is her first summer. She has a way
of measuring things as her eye explores
and defines each wave on a summer's day

with the luxury of unencumbered sight. I say
boat but all she sees are endless waters —
my daughter's eyes are blue as Georgian Bay.

Her little hand points to a gull, the sway
and lilt of its wings on wind. All that matters
as she defines each wave on a summer's day

and sparkles with the glint of tiny stars
is that she is fed and dry and happily ours —
my daughter's eyes are blue as Georgian Bay
and define each wave on a summer's day.

⊷⟹

MOLLY PEACOCK (b. 1947)

Little Miracle

No use getting hysterical.
The important part is: we're here.
Our lives are a little miracle.

My hummingbird-hearted schedule
beats its shiny frenzy, day into year.
No use getting hysterical —

it's always like that. The oracle
a human voice could be is shrunk by fear.
Our lives are a little miracle

— we must remind ourselves — whimsical,
and lyrical, large and slow and clear.
(No use getting hysterical!)

All words other than *I love you* are clerical,
dispensable, and replaceable, my dear,
Our inner lives are a miracle.

They beat their essence in the coracle
our ribs provide, the watertight boat we steer
through others' acid, hysterical
demands. Ours is the miracle: *we're here.*

Liz Howard (b. 1985)

A Wake

Your eyes open the night's slow static at a loss
to explain this place you've returned to from above;
cedar along a broken shore, twisting in a wake of fog.

I've lived in rooms with others, of no place and no mind
trying to bind a self inside the contagion of words while
your eyes open the night's slow static. At a loss

to understand all that I cannot say, as if you came
upon the infinite simply by thinking and it was
a shore of broken cedar twisting in a wake of fog.

If I moan from an animal throat it is in hope you
will return to me what I lost learning to speak.
Your eyes open the night's slow static at a loss

to ever know the true terminus of doubt, the limits of skin.
As long as you hold me I am doubled from without and within:
a wake of fog unbroken, a shore of twisted cedar.

I will press myself into potential, into your breath,
and maybe what was lost will return in sleep once I see
your eyes open into the night's slow static, at a loss.
Broken on a shore of cedar. We twist in a wake of fog.

David O'Meara (b. 1968)

Ever

Maybe
one day we'll be together in Krakow,
we'll see.

Could we
reach Savannah by Friday, if we drove?
Maybe.

You, me,
from the streets of Samarkand to Peggy's Cove;
we'll see

Delphi,
Angkor Wat, the markets of Asia, the Louvre,
maybe

shade-trees
on the Euphrates if time is kind enough,
we'll see.

Will we
ever live in Montreal again? Maybe not, love.
Maybe.
We'll see.

DAVID WALTNER-TOEWS (b. 1948)

from Coming up for Air

Woods

I do not know whose woods those are. I do not care
to know. We fly above them, see the fox along the trees escape
into the shadows, pausing. We glide along the river's graceful turn

of phrase among the stuttering urban landscapes,
above the maples, poplars, oak, the green-roofed barns.
To know we fly above them, see the fox along the trees, escape

into clouds: enough. Let them stand arms akimbo, wish us good, or harm.
We are above all that — the truckers and the market — our heads
above the maples, poplars, oak, the green-roofed barns,

where farmers walk from shadows, smooth sun-warmed wood,
hitch Clydesdales to the plough. It is illusory to think
we are above all that — the truckers and the market — that heads

can somehow dis-attach from stomachs, that without bread and drink
there can be dreams. My hopes for earth's redemption yawn,
hitch Clydesdales to the plough. It is illusory to think

it matters more who owns the woods than that the woods are
there. I do not know whose woods those are. I do not care.
There can be dreams. My hopes for earth's redemption yawn
into the shadows, pausing. We glide along the river's graceful turn.

SANDY SHREVE (b. 1950)

More of the Just

The mother who comforts the tearful child who bloodied her son's nose.
The estranged friends who get over it.
The citizens of warring countries who refuse to take up arms.

The flash mob dancers.
The driver who screeches to a halt in the crosswalk and blanches.
The estranged friend who calls first and the one who gladly answers.

The teenager who shovels her elderly neighbour's driveway, anonymously.
The publisher who chooses not to sell to the chains.
The driver who apologizes to the children he just missed.

The ham radio operator who keeps the Morse Code alive.
The husband who reads poetry to his ailing wife.
The publisher who sells, instead, to the staff and the staff, who form a co-op.

The sand artists.
The ones who walk down city streets smiling at strangers.
The husband who doesn't get the poems, but reads them anyway, beautifully.

The father who teaches the winter sky to his neighbour's kids.
The mother who comforts her bloodied son without laying blame.
The ones who stop and talk with street people.
The citizens of countries at war who march arm in arm for peace.

... AND MORE

There are numerous other forms, far more than space in this anthology allows us to include. This chapter offers a taste of just a few. For more forms, see references in the Bibliography, particularly Robin Skelton's *The Shapes of Our Singing*.

Acrostic

An acrostic makes a vertical word, phrase or sentence with the first letter or word of each consecutive line in a poem. The poem can be any length and in any form, and is not necessarily rhymed or metred. Adam Sol bases "Acrostic Lament" on the first letter of each line to spell out the alphabet. But he takes the form a bit farther, with most lines also featuring several words beginning with that initial letter ("Behold the broken bone of my bold city"). In Stephen Scobie's "Queen Mary, She's My Friend," the first words make up the refrain from Bob Dylan's song, "Blowing in the Wind." Christian Bök's "The Nocturne of Orpheus" is a double acrostic, in which the first and last letter of each line spells out the dedication to *The Xenotext — Book 1*. Other approaches are also possible. For example, the acrostic element, be it a first letter of a word or an entire word, can be somewhat disguised if it is placed in the middle or at the end of each line.

Adam Sol (b. 1968)

Acrostic Lament

Ah, she is awry! And all her beauty is anguish!
　　Behold the broken bone of my bold city,
City that once clamored and careened like a caffeinated Doberman.
　　Dust is now her dessert, death her deal.
Even the elms embrace ash and filthy embers;
　　Forgotten are her favorites, aflame her great fortress.
Gone are the good, the governed, the greedy, and the gallant!
　　Heavy-hearted, her heroines inquire, "How did this happen?" O!
I am ill with imagery, with the imagined, the imminent, and "this just in."
　　Jarred, even rage escapes me. I am havocked.
Killers and kings alike are keeled over with shock. Yea, our loss is
　　kaleidoscopic,
　　Looming large like some magnificent Leviathan,
More mountain than monster, a new feature of our minds and memory.
　　Never again will nerds, nymphs, or nurses need reminding.
O, my people! My oatmeal-eaters and olive pressers!
　　Petty and pathetic seem the predictions I pandered from Quarry to Passaic.
Quaint and quirky my omens! How quickly my regular rants and
　　Ridiculous ravings have assumed sinister resonances!

Still, I will say my piece amidst these stones. Stay sturdy, fellow citizens!
　　Tomorrow the Twin Towers will again teach us transcendence.
Unfasten the umbrellas of your souls! Unleash your uncles' vitality!
　　Verily will our valiant wills be revamped into vigor.
Wherever we wander we will wage war on excuses and weariness.
　　Except for our expressions, we will nix our excesses and yearn for examples.
Young girls will yell in yellow jumpers. Yea, Your city will rise,
　　Zestier than it was, wiser and more zaftig, zealous to be Zion!

⊷⟹

STEPHEN SCOBIE (b. 1943)

Queen Mary, She's My Friend

The question includes its own
answer: in my beginning is
my end. Remember Queen Mary, making
friends with the headsman's axe. What
is the end? All of her future days,
blowing like smoke from a casual fire
in the forest of her heart.
The axe lifts over Fotheringay. A soft
wind from the north touches her cheek as she climbs
the steps to the scaffold. There is no
answer, she thinks, and no beginning. But where
is all this smoke coming from,
blowing into her eyes? She can't see, not even the block.
"In my end is my beginning."
The axe answers all of her questions.
Wind ruffles the hair of her head as it falls.

CHRISTIAN BÖK (b. 1966)

The Nocturne of Orpheus

THIS COVENANT OF LOVE IN A DIRGE FOR A GOD
HAS DELIGHTED AN ANGEL WHO OBEYS MY PLEA,
EACH SONNET A RHYTHM FOR HER TO DECIPHER,
MAKING LEGIBLE A KEY IN HER DREAM OF DUSK:
A REDNESS THAT DARKENS THE HUE OF A TULIP
IS RICHENING HER VIEW ON THE HILL OF A LEA,
DAPPLING HER VISTA AT THE END OF MY VIGIL,
EVEN IF HAVOC CALLS FORTH RUIN TO KILL ME.
NO CHURCH, NO CHAPEL, IS A REFUGE IN A STORM,
IF WE BEG TO BE WARM, YET LET DIE THE CANDLE.
NO HERDER, NO HERMIT, ENCHANTED BY THE SEA,
HAS HITHERTO KNOWN THE ENNUI OF A COWARD,
EVEN WHEN INFERNOS IN HELL BURN THE HERO:
RADIANT AS FLINT, BE THE ACHE OF MY SORROW.

Anglo-Saxon

The earliest known English poetry (750–1100 AD) was in Anglo-Saxon, an older form of the language so different from what we speak today it must be translated to be understood. It was accentual verse (not accentual-syllabic) with four strong stresses to a line. There was a pause (caesura) in the middle with two strong stresses on either side. In each of the resulting half-lines the stressed and unstressed syllables were arranged according to five possible patterns. In all cases, one or both of the stressed syllables in the first half-line began with the same sound (alliteration) as the first stressed syllable after the caesura. This was the only alliterated syllable in the second half-line.

A good example is line 3 of Cassidy McFadzean's poem: "<u>skulls</u> with <u>d</u>rooping || <u>d</u>ecorated <u>hoods</u>," (underlined words are the strongly stressed syllables and the alliterated sound is "d."). Cassidy follows the tradition with few variations, as in line two where the alliterated syllables are unstressed, rather than stressed ("*pre<u>serve</u>* their *<u>pal</u>lor* || *protect* whey-<u>faces</u>"). Traditionally, when the alliteration was based on consonants the sounds had to be exactly alike, but when based on vowels they did not have to match.

CASSIDY MCFADZEAN (b. 1989)

Riddle: These men dig fingers[55]

These stout monks   meditate in shade,
  preserve their pallor,   protect whey-faces
and bulging crowns.   They cover their bald
  skulls with drooping   decorative hoods,
  stately as top hats   shielding the sun
  or drenched in hail,   hanging snoods.
These men dig fingers   dirtcovered into earth,
fat bodies heave as   the hems of their skirts,
    tatter in the soil,   toes wriggling,
  like mice tails,   tantalized by prayer.
The monks remain   through the rain and grime
  as their hats wither,   wilting and darkened.
    They keep tongues   keen, singing
as they head indoors   to the heat of the sauna
  harkening to sow   a sweet melody of
sustenance filling our   stomachs with warmth.
What are these creatures?   Call out their names.

⇥

Doublet

In "A Doublet/Compost Poem," Barbara Nickel has transformed a word-game devised by Lewis Carroll into a form poem.

Carroll invented the game to entertain bored children on Christmas Day, 1877. The idea is simply to choose any two words of the same length (Carroll called these the doublet), then change one into the other. To do this, you pick one of the words and substitute just one letter to create a new word. This step is repeated until you have the other word of the doublet. Each new word (called a link) must be a real one, the new letter must be in the same position in the word as was the altered letter, and all other letters must stay in the same position as they held in the preceding word. The list (called a chain) you create can be any length, but the idea is to make it as short as possible.[56]

Nickel has played this game with the doublet "rind" and "dirt" — then taken it a step further by incorporating each word of the chain into a line of her children's poem.[57] Notice, too, that the words in her series fall into rhymed pairs (all but the last, are full rhymes).

---

56 Lewis Carroll, in the preface to *Doublets, A Word-Puzzle* by Charles Lutwidge Dawson (London: Macmillan & Co., 1879).

57 Nickel, in private correspondence with the editors, says she first learned about the doublet as a poetic form from Avis Harley's book, *Fly With Poetry: An ABC of Poetry.* (Honesdale, PA: Wordsong/Boyds Mills Press, 2000).

BARBARA NICKEL (b. 1966)

— After Avis Harley's "How Can You Change 'Sleep' Into 'Dream'"

A Doublet/Compost Poem:

How can you change "rind" into "dirt"?

Instead of throwing my grapefruit rind   into the trash,
           I could change my mind.
              This rind of mine needs worms and earth,
                    nine   weeks maybe to turn
            into a nice   heap of fruity mush for the garden.
              No   dice   rolling here! Not chance but choice; our
         planet is in dire   need of rinds, rinds turning like wheels and
    minds and orange moons, rinds
              turning
            into
               dirt.

Limerick

The limerick, an English folk form derived from the madsong (any song sung by a fool), is a popular — often bawdy — type of light verse. As Alan Wilson's "Particle Limericks" show, however, its intrinsic invitation to humour also offers poets a light-hearted way to tackle more serious subjects, so it makes sense that there is a tradition of using the limerick to write about science. The final punch line is sometimes a variation of line 1.

The standard form is straightforward — a five-line stanza consisting of a regular pattern of iambs and anapests rhyming *aabba*. Lines 1, 2 and 5 have three strong stresses ("There <u>was</u>| a neu<u>tri</u>|no from <u>Kent</u>,") and lines 3 and 4 have two ("With<u>out</u> |any <u>mass</u>"). A madsong stanza has the same metre but rhymes *abccb*.

ALAN WILSON

Particle Limericks

1
There was a neutrino from Kent,
who said, *Why pay any more rent?*
Without any mass,
not even an ass,
I might as well sit in a tent.

2
A drinking electron got tight,
charged randomly into the night,
with a sizzling sound,
he spun to the ground,
and threw up a bundle of light.

3
There was an unstable muon,
who realized something was wrong.
If I don't ditch some mass,
get rid of it fast . . .
But too late — the muon was gone.

Sapphics

The traditional Sapphics stanza is a quatrain named after the Greek poet Sappho who lived in the early seventh century BC. It is organized into a pattern of eleven long and short vowel sounds in the first three lines and five long and short vowel sounds in the fourth. This pattern has been adapted to English by substituting strong stresses for long vowels and soft ones for short. Each of the first three lines must be eleven syllables arranged in a stress pattern of strong / soft / strong / soft (or strong) / strong / soft / soft / strong / soft / strong / soft. The fourth line must be five syllables arranged in a stress pattern of strong / soft / soft / strong / soft.

In English, then, Sapphics might be considered a hybrid form, straddling syllabic verse (based on a set syllable count for each line) and accentual-syllabic verse (based on a set pattern of stresses and syllables for each line).

Don McKay strictly applies both the syllable count and stress pattern in every line, while Jay Macpherson varies the pattern only in her eleven-syllable lines.

DON McKAY (b. 1942)

Recipe for Divertimento in D, K: 136

1. *Allegro*
Gather tictocks, stir in a pot and feed to
tigers. Run these cats round a tree until they
turn to butter. Spread on a muffin. Makes an
excellent breakfast.

2. *Andante*
Let the clock remember the summer sadly.
Simmer. Tie this phrase to the seagull soaring
past. When seagull reaches the far horizon
lower the curtain.

3. *Presto*
Catch two chipmunks. Marinate. Open sleeping
clock and toss in merrily. Add the gusto.
Keep the sneezing regular, duple, hearty.
Tickles the angels.

Jay Macpherson (1931–2012)

from **The Way Down**

Some Ghosts & Some Ghouls

While we loved those who never read our poems,
Answered our letters, said the simple things we
Waited so long for, and were too polite to
   See we were crying,

Irony fed us: for the days we watched our
Chances to please them, nights in rumpled beds lay
Gored by their phantoms, guilty most of suffering,
   We were rewarded.

While we admired how ignorance became them,
Coldness adorned, they came at length to trust us,
Made us their mirrors: last their hopeless loves to
   Us they confided.

They were our teachers: what we are, they made us.
Cautious our converse, prudent our behaviour,
Guarded our faces: we behind them lurking,
   Greedy, devourers.

Syllabic Poem

English is an accentual-syllabic language, that is, one in which each word is made up of a series of syllables that are each given strong or soft stresses when spoken. Most metred poems in English measure the number of syllables, as well as the pattern of stresses on those syllables.

Another system, however, considers only the number of syllables in a line, regardless of where the stresses fall. This is called syllabics. It gained some popularity in the early twentieth century when, in England, Robert Bridges and his daughter Elizabeth Daryush, and in the US, Marianne Moore (independently of each other) developed the form for English poetry. The idea is to de-emphasize metred patterns to create a subtle form of poetry, relying as much on the visual as the aural for effect. It is the closest a poet can come to free verse yet still maintain a certain writing "discipline."

As Lewis Turco explains in *The New Book of Forms*, there are three main syllabic options:

- using the same number of syllables in every line,
- establishing a syllable pattern in the first stanza (which may vary from line to line), and following it in each subsequent stanza, and
- varying the number of syllables per line within certain limits (e.g., each line has a minimum of seven and a maximum of nine syllables).

How syllables are counted can vary, especially given regional inflections and differences in pronunciation. So you might count "buoy" as one syllable, or two.

Another well-known syllabic pattern, probably of French medieval origin, is the five-line *cinquain*. American poet Adelaide Crapsey adapted it to English, giving it a pattern of 2, 4, 6, 8 and 2 syllables per line. Nancy Bennett's "The Ghost of His Hand" is a fine example of why the *cinquain*'s intensity is often compared to the Japanese haiku.

DANIEL DAVID MOSES (b. 1952)

The Hands

Yes, our faces are ten blanks
but bearded with the ghosts of
quarter moons. So we are wise,
wiser than you who go clothed
in fur, than you who have eyes.

RUSSELL THORNTON (b. 1959)

The Cherry Laurel

The women who would gather in the vale
chewed cherry laurel leaves. When the poison
took hold and ushered them into frenzy,
they would see the vale was a hovering
of matter, a glittering haze. The earth
their bare feet danced on, and that had brought forth
everything around them, would, if they
threw off the names they had used for themselves,
begin to reveal to them what there was
of eternity in the world.
                          The vale
could open into a being, human,
yet other, whose name was a limitless,
pure embrace in an instant with no end;
then could close again and be a chaos
of innumerable identities
interspersed with abyss upon abyss.
It could pour blind currents of life, of death,
through the women's living skulls, and plunge them
into metamorphoses — so they might
suddenly know more than any mortal,
having become the vale itself, knowing.
Some would never return from such knowing,
and collapse and die. But others would now
be called Daphne, the name for the laurel,
and be priestesses.

The light of the vale
is in love with those frenzied ones — the rays
sent as from Apollo still following
the woman who ran from him and escaped
when she was changed into a tree. The fate
of even Apollo's love is held here
in the laurel branches. Here, your own fate,
though you do not know that fate, now fills you,
while the light, the vegetation, and rock,
so bright, so mysteriously exact,
are a moving stillness about to speak.

— Vale of Tempe/Larissa, Greece

NANCY BENNETT (b. 1962)

The Ghost of His Hand

Shallow
Bruises blush blue
Hidden by my sweet smile
Bruises fade but their ghosts always
Linger

Visual

Almost all cultures have a tradition of merging sound — the spoken quality of poems — into shape, to highlight the physical qualities of language. A visual poem is "drawn" on the page to depict the thing it describes and reinforce meaning. Visual poetry has many names (with small differences in definition), including concrete, shaped, pattern, spatial and calligramme. In *poetic designs*, Stephen Adams makes a useful distinction between shaped and visual poems. The former have a particular visual shape but, like Barbara Nickel's children's poem "Reduce your eco-foot-print," are still to be read. (Nickel's poem, intriguingly, also works as a list poem.) Visual poems are made up of letters but, like art, are primarily meant to be looked at.

bp Nichol's "Blues" is an example of a visual poem. He lays out the word "love" in various patterns and leaves it at that, so we are free to speculate on the "evol"utions of love, its ("eeeeeee") maddening and even its "evol" or dark sides. This poem might be saying, "I love in every which way," or "Love turns me upside down and all out of whack, or. ..." It has as many interpretations as any piece of visual art.

BP NICHOL (1944–1988)

Blues

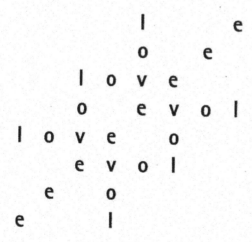

BARBARA NICKEL (b. 1966)

Reduce your eco-
foot-
print

Walk, bike, scooter,
bus, carpool even if it's
raining and you've lost your
other boot and you're late and
you've got too much to carry;
pogo-stick, meander, hike,
jog, puddle-jump, sing, pick-
up-litter-as-you-go, skip,
read-as-you-walk, hop-
scotch, leap, roller-
blade even if you ate
too much for break-
fast and it's snow-
ing and you forgot
your homework; smell
the tar, smell the cut
grass, the witch hazel
tree, blue hyacinths and
the fresh, wet earth
you're saving step
by little step.

— Barbara Nickel

COMING TO TERMS

Prosody is the study of the technical devices of form — especially line, metre (and rhythm), repetition and rhyme — that, together, make poetry distinct from prose. The word is derived from the Latin, *prosodia*, which refers to the stresses on syllables — hardly surprising, given the central importance of stress and metre in English language poetry until the advent of free verse in the twentieth century. Of course many of these techniques are also useful — even vital — for the free-verse poet, but here we will focus only on their use in formal poetry.

We have divided this section into four parts, each addressing one of the above devices. For ease of reference, the terms here, along with those used in the chapter introductions, are also listed in the index.

We have used standard poetic notation: metre is indicated by a line under strongly stressed syllables; feet are indicated by a single vertical line; caesurae by a double vertical line; line breaks by a slash; stanza breaks by a double slash; and rhyming sounds or words by italics.

Line

One key distinction between prose and poetry is that the latter (with the exception of the prose poem) is based on the line rather than the paragraph. Moreover, the line acts somewhat like a conductor's baton, in that it draws together all the other elements — including rhyme, metre and repetition — to complete the poem's overall music. The white space at the end of a line is breath, a pause. Even visual poems like bp Nichol's "Blues" rely on this key element to create its shape and impact.

A poem's tone, pace, meaning and emotion are all influenced by its lines: whether they are long or short; where they break in relation to syntax; how they interact with phrases, sentences and stanzas; the way they end in relation to rhyme and metre (e.g., softly with an unstressed syllable, emphatically with a stressed rhyme) and so on. The following are some devices involved in constructing the poetic line.

CAESURA: From the Latin for "cutting," a caesura (also spelled ce-sura) is a pause marking the natural rhythms of speech in a line of poetry. Usually near the middle of the line, it is often indicated by punctuation, as in "A gentle rain. Tanks rumble down the golden streets" from Leigh Nash's "And With Good Reason."

END STOPPED:	A line of poetry in which grammar and sense are complete (i.e., not carried over to the following line), so the reader naturally pauses before reading on. Often signified by a punctuation mark. For example, in the last stanza of Eli Mandel's villanelle, all four lines are end-stopped, as in: "Mostly you circle round and round the park."
ENJAMBED:	A phrase or sentence that is not complete in one line and must be carried over to the next, as in the following from Sir Charles G.D. Roberts' "The Skater": "Till the startled hollows awoke and heard // A spinning whisper, a sibilant twang."
HETEROMETRIC:	Stanzas with lines that have different metres. For example, see Annie Charlotte Dalton's "The Praying Mantis," where lines one and two of each stanza have four strong stresses and lines three and four have three.
INDENTATION:	Often used to indicate a slight pause in reading or to suggest a change in rhyme scheme; for instance if four lines are rhymed *abab*, the *b* lines may be indented. Indentation may also indicate different metres. John McRae gives the *b* rhymed lines a slight indentation, and the unrhymed refrain lines a larger indentation, in his rondeau, "In Flanders Fields."
ISOMETRIC:	Stanzas with all lines in the same metre. For example, Alexandra Oliver's sonnet, "Meeting the Tormentors in Safeway," where each line is in iambic pentameter. Mark Strand and Eavan Boland in *The Making of a Poem* point out that isometric poetry was the norm until the end of the Middle Ages, when poets began to experiment with varying line lengths.
PARENTHESIS:	Parenthesis in the poetic line is used to indicate an aside or insert information without disrupting the overall syntax. Its mild interruption offers a succinct way to add depth and complexity to content, particularly when the option of going off on a tangent would intrude on what is being said. Glenn Kletke uses this throughout "O Grandfather Dust." In these lines, for instance, the device adds descriptive detail to a list: "… pail / of well water (cold, so cold), tin dipper, sky dipper, Milky Way." And it adds emotional emphasis, a whiff of death, in the lines: "… how later in the morning you would carry to her / (O grandmother ashes!) prairie smoke …"

Metre

Metre is the foundation for the music in traditional poetry. The English language is rich in the number of systems it has for finding the metre — the measure — in a line. The five systems are: accentual (a pattern based only on strong stresses, as in Anglo-Saxon); syllabic (a pattern based only on the number of syllables, as in haiku); accentual-syllabic (the most common, a combination of both stress and syllable, as in iambic pentameter); quantitative (an adaptation of Greek and Latin metres to English); and free verse (the absence of any regular pattern).

For a detailed explanation of metre, readers can explore the references listed in the Bibliography. Very briefly, metrical patterns are divided into "feet." If syllables are like notes of music, then the "foot" is the musical bar sign that helps us locate ourselves in the patterns we're writing or reading and the metrical pattern is the time signature of the piece.

Most feet have just one strong stress plus whatever soft stresses it needs to complete its pattern. There are four primary feet for measuring metre, all based on the concept that each syllable in English has a certain amount of emphasis, or stress, when it's spoken. These are: the iamb (a soft/strong stress as in bestow), trochee (strong/soft as in ho-ly), anapest (soft/soft/strong as in un-der-stand), and dactyl (strong/soft/soft as in gin-ger-bread). Several others that may be used are listed in the definitions below.

Usually the overall pattern is the best gauge of a poem's metre. To "scan" a poem is to read or analyze its metric pattern (scan comes from the Latin *scandere*, to climb, which rightly suggests that scanning is not always an easy stroll, even if it's an enjoyable one). But poetry is nothing if not flexible, and often a poem's pattern is open to interpretation. Even the experts can hold widely varying views and sometimes passionately debate the "proper" way to scan certain feet or lines. In the end, the point isn't to debate the "right" or "wrong" way to scan a particular poem, but rather, for writers and readers to use metre as a tool to enjoy the music of poetry.

Metrical patterns create the underlying beat behind the overall rhythm of words and lines, while the rhythm of the voice as it reads a line of poetry is often quite different from the poem's metre. Think of music: if metre is the bass player then rhythm is the voice of the singer. In poetry, rhythm is the way we speak — it is tone, inflection, intent. The interplay and tension between these two — metre and vocal rhythm — creates much of the complex beauty of metred forms.

Opposite are the definitions of several terms related to metre.

Metrical Patterns:
There are two main schools of thought regarding how to scan for metre. One shares Robert Frost's view that there are only two kinds of English foot, iambic and loose iambic; the other maintains that a wider range of feet are necessary to accurately depict a poem's metre. By that school's definition, and to give the reader as broad a range of terms as possible, the following list describes a number of feet that may be found in English poetry. Traditionally, a soft stress (breve) in a pattern is indicated by ˘ and a strong stress (macron) by ′.

AMPHIBRACH: (˘ ′ ˘) A three-syllable foot, with the strong stress in the middle, flanked by two softly stressed syllables. For example, in F.R. Scott's "Metric Blues," the lines "The <u>met</u>|ric <u>tal</u>|on/'s <u>got</u> | you <u>gal</u>lon" can be scanned as three iambs and an amphibrach. (The last foot could also be scanned as an iamb with a tag.)

AMPHIMACER: (′ ˘ ′) A three-syllable foot, with two strong stresses flanking a softly stressed syllable, as in the final foot of line 3 in each stanza of Pauline Johnson's "The Train Dogs" (e.g., "<u>Shag</u>gy and | <u>swift</u> comes the | <u>yelp</u>ing <u>band</u>." (Also called cretic.)

ANACRUSIS One or more unstressed syllables at the beginning of a line that are not part of the first foot, as in this otherwise iambic line from Bliss Carman's "Low Tide at Grand Pré": "By an <u>ec</u> | sta<u>sy</u> | of <u>dream</u>." (In this example, the first foot could also be scanned as an anapest.)

ANAPEST: (˘ ˘ ′) A three-syllable foot, with the strong stress on the third. It often provides a light, speedy rhythm to a line, as in this one from Earle Birney's "From the Hazel Bough": "She was <u>plump</u> | as a <u>finch</u>."

CATALECTIC: (′) A final metrical foot in a line that, based on the prevailing pattern of metre in the poem, is incomplete, as in "Free" in the final line of stanza 9 in Steven Price's ballad: "When <u>out</u> | he <u>stepped</u>. | <u>Free</u>."

DACTYL: (′ ˘ ˘) A three-syllable foot, with the strong stress on the first. Marjorie Pickthall opens the following line from "Ebb Tide" with two dactyls: "<u>Borne</u> from the | <u>fight</u> and the | <u>full</u> en|<u>deav</u>our."

DOUBLE IONIC: (˘ ˘ ′ ′) When pyrrhic feet and spondees appear back to back they are called double ionic, as in this example from Tim Bowling's "Morenz": ("The <u>break</u>, | the <u>cast</u>, | the <u>fe</u>|ver, the |

held <u>breath</u>"). In this way, they "add up" to two iambs, creating an emphasis that doesn't wholly depart from the iambic pattern.

IAMB: (˘ ´) A two-syllable foot with the strong stress on the second. For example, the following line from Annie Charlotte Dalton's "The Praying-Mantis" has four iambs: "Strange <u>crea</u> | tures <u>walk</u> | and <u>breed</u> | their <u>kind</u>." *The Oxford Companion to the English Language* says the iamb is "the most frequently used foot in English verse."

PYRRHIC: (˘ ˘) A foot consisting of two softly stressed syllables, it usually appears with a spondee, as "ver, the" in the line, "The <u>break</u>, | the <u>cast</u>, | the <u>fe</u>|ver, the | <u>held</u> <u>breath</u>" in Tim Bowling's "Morenz" (see also double ionic).

SPONDEE: (´ ´) A foot consisting of two strong stresses, usually used for emphasis, as in the first of these two lines from F.R. Scott's "Metric Blues": "<u>Frown</u>, <u>pound</u>, / you're <u>quite</u> / un<u>sound</u>" (see also double ionic).

TAG: (˘) A soft stress at the end of a metred line that allows for colloquial speech. The tag is counted as part of the last foot. For example, the anonymous "Bugs" alternates iambic trimeter and tetrameter lines and every trimeter line ends with a tag. In the final line, "That <u>eats</u> | with<u>out</u> | per<u>mis</u>sion," the tag is the final (softly stressed) syllable, "sion," and is considered part of the final iambic foot. (Alternatively, this foot could be called an amphibrach.)

TROCHEE: (´ ˘) A two-syllable foot, with the strong stress on the first. For example, lines 2, 4, 5, 7 and 8 of Elise Partridge's triolet, "Vuillard Interior" all begin with trochees: "<u>o</u>ver," "<u>un</u>der," "<u>o</u>ver," "<u>knot</u>ting," "<u>in</u>to."

Poets frequently use substitution to give the power of the unexpected to regularly metred lines.

SUBSTITUTION: The prevailing metrical pattern is often varied by substituting a different foot for the one generally used. This can be very powerful, as in P.K. Page's "Water and Marble." Page writes in an overall iambic pattern as the speaker talks about the power of her lover, as in the line: "and <u>when</u> | his <u>name</u> | is <u>spo</u>|ken <u>pale</u> | still <u>sky</u>"). Occasionally, though, she opens a line with a trochee, breaking the iambic pattern, as in "tre̲mbles | and bre̲aks | and mo̲ves ..." Just as the speaker trembles, so the pattern trembles, too, and almost breaks — sound and sense, powerfully working together. (Also called variation.)

Lines of metred poetry are named for the number of feet per line, e.g.:

- One foot: monometer
- Two feet: dimeter
- Three feet: trimeter
- Four feet: tetrameter
- Five feet: pentameter
- Six feet: hexameter (called an alexandrine when all six feet are iambs)
- Seven feet: heptameter
- Eight feet: octameter

Repetition

Poets use repetition in a variety of ways, particularly to intensify emotion; perhaps recurring words and phrases remind us at some physical level of the repetition of the heartbeat, of seasons and tides. The use of this seemingly simple yet challenging tool can — when used well — build suspense, add emphasis, suggest inevitability, exhibit obsessiveness and so on.

Repetition also provides the foundation for a number of fixed forms, including the blues, fugue, ghazal, glosa, incantation, madrigal, palindrome, pantoum, the entire rondeau family, sestina, terzanelle, triolet and villanelle; how it is employed in those forms is discussed in the various chapter introductions.

There are numerous technical terms for this device, each denoting a different type of recurrence for words, lines, phrases, sentences or stanzas. Some of the most commonly used are described below.

Refrain

"Refrain" is often broadly used to refer to any regularly repeated line(s) that provide a chorus effect in a poem. However, refrain is one of several terms that can have more precise meanings:

BURDEN:	A complete stanza that is repeated regularly throughout a poem, as in Ryan Knighton's "Ballad of Echolocation."
INCREMENTAL REPETITION:	Complete stanzas that are repeated, but with significant alterations each time they appear; the changes, as they accrue, help to build the poem's emotion and give it momentum, as in the madrigal.

REFRAIN:	Part of one stanza that is regularly repeated in each successive stanza. For example, the lines "Grey Rider of the Shee?" and "To-night, O Vanathee" in Norah M. Holland's "The Grey Rider" are refrains. (Sometimes also used synonymously with "burden" and "repetend.")
REPETEND:	A line or phrase that is irregularly repeated, sometimes with variations, throughout a poem. This technique is a key feature of the fugue, for example, the lines "And the season advances" in Herménégilde Chiasson's poem of the same title.

Words and Phrases

ANADIPLOSIS:	A word or phrase used at the end of one line and repeated at the beginning of the next. For example, the word "dead" in the first two lines of A.J.M. Smith's "News of the Phoenix": "They say the Phoenix is dying, some say dead. / Dead without issue is what one message said."
ANAPHORA:	Word(s) repeated at the beginning of consecutive lines. For example, "I jab my tools in water / I jab them in charcoal, / I jab them at the bottle's neck" from John G. Fisher's "Back on the Job." Used persistently throughout a poem, this device has an incantatory effect, as in Renée Saklikar's "from the archive, a continuance." Anaphora also refers to this kind of repetition within lines when the word(s) start successive phrases or sentences. For example, the phrase "dead in" at the beginning and in the middle of most lines in Thuong Vuong-Riddick's "My Beloved is Dead in Vietnam."
EPANALEPSIS:	Use of the same word(s) at both the beginning and the end of a single line, as in E.J. Pratt's "The Lee-Shore": "Keep away from the land, keep away."
EPISTROPHE:	Word(s) repeated at the end of consecutive lines. For example, the word "marble" ends the last four lines of P.K. Page's "Water and Marble": "… in a dome of marble / and winter seals its floury drifts in marble / all matter doublelocks as dense as marble / and I, in other's eyes, am cut from marble." Epistrophe also refers to this kind of repetition within lines when the word(s) end successive phrases and sentences. For example, in stanza 2 of "Fugue," Robyn

Sarah ends these two sentences with the word "children": "… They are taking / it all with them: rugs, / pianos, children. Or they are leaving / it all behind them: cats, / plants, children."

EPIZEUXIS: Insistent, multiple repetition of the same word or phrase within a line, often to add emotional intensity, as in "Yeats. Yeats. Yeats. Yeats. Yeats. Yeats. Yeats." from John Thompson's ghazal "IX."

ITERATIO: A word or phrase repeated only once, without interruption, within a line. Kenneth Leslie uses this to achieve a thoughtful tone in line 2 of "Sonnet": "silver of life, life's silver sheen of glory."

POLYPTOTON: A word repeated almost immediately but in a different form, as in "faces a faceless …" in Maxianne Berger's "Empty Chairs."

SYMPLOCE: Repetition at both the beginning and end of successive lines, where the word(s) repeated at the start are different from the word(s) repeated at the end. Tim Bowling uses this device in lines 1 and 2 of "Morenz": "The crowds, the cheers, the broken leg, the death./ The crowds, the tears, the open casket, the death." (This is a combination of anaphora and epistrophe.)

Rhyme

A central feature of most form poetry, rhyme is the matching of like sounds in words. It occurs not only at the ends of lines, but within them. (It is worth noting that, as Stephen Adams points out, "free verse can also call on rhyme as a structuring device."[58])

For centuries, its detractors have condemned rhyme for much the same reasons as John Milton did in his defence of using blank verse (unrhymed iambic pentameter lines) in "Paradise Lost." In his preface to that poem, Milton called rhyme "the invention of a barbarous age, to set off wretched matter and lame metre" and argued that "true musical delight … consists only in apt numbers,

---

58 Stephen J. Adams, *poetic designs* (Peterborough, Ontario: Broadview Press, 2000), p. 177

fit quantity of syllables, and the sense variously drawn out from one verse into another, not in the jingling sound of like endings ..."[59]

Of course, Milton knew a good rhyme when he saw one, and used the device well in numerous poems. His argument was against poor rhyme, the kind that "jingles." Handled well, rhyme does not have to intrude or distract. As Alexander Pope said in his *An Essay on Criticism*, "The sound must seem an echo to the sense." More recently, Edward Hirsch, in *A Poet's Glossary*, describes it this way: "There is something charged and magnetic about a good rhyme ... as if the poet had called up the inner yearning of words to find each other."[60] When that is the case, rhyme can profoundly influence the music, tone and emotional impact of a poem.

Rhyme schemes also play a role in how stanzaic poems are structured — and the pattern, once established, tends to be repeated throughout.

Rhyme is usually categorized by its sound and its position in words, lines and stanzas. Rhyming sounds or words in the examples that follow are indicated by italics.

Sound

ALLITERATION: Repetition of initial sounds of words in close proximity, for example, "... *h*uman, *h*ers, and anchored in them, *h*is" in John Reibetanz's "Head and Torso of the Minotaur." Alliteration is also a structuring element in Anglo-Saxon poetry (see "... and More" chapter). (Also called head or initial rhyme.)

ASSONANCE: Repetition of vowels that sound the same in words, for example, the letter *i* in "... beh*i*nd us. We arr*i*ve" in Diana Brebner's "The Golden Lotus."

CONSONANCE: Repetition of consonants that sound the same in words, for example, the letters *ns* in "te*ns*ed" and "agai*ns*t" in Charles Bruce's "Eastern Shore."

EYE: An exception to rhyme based on sound, this is based on the spelling of words; i.e., they look similar but sound different. For example, *appears* and *pears* in the closing couplet of Diana Brebner's "The Golden Lotus." In many cases eye-rhymes probably sounded alike at one point, but lost that quality as pronunciations changed.

---

59   John Milton, *Paradise Lost and Other Poems* (Markham: Penguin Books Canada, 1981), p. 34
60   Edward Hirsch, *A Poet's Glossary*, p. 528.

FULL:	Words where all sounds but the first are the same, for example, dr*oop* and h*oop* in Dennis Lee's "Alligator Pie." (Also called perfect, true or pure rhyme.)
IDENTICAL:	Rhyming by repeating the same word, giving added emphasis to content; for instance, "me" in Leonard Cohen's "Twelve O'Clock Chant." Identical rhyme is one of the traditional elements at the end of the second line of each ghazal couplet and is often an important feature in blues poems. (See also, rich rhyme.)
MACARONIC:	The rhyming of words from different languages, for example, "Beaucaire" and "there" in Catherine Owen's "Villanelle."
MONORHYME:	The use of the same full rhyme sound throughout all or part of a poem. R. Nathaniel Dett features monorhyme in the second and fourth lines of all stanzas in "Conjured" ("pitch," "witch," "itch," "stitch," "hitch," "switch," "ditch," "twitch," "which.")
NEAR:	Words that contain one or more similar sounds, but are otherwise different; for example, "pot*atoes*" and "t*able*s," "*L*odge" and "Green*laws*" and "c*ash*" and "gl*ass*" in Brian Bartlett's found poem, "What He Chose to Record." Usually these rhymes rely on assonance or consonance. (Also called approximate, half, imperfect, off, oblique or slant rhyme.)
ONOMATOPOEIA:	Words that make the sound of what they stand for; for example, "Buzzin'" in George Elliot Clarke's "King Bee Blues": "I'm an ol' king bee, honey, / Buzzin' from flower to flower."
RICH RHYME:	Words that sound exactly the same, but are homophones — spelled differently and with different meanings; for example, the end rhyme in Phyllis Webb's "The Second Hand": "tying our hearts in a lover's *knot*, // now, whether we flower or *not*." (From the French term, *rime riche*. Also known as identical rhyme when the rhyming words are homographs — same spellings but with different meanings, as in *fall* (autumn) and *fall* (drop) in the penultimate stanza of Eric Ormsby's "Jaham Sings of the Fear of the Moon.")

Position in Words

ONE-SYLLABLE: Words that rhyme on the final strongly stressed syllable in the line, as in _mouse_, _grouse_ and _house_ in Glenn Kletke's "O Grandfather Dust" or _Tennessee_ and _McGee_ in Robert Service's "The Cremation of Sam McGee." Also called masculine rhyme.

TWO-SYLLABLE: Words that rhyme across two syllables, including on the soft stress that ends a line; for example, _wonder_ and _thunder_ in Marjorie Pickthall's "Ebb Tide." Also called feminine or double rhyme.

TRIPLE RHYME: Words that rhyme across three syllables, as in vulg_arity_ and cl_arity_ in Sharon Thesen's "The Broken Cup."

APOCOPATED: The final syllable of one of the words is left out of the rhyme; for example, "_sheath_ed" and "_death_" in Brian Bartlett's "What He Chose to Record."

BROKEN: More than one word is used to complete the rhyme; for example, "V_enus_" and "betw_een us_" in Richard Outram's "Tourist Stricken at the Uffizi." (also called mosaic rhyme).

WRENCHED: The strongly stressed syllable of one word rhymes with a softly stressed syllable in another, for example, _caught_ and _on_slaught in Phyllis Webb's "The Second Hand."

Position in Lines

END: Any instance where the rhyme falls on the last word in lines, as in the opening stanza of Sir Charles G.D. Roberts' "The Skater": "My glad feet shod with the glittering _steel_ / I was the god of the wingèd _heel_." (Also called terminal rhyme.)

INTERNAL: Rhyme within a line; for example, "A pal's last _need_ is a thing to _heed_, so I swore I would not fail" in Robert Service's "The Cremation of Sam McGee."

CHAIN: The last syllable of one line rhymes with the first syllable in the next, as in "See how long you l_ast_ / C_ask_et-like that boiler loomed," in Steven Price's ballad.

Position in Stanzas

COUPLET: A rhyme scheme where words at the ends of two consecutive lines rhyme (_aa_), as in these lines from Barker Fairley's "Bach Fugue": "This is the first of the themes, the lecturer _said_, / Please be at pains to fix it in the _head_."

CROSSED:	A rhyme scheme where end words of alternate lines rhyme (*abab*), as in the first four lines of Archibald Lampman's "The City of the End of Things": "Beside the pounding cata*racts* / Of midnight streams unknown to *us* / 'Tis builded in the leafless t*racts* / And valleys huge of Tartar*us*." (Also called alternating or interlocking rhyme.)
ENVELOPE:	A rhyme scheme where rhyming end words of two or more lines are enclosed by rhyming words in the line before and after them (*abba*). For example, Pauline Johnson's "The Train Dogs" uses envelope rhyme: "Savage of bread and of *bone*, / Shaggy and swift comes the yelping *band*, / Freighters of fur from the voiceless *land* / That sleeps in the Arctic z*one*." (Also called inserted rhyme or kissing rhyme.)
INTERMITTENT:	A rhyme scheme where only the end words of alternate lines rhyme, as in the ballad stanza (*abcb*); for example, the rhyme scheme in all but the last two lines of John G. Fisher's "Back on the Job": "I jab my tools in water / I jab them in charc*oal*, / I jab them at the bottle's neck, / But there! I've missed the h*ole*."
INTERLACED:	A rhyme scheme with two rhymes in consecutive lines — the first rhyme is on words at the mid-line pause (caesura) and the second is on the end words. For example, these lines in Marilyn Bowering's "Widow's Winter": "Bless the r*ed* door open w*ide*. / Bless the d*ead* who play ins*ide*." (Also called caesural rhyme.)
LEONINE:	A rhyme that occurs within the line. The word before the caesura rhymes with the last word of the line, as in the opening line of Robert Service's "The Cremation of Sam McGee": "There are strange things d*one* in the midnight s*un*."
TERZA RIMA:	A particular rhyme scheme for three-line stanzas, rhyming *aba bcb cdc*, etc, as in Sharon Thesen's "The Broken Cup." The envelope in one stanza encloses the middle line, which goes on to become the enclosing rhyme in the next stanza.
THORN:	An unrhymed line or lines in stanzas that are otherwise rhymed, as in "creatures" at the end of stanza 1 in Irving Layton's "Keine Lazarovitch." (Thorn lines are represented by an "x" in rhyme schemes — so, in Layton's poem, the rhyme scheme is *aaax bbbc dddc eeef gggf*.)

NOTES TO THE POEMS

"The Grey Rider" by Norah M. Holland: In her book, *Spun-Yarn and Spindrift*, Holland says that *Shee* and *Sidhe* mean "fairies;" *Vanathee* means "woman of the house."

"Back on the Job" by John G. Fisher: *The Tribune* in Toronto introduced this poem with: "The following original lines are reproduced in *The Tribune* at the request of Mr. Frank J. Crofton. They were penned by John G. Fisher, a veteran member of the Glass Blowers' Association, who returned to active work in the trade recently, after an absence of about 20 years." (Quoted from *The Poetry of the Canadian People, 1720–1920: Two Hundred Years of Hard Work*, edited by N. Brian Davis, Toronto, ON: NC Press Ltd., 1976, p. 175).

"XVIII .ii" by Steven Price is from *Anatomy of Keys*, his book-length meditation on the life of Harry Houdini.

"The Ballad of Echolocation" by Ryan Knighton: In correspondence with the editors, Knighton said the sound of his cane tapping the pavement was the impetus for the metre — and the source of the title — for this poem.

"Jeremiah's Blues on the GW Bridge" by Adam Sol: Jeremiah, from Sol's verse-novel *Jeremiah, Ohio*, is a contemporary homeless wanderer, inspired by the Biblical prophet and doomsayer of the same name.

"Metric Blues" by F.R. Scott: *Lhude* means loud. Scott's poem is an example of poets being inspired by each other's work. In this case "lhude" was earlier used by Ezra Pound in "Ancient Music" ("Winter is icummen in, / Lhude sing Goddamm"). Pound's poem in turn is a parody of the anonymous Anglo-Saxon madsong, "Cuckoo Song" (c. 1250), which begins: "Sumer is icumen in, / Lhude sing cuccu!" Notice that though the poem is ostensibly a lament about having to shift from Imperial to metric measure, it manages to mention "pound" twice, and of course, "pound" could refer to both the person and the measure.

"Quodlibets" by Robert Hayman: In the anthology *The Poets of Canada*, editor John Robert Colombo says this is the first original verse published on the North American continent and notes that "a *quodlibet* (Latin for 'what it pleases') is a debating point" (p. 25–26). Musically, the quodlibet is defined by Penguin's *A New Dictionary of Music* as a "piece containing several popular tunes put together in unusual and (usually) ingenious fashion — such as that which ends Bach's 'Goldberg Variations,' incorporating two well-known tunes of his day."

"Pavillion Misrepresents Outlook" by F.R. Scott: The words were found in an article in *The Gazette*, Montreal, July 11, 1967.

"What He Chose to Record" by Brian Bartlett: All words and sentences were taken from the 1889–1918 diaries of the poet's great-grandfather, C.B. (Crawford Buntin) Lawrence, of Bayside, New Brunswick.[61]

from "The Garbage Poems" ("For the boys cliff-jumping by the memorial stone") by Anna Swanson: In 2015 when Swanson was in Flatrock, Newfoundland, she stayed in a small house near a swimming hole that at night was "populated by teenagers who drank beer and energy drinks and jumped off cliffs and poured entire containers of Sunlight dish soap into the waterfall to make bubbles." In the mornings she would collect the trash, and swim there. The poem is from a series called "The Garbage Poems" that's limited to the words she found on those cans and labels.

"Zong! #24" by M. NourbeSe Philip:[62] In 1781 a ship carrying 470 slaves sailed from West Africa to Jamaica on a ship called the *Zong*. As was usual, the cargo was insured. Due to the captain's navigational errors, the trip took far longer than usual and when they ran out of water, the captain, Luke Collingwood, threw 150 of his "negro" cargo overboard, believing that if they died natural deaths on board, the insurance company wouldn't pay the owners. In due course the ship's insurers were ordered to pay the shipping company for the loss of "cargo," but the decision was appealed to the British Court of Queen's Bench. The final report, *Gregson vs. Gilbert*, or the *Zong* case, is the only record remaining and forms the text from which NourbeSe Philip drew the poems in her book *Zong!* (This decision was also key to the eventual British decision to end the trans-Atlantic slave trade.)

Distressed at the knowledge that the drowned people had no recorded names, NourbeSe Philip decided "They must be named." The names below the horizontal line at the bottom of the pages of the poem, she tells us, are "ghostly footnotes." She adds that the "idea at [the] heart of the footnotes in general is acknowledgement — someone else was here before — in *Zong!* footnote equals the footprint. Footprints of the African[s] on board the *Zong*."

from "the place of scraps" by Jordan Abel: Abel's book revolves around a key work, *Totem Poles*, by Marius Barbeau, an early-twentieth-century

---

61 Brian Bartlett, *The Watchmaker's Table* (Fredericton, NB: Goose Lane Editions, 2008), p. 131–132

62 All quotes by Marlene NourbeSe Philip, are from the *Notanda* (Latin, the legalese for Notes) at the end of her book, *Zong!* — *As told to the author by Setaey Adamu Boateng* (Middletown, CT: Wesleyan University Press, 2008).

anthropologist who studied First Nations cultures in the Pacific Northwest, including Abel's ancestral Nisga'a Nation. Beginning with Barbeau's own words, Abel uses erasure to "mine" the original text and thus explore the complicated relationship between First Nations cultures and ethnography.

"Late Love Song, With an Orange: A Cento" by Maureen Hynes: The sources used in this poem are:

(1) Jane Munro, "Old Man Vacanas #3," *Blue Sonoma*, London, ON: Brick Books, 2014.

(2) Sue Goyette, "Thirty-One," *Ocean*, Kentville, NS: Gaspereau Press, MMXIII.

(3) Joanne Kyger, "[When I used to focus on the worries, everybody ...]" from *About Now: Collected Poems*, published by the National Poetry Foundation, 2007.

(4) Muriel Rukeyser, "Then I saw what the calling was," *A Muriel Rukeyser Reader*, New York, NY: W.W. Norton, 1994.

(5) Erin Mouré, "Agarimo, May," *Little Theatres (teatrinos) or/ou Aturoxos Calados*, Toronto, ON: House of Anansi, 2005.

(6) John Berryman, "Sonnet 13," from *Berryman's Sonnets*, New York, NY: Farrar, Straus & Giroux, LLC, www.fsgbooks.com, 1969.

(7) Mary Ruefle, "Proscenium Arch," *Selected Poems*, Seattle & New York, NY: Wave Books, 2010.

(8) Joanne Kyger, "[When I used to focus on the worries, everybody ...]" from *About Now: Collected Poems*, published by the National Poetry Foundation, 2007.

(9) Hillary Gravendyk, "Apologies with bees in it," Harm, Richmond, California: Omnidawn, 2012, http://ronsilliman.blogspot.ca/2014/05 blog-post_12.html.

(10) Laura Kasischke, "Landscape with one of the earthworm's ten hearts," *Space, in Chains*, Port Townsend, WA: Copper Canyon, 2011.

(11) Catherine Graham, "The Animal Game," *Her Red Hair Rises With the Wings of Insects*," Hamilton, ON: Wolsak and Wynn, 2014.

(12) Brenda Shaugnessy, "Card 19: The Sun," *Our Andromeda*, Townsend, WA: Copper Canyon, 2012.

(13) Maleea Acker, "iv. Calle Alcudia," *Air-Proof Green*, St. John's, NL: Pedlar Press, 2013.

(14) Jean Valentine, *"Old love, I want to phone you,"* *Break the Glass*, Port Townsend, WA: Copper Canyon, 2010.

(15) Adrienne Rich, "There is no one story and one story only," *The School Among the Ruins: Poems 2000–2004*, New York, NY: W.W. Norton, 2004.

(16) Catherine Graham, "Small Hidden Door," *Her Red Hair Rises With the Wings of Insects,*" Hamilton, ON: Wolsak and Wynn, 2014.

(17) Barry Dempster, "One Minute," *Love Outlandish,* London, ON: Brick Books, 2009.

(18) Nicole Brossard, *Lovhers,* translated by Barbara Godard, Toronto, ON: Guernica, 1980.

(19) Alicia Suskin Ostriker, "Vocation," *No Heaven,* Pittsburg, PA: University of Pittsburgh, 2005.

(20) Barry Dempster, "Come Live With Me," *Love Outlandish,* London, ON: Brick Books, 2009.

(21) Mary Ruefle, "Why I am not a good kisser," *Selected Poems,* Seattle & New York, NY: Wave Books, 2010.

(22) Maleea Acker, "Pixel," *Air-Proof Green,* St. John's, NL: Pedlar Press, 2013.

(23) Erin Mouré, "Apples," *Little Theatres (teatrinos) or/ou Aturoxos Calados,* Toronto, ON: House of Anansi, 2005.

(24) Mary Ruefle, "Kiss of the Sun," *Selected Poems,* Seattle & New York: Wave Books, 2010.

(25) Dionne Brand, "VII," *Inventory,* Toronto, ON: McClelland & Stewart, 2006.

"Ghazal V" by Kuldip Gill: In her book, *Dharma Rasa,* Gill provides the following translations: *doria* — "decorative wool or cotton extensions for braids;" *baisaki* — "spring festival;" *gulabi* — "rose colour;" *khoti* — "a small room sometimes on a rooftop;" *doli* — "very sad wedding songs, also the cart that carries a bride away." p.101–103. It's also our understanding that "Vasanti" was a name Gill sometimes used in reference to herself, so the last couplet is a signature couplet.

"IX" from *Stilt Jack* by John Thompson: *Captain Kangaroo* was the longest running children's television series in history. Bob Keeshan, who also played the role of Clarabell the Clown on the *Howdy Doody Show,* was the gentle Captain Kangaroo (named for all his many pockets) who appeared on TV every weekday morning from 1955–1984. "Smokin' cigarettes and watchin' Captain Kangaroo" is a line from the song "Flowers on the Wall," written by the Statler Brothers.

"Planet Earth" by P.K. Page: This, the title poem in her collection, *Planet Earth: Poems Selected and New,* was selected in 2001 to mark the United Nations International Year of Dialogue Among Civilizations and was read aloud simultaneously at the UN in New York, a science station in the Antarctic, on a boat in the West Philippines Sea and on Mount Everest.

"Hymn for Portia White" by George Elliot Clarke: Portia White (1911–1968) was a classical singer and brilliant interpreter of Black spirituals. Of Afri-cadian (African-Acadian) descent, she was born in Truro, Nova Scotia, the third of 13 children. Her father, the descendant of slaves and an ordained minister, was the first Black student to graduate from Acadia University. As the family was very poor, the community (including the mayor of Halifax, the president of the Halifax Ladies' Musical Club and the lieutenant-gov-ernor), set up and contributed to the Nova Scotia Talent Trust, created in 1944 to support White's early musical training and later singing career. The trust still exists to support young artists.

"Shouting Your Name Down the Well" by David W. McFadden: In correspond-ence with the editors, David McFadden said the title of his sequence refers to a Japanese tradition of calling the spirit of the recently deceased back to earth by shouting their name down the well. "Takuboku" refers to the Japanese poet Ishikawa Takuboku (1886–1912).

"To Lighten Heavy Loads" by Aua: This is among the Inuit songs collected and translated by Danish explorer Knud Rasmussen, who included them in his *Report of the Fifth Thule Expedition, 1921–1924*. In his introduction to *Poems of the Inuit*, John Robert Colombo notes that "The Inuktitut word for breath, *anerca*, also means poetry." (p. 14) He quotes Rasmussen on "To Lighten Heavy Loads": "Aua himself had, as a young man, learnt certain charms of this sort from an old woman named Qeqertuanaq, in whose fami-ly they had been handed down from generation to generation dating back to 'the very first people on earth.' And by way of payment Aua had undertaken to feed and clothe her for the rest of her life. They had always to be uttered in her name, or they would be of no avail." (p. 111)

"from the archive, a continuance" by Renée Sarojini Saklikar: The poem is from Saklikar's book-length poem, *children of air india*, which probes the horror and aftermath of the bombing of Air India Flight 182 on June 23, 1982. The bombing killed 329 people, the majority of them Canadian citizens of Indian ancestry. Eighty-two of the victims were children. It was Canada's worst mass murder and the deadliest terrorist attack involving an airplane until the September 11, 2001, attacks in New York, yet only one person has ever been convicted of involvement in the crime.

"Morenz" by Tim Bowling: Howie Morenz (1902–1937) is widely considered the National Hockey League's first superstar. Morenz, whose speed and puck handling were legendary, was known variously as the "streak on skates," "the Stratford streak," and the "Canadien Comet." He spent 12 of his 14 years in the NHL (1923–1937) with the Montreal Canadiens, scoring just over 290 career goals in that league (in 1929–1930, he scored an amazing 40 goals in 44 games). He died suddenly a few weeks after breaking his leg during an NHL game at the Montreal Forum, as a result of complications related to the injury. A three-time Hart Trophy winner, Morenz was one of the first players to be elected to the Hockey Hall of Fame when it was created in 1945.

"His Flute, My Ears" by Gregory Scofield: The final stanza in this poem closes with a translation of the Cree phrases.

"Empty Chairs" by Maxianne Berger: Berger says she varied her pantoum by altering the repeated words, phrases and lines, "through polyptotonic variation to play on the contrasts set up by the poem's premise." (In correspondence with the editors.)

"blues" by Christine Wiesenthal: The poem plays with feeling sad but also "bluing" — a process traditionally used to prevent whites from going yellow in the wash.

"Fiddle bids us" by Marilyn Dumont: "set us below": to set people below means to look down on them.

"The Edge" by Fred Cogswell: *loup-garou* means werewolf.

"Flirrup" by Mary Dalton: In her "Note on the Poems" in her book, *Merrybegot*, Dalton comments: "At the risk of incurring the scorn of critics such as the contemporary of John Clare who sneered at his incomprehensible words in *The Shepherd's Calendar*, I have chosen not to include a glossary. Generally the context in which a word or idiom appears will guide the reader and the DNE [*Dictionary of Newfoundland English*] to be found in print and on-line at www.heritage.nf.ca/dictionary will almost always be helpful to someone wanting to follow the words."

from "SIGINT" by Ken Babstock: SIGINT is a military abbreviation for Signals Intelligence, commonly referred to as "spying." Ken Babstock explains in his notes to the book that these sonnets "'occur' inside the abandoned NSA surveillance station on the summit of Teufelsberg ('Devil's Mountain') in Berlin, Germany. A man-made mountain, Teufelsberg is the result of the Allies' decision to pile massive quantities of the postwar rubble of Berlin on top of a Nazi military-technical college, designed by Albert Speer and left unfinished after the war. As part of ECHELON, this NSA listening station was constructed in 1963, intercepting all telecommunications and satellite signals from the east. It was abandoned and left derelict after the fall of the Berlin Wall and the departure of the NSA in 1991. The cluster of buildings and radar domes remains empty." Babstock goes on, "The sonnets source vocabulary from Walter Benjamin's records of his son's language acquisition between the ages of two and six," but that source text is abandoned at the sonnet's volta. Babstock further explains: "The italicized 'incident reports' that appear in lieu of a traditional sonnet's closing couplet imagine collisions between light aircraft and common swifts in what would have been Soviet airspace." In the full text, "the collisions begin in Siberia at 'A' and travel westward (through a malfunctioning clock) to Berlin and 'Z.'"[63]

"From the Hazel Bough" by Earle Birney: The Celts believed hazelnuts gave one wisdom and inspiration, and since the fifteenth century in Europe (and later North America), hazel boughs and witch hazel have been used to dowse (find) water, gems or minerals deep underground.

"Low Tide on Grand Pré" by Bliss Carman: *Acadie* refers to Acadia, the areas in what are now New Brunswick and Nova Scotia that were settled by the French in the seventeenth and eighteenth centuries. Grand Pré is the site of Longfellow's romantic poem "Evangeline," based on Le Grand Dérangement, the name given by the Acadians to their tragic expulsion from the country by the British in 1755. The exiles were allowed to return after New France was ceded to England in 1763. Most of today's Acadians live in New Brunswick, Nova Scotia and Prince Edward Island as well as parts of Quebec and Maine.

"Cell Sequencing" by Madeline Bassnett: Bassnett invented this nonce form based on the idea of cell division and death. Each stanza uses the same words but fewer of them than in the preceding stanza, the idea being to reflect the reality of replication and reduction. The poem ends with a monostich stanza — one line recognizing the cell as the basic building block of human bodies. As Bassnett told us, "even reduced, it is waiting to reproduce."

"Woods" by David Waltner-Toews: Waltner-Toews says, "This poem is from a sequence of five terzanelles and a sonnet written from the point of view of an ultra-light, and dedicated to Carl Hiebert, who took me up with him. Confined to a wheelchair since 1971, Carl flew his open-cockpit ultralight aircraft 5,000 miles across Canada, landing at Expo '86 in Vancouver. The five elements in the Chinese calendar are earth, metal, water, wood and fire. The Greek tradition had earth, air, fire and water. I have amalgamated the two groups." (In correspondence with the editors.)

63 Ken Babstock, *On Malice* (Toronto, ON: Coach House Books, 2014), p. 93.

"More of the Just" by Sandy Shreve: This poem is after Steven Heighton's "Some Other Just Ones" (in his collection, *Patient Frame*) and Jorge Luis Borges' "The Just" (in his *Selected Poems*).

"Queen Mary, She's My Friend" by Stephen Scobie: The acrostic is on the first word of each line and forms a refrain from Bob Dylan's "Blowing in the Wind."

"Riddle: These men dig fingers" by Cassidy McFadzean: The answer to the riddle is "mushroom."

"Particle Limericks" by Alan Wilson: Alas for Wilson's first limerick, Canadian astrophysicist Arthur B. McDonald and Japanese physicist Takaaki Kjita, proved that neutrinos do, in fact, have mass (and won the 2015 Nobel Prize in Physics for that work). The poem, nonetheless, remains a pleasure!

BIBLIOGRAPHY

The following is a selection of useful texts on fixed forms and prosody:

Adams, Stephen, *poetic designs: an introduction to meters, verse forms, and figures of speech*, Peterborough, ON: Broadview, 1997 (reprinted 2000)

Agha, Shahid Ali, ed., *Ravishing DisUnities, Real Ghazals in English*, Hanover and London: Wesleyan University Press, 2000

_____, *Call Me Ishmael Tonight: A Book of Ghazals*, New York, NY: W.W. Norton, 2003

Allen, Lillian, "Black Voice — Context and Subtext." The Anne Szumigalski Memorial Lecture in *Prairie Fire*, Winter 2014-15, Vol. 35, No. 4

Beckson, Karl and Arthur Ganz, eds., *A Reader's Guide to Literary Terms*, Harvard: The Noonday Press: 1960

Brogan, T.V.F., ed., *The New Princeton Handbook of Poetic Terms*, Princeton, NJ: Princeton University Press, 1994

Burt, Stephen and David Mikics, eds., *The Art of the Sonnet*. Cambridge, MA: Belknap Press, 2010

Carter, Barb, "The Prose Poem: Favours of the Moon and Other Moon Shine. An Interview with Eve Joseph and Patricia Young." *The New Quarterly*, Summer 2015

Carter, Terry Ann, "A History of Haiku in Canada (in Two Parts)." www.brick-books.ca/a-history-of-haiku-in-canada-in-two-parts-by-terry-ann-carter/ Posted May 14, 2015. Accessed August 16, 2015

_____, *Lighting the Global Lantern — A Teacher's Guide to Writing Haiku and Related Literary Forms*, Frontenac, ON: Wintergreen Studios Press, 2011

Cuddon, J.A., *The Penguin Dictionary of Literary Terms and Literary Theory*, 3rd edition, London: Penguin, 1991

Finch, Annie, and Kathrine Varnes, eds., *An Exaltation of Forms: Contemporary Poets Celebrate the Diversity of Their Art*, Ann Arbor, MI: University of Michigan Press, 2002

Fuller, John, *The Sonnet*, London: Methuen & Co., 1972

Fussell, Paul, *Poetic Meter & Poetic Form* (Revised Edition), New York, NY: Random House, 1979

Hecht, Anthony, *Melodies Unheard: Essays on the Mysteries of Poetry*, Baltimore, MD: Johns Hopkins University Press, 2003

Higginson, William J., with Penny Harter, *The Haiku Handbook: How to Write, Share, and Teach Haiku*, New York, NY: Kodansha International, 1985

Hirsch, Edward, *A Poet's Glossary*. Boston, New York, NY: Houghton Mifflin Harcourt, 2014

_____, *How to Read a Poem — and learn to fall in love with poetry*, A DoubleTakeBook, Centre for Documentary Studies in association with A Harvest Book, Harcourt Inc., 1999

Hirschfield, Jane, *Nine Gates, Entering the Mind of Poetry*, New York, NY: Harper Collins, 1997

Hollander, John, *Rhyme's Reason*, New Haven, CT: Yale University Press, 1981

Holman, C. Hugh, *A Handbook to Literature* (Fourth Edition), Indianapolis, IN: Bobbs-Merrill, 1981

Lehman, David, ed., *Ecstatic Occasions, Expedient Forms: 65 Leading Contemporary Poets Select and Comment On Their Poems*, New York, NY: MacMillan and London: Collier MacMillan, 1987

Levin, Phillis. *The Penguin Book of the Sonnet: 900 Years of a Classic Tradition in English*, New York, NY: Penguin, 2001

Mason-John, Valerie and Kevan Anthony Cameron, *The Great Black North — Contemporary African-Canadian Poetry*, Calgary, AB: Frontenac House, 2013

Matthews, Harry and Alastair Brotchie, *Oulipo Compendium*, London: Atlas, 1998

Oliver, Mary, *A Poetry Handbook*, Harcourt Brace, 1994

_____, *Rules for the Dance: A Handbook for Writing and Reading Metrical Verse*, Boston, MA: Houghton Mifflin, 1998

Oppenheimer, Paul, *The Birth of the Modern Mind: Self, Consciousness, and the Invention of the Sonnet*, New York, NY: Oxford University Press, 1989

Packard, William, *The Poet's Dictionary — A Handbook of Prosody and Poetic Devices*, New York, NY: Harper Perennial, 1994

Padgett, Ron, ed., *The Teachers and Writers Handbook of Poetic Forms*, New York, NY: Teachers and Writers Collaborative, 1987

Pinsky, Robert, *The Sound of Poetry: A Brief Guide*, New York, NY: Farrar, Straus & Giroux, 1998

Rhodes, Shane, "Reuse and Recycle: Finding Poetry in Canada." *Arc Poetry Magazine*, Winter 2013 (p. 47–57)

Skelton, Robin, *The Shapes of Our Singing: A Guide to the Metres and Set Forms of Verse from Around the World*, Spokane, WA: Eastern Washington University Press, 2002

Steele, Timothy, *all the fun's in how you say a thing,: an explanation of meter and versification*, Athens, OH: Ohio University Press, 1999

Strand, Mark and Eavan Boland, *The Making of a Poem, A Norton Anthology of Poetic Forms*, New York, NY: W.W. Norton and Company, 2000

The Prose-Poem Project — A Literary Journal Devoted to the Prose Poem (vol 3 issue 2 spring 2013) accessed online at www.prose-poems.com

Turco, Lewis, *The Book of Forms: A Handbook of Poetics Including Odd and Invented Forms*, Revised and Expanded Edition, Hanover, NH: University Press of New England, 2012

_____, *The New Book of Forms: A Handbook of Poetics*, 3rd edition, Hanover, NH: University Press of New England, 2000

White, Gertrude M. and Joan G. Rosen, *A Moment's Monument: The Development of the Sonnet.* New York, NY: Charles Scribner's Sons, 1972

Williams, Miller, *Patterns of Poetry: An Encyclopedia of Forms*, Baton Rouge and London: Louisiana State University Press, 1986

Wilson, Sheri-D, ed., *The Spoken Word Workbook: Inspiration from poets who teach*, Calgary/Banff: The Calgary Spoken Word Society and The Banff Centre Press, 2011

PERMISSIONS

Caitlin Press was unable to contact the estates of Milton Acorn, Charles Bruce, Fred Cogswell, Robert Finch, Phyllis Gotlieb, Kenneth Leslie and Eli Mandel, despite our best efforts. We ask that the executors of their estates please get in touch with Caitlin Press to discuss permission and remuneration for future editions of *In Fine Form*.

Ballads

"Still Life" by Anne Wilkinson is reprinted from *Heresies: The Complete Poems of Anne Wilkinson 1924–1961*. "1838" from *The Gods* by Dennis Lee. Copyright the author. "The Grey Rider" by Norah M. Holland is reprinted from *Spun-Yarn and Spindrift*. "The Contract Mucker" by Wilson H. Tomson is reprinted from *The Poetry of the Canadian People 1720–1920: Two Hundred Years of Hard Work* (NC Press, 1976). "Back on the Job" by John G. Fisher is reprinted from *The Poetry of the Canadian People 1720–1920: Two Hundred Years of Hard Work* (NC Press, 1976). "The Lee Shore" by E.J. Pratt is reprinted from *E.J. Pratt: Complete Poems* (University of Toronto Press, 1989). "The Creation of Sam McGee" by Robert Service is reprinted from *In Fine Form: The Canadian Book of Form Poetry* (Polestar, 2005 / Caitlin Press, 2013). Excerpt from *Anatomy of Keys* by Steven Price (Brick Books, 2006) is used with permission of the poet and the publisher. "The Ballad of Echolocation" from *Swing in the Hollow* by Ryan Knighton (Anvil Press, 2001) is used with permission of the publisher.

Blues

"Jeremiah's Blues on the GW Bridge" from *Jeremiah, Ohio* copyright 2008 by Adam Sol. Reprinted by permission of House of Anansi Press Inc., Toronto. (www.houseofanansi.com) "Conjured" by R. Nathaniel Dett is reprinted from *Album of a Heart*. "King Bee Blues" from *Whylah Falls* by George Elliott Clarke (Gaspereau Press, 2010) is used with permission of the poet and publisher. "Jump Rope Rhyme of the 49er Daughters" from *49th Parallel Psalm* by Wayde Compton (Arsenal Pulp Press, 1999) is used with permission of the poet and the publisher. "Metric Blues" by F.R. Scott is reprinted with permission of William Toye. "Self-Sufficient Blues" from *Why I Sing the Blues* by Maureen Hynes (Smoking Lung Press, 2001) is used with permission of the poet.

Epigram

Excerpt from *Quodlibets* by Robert Hayman is reprinted from *The Poets of Canada* (Hurtig Publishers, 1978). "News of the Phoenix" by A.J.M. Smith is reprinted with permission of William Toye. "Aunt Jane" by Alden Nowlan is used with permission of the poet's estate. "Very Short Poem" from *Collected Poems by Raymond Souster* by Raymond Souster (Oberon Press, 1981/2003) is used with permission of the publisher. "Tourist Stricken at the Uffizi" from *Turns and Other Poems* by Richard Outram (Chatto & Windus with Hogarth Press, Anson-Cartwright Editions, 1975) is used with permission of the poet's estate. "Cowichan Valley Poem" from *Washita* by Patrick Lane (Harbour Publishing, 2014) is used with permission from the poet and the publisher. "You Fit into Me" by Margaret Atwood, used by permission of the Author. Available in the United States in SELECTED POEMS I, 1965 – 1975, published by Houghton Mifflin, ©Margaret Atwood 1976; and in Canada, SELECTED POEMS, 1966 – 1984, published by Oxford University Press, ©Margaret Atwood 1990. Excerpt from "Winter Epigrams" by Dionne Brand is used with permission of the poet.

Found Poem

"Pavilion Misrepresents Outlook" by F.R. Scott is reprinted with permission of William Toye. The excerpt from "What He Chose to Record (#1)" was originally published in *The Watchmaker's Table* copyright © 2008 by Brian Bartlett. Reprinted by permission of Goose Lane Editions. Excerpt from "The Garbage Poems" by Anna Swanson is used with permission of the poet. Excerpts from *the place of scraps* by Jordan Abel (Talonbooks, 2013) is used with permission of the poet and the publisher. "Zong! #24" from *Zong!* by M. NourbeSe Philip (Weslyan University Press / The Mercury Press, 2008) is used with permission of the poet and Weslyan University Press. "Late Love Song, With an Orange: A Cento" by Maureen Hynes is used with permission of the poet.

Fugue and Madrigal

"Nothing" from *Novel Gas, Penny Black* by David O'Meara (Brick Books, 2008) is used with permission of the poet and the publisher. "Walk On" by Barbara Pelman is with permission of the poet. "The Praying-Mantis" by Annie Charlotte Dalton is reprinted from *Poetry by Canadian Women* (Oxford University Press, 1989). "And the Season Advances" was originally published in *Climates* copyright © 1996 Herménégilde Chiasson, translation copyright © 1999 by Jo-Anne Elder and Fred Cogswell. Reprinted by permission of Goose Lane Editions. "Fugue" was first published in *The Space Between Sleep and Waking* by Robyn Sarah (Villeneuve, 1981). Reprinted with permission of author. The poem will be included in a Selected Poems to be published by Biblioasis in 2017. "One" is excerpted from *Cardinal in the Eastern White Cedar* by Roo Borson. Copyright © 2017 Roo Borson. Reprinted by permission of McClelland & Stewart, a division of Penguin Random House Canada Limited. "i am graffiti" from *This Accident of Being Lost* copyright 2016 by Leanne Simpson. Reprinted by permission of House of Anansi Press Inc., Toronto. (www.houseofanansi.com) "Madrigal, a Lullaby for Xan" from *Human Bodies: New and Collected Poems, 1987–1999* by Marilyn Bowering is used with permission of the poet and Dundurn Press. "Night Piece" from *The Edge of Time* by Robin Skelton (Ronsdale Press, 1995) is used with permission of the publisher.

Ghazal

"Landscapes and home/Ghazal 22" by Yvonne Blomer is used with permission of the poet. "Ghazal V" by Kuldip Gill from Dharma Rasa, Nightwood Editions 1999, (www.nightwoodeditions). "Tonight the Sky is My Begging Bowl" by Sina Queyras is used with permission of the poet and Coach House Books. "Of Night" is excerpted from The Second Blush by Molly Peacock. Copyright © 2008 Molly Peacock. Reprinted by permission of McClelland & Stewart, a division of Penguin Random House Canada Limited. "You Can't Lead a Horse" from The Other Side of Ourselves by Rob Taylor (Cormorant Books, 2001) is used with permission of the poet and the publisher. "IX" from Stilt Jack copyright 1978 by John Thompson. Reprinted by permission of House of Anansi Press Inc., Toronto. (www.houseofanansi.com) "And With Good Reason" by Leigh Nash was originally published in issue 73 of *Arc Poetry Magazine* and is used with permission of the poet.

Glosa

"Planet Earth" from *Planet Earth — Poems Selected and New* by P.K. Page (Porcupine's Quill, 2002) is used with permission of the publisher. "Sixteen" by Sadiqa de Meijer was originally found in *A Crystal Through Which Love Passes: Glosas for P.K. Page* (Buschek Books, 2013) and is used with permission of the poet. "Tree Song" by Kate Braid is used with permission of the poet. "Country Mice" from *Where the Words End and My Body Begins* by Amber Dawn (Arsenal Pulp Press, 2005) is used with permission of the poet and the publisher. "Norberto Hernandez — Photographed Falling September Eleventh" by David Reibetanz is used with permission of the poet. "What do you want?" by Brenda Leifso is used with permission of the poet. "O Grandfather Dust" by Glenn Kletke is used with permission of the poet. "Solstice" from *Late Moon* by Pamela Porter (Ronsdale Press, 2013) is used with permission from the publisher.

Haiku and Other Japanese Forms

Excerpt from "Spring" from *Even a Stone Breathes: Haiku and Senryu* by Winona Baker (Oolichan Books, 2000) is used with permission of the publisher. "[untitled]" from *a hundred umbrellas* by Naomi Beth Wakan (Haiku Arbutus and Friends, 2015) is used with permission of the poet. Excerpt from "Three Political Falltime Haiku" from *Vermeer's Light: Poem's 1996-2006* by George Bowering (Talonbooks, 2006) is used with permission of the publisher. "Hymn for Portia White" from *Lush Dreams, Blue Exile* by George Elliot Clarke (Pottersfield Press, 1994) is used with permission of the poet and the publisher. "[untitled]" by George Swede originally appeared in *Lighting the Global Lantern* (Wintergreen Studios, 2011) and is used here with permission of the poet. "[untitled]" by Marco Fraticelli originally appeared in *Lighting the Global Lantern* (Wintergreen Studios, 2011) and is used here with permission of the poet. "Haiku Monument for Washington, D.C." is excerpted from *Asphodel* by Michael Redhill. Copyright © 1997 Michael Redhill. Reprinted by permission of McClelland & Stewart, a division of Penguin Random House Canada Limited. "[untitled]" by LeRoy Gorman is used with permission of the poet. Excerpt from "Part Five: Maestro" from *Hallelujah Haiku, Senryu, Tanka* by Terry Ann Carter (Buschek Books, 2012) is used with permission of the poet. "Shouting Your Name Down the Well" from *Shouting Your Name Down the Well* by David W. McFadden (Mansfield Books, 2014) is used with permission of the publisher. Excerpt from "Hortus Urbanus / Urban Garden" by Colin Morton is used with permission of the poet. "The Broad Plain – Station 8 – Hiratsuka" from *Ink Monkey* by Diana Hartog (Brick Books, 2006) is used with permission of the poet and the publisher. "Father/Mother Haibum #5" from *Waiting for Saskatchewan* by Fred Wah (Turnstone Press, 1985) is used with permission of the publisher. "1961" from *On the Road to Naropa My Love Affair with Jack Kerouac: A Haibun Memoir* by Terry Ann Carter (Inkling Press, 2015) is used with permission of the poet.

Incantation

Excerpt from "Magic Words" by Aua is reprinted from *Poems of the Inuit* (Oberon Press, 1981). "My Beloved is Dead in Vietnam" from *Two Shores / Deux rives* by Thuong Vuong-Riddick (Ronsdale Press, 1995) is used with permission of the poet and the publisher. "Widow's Winter" by Marilyn Bowering is used with permission of the poet. "from the archive, a continuance" by Renée Sarojini Saklikar from *children of air india: un/authorized exhibits and enterjections*, Nightwood Editions, 2013, (www.nightwoodeditions.com). "What Women Want" from *Leona Gom: The Collected Poems by Leona Gom* (Sono Nis Press, 1991) is used with permission of the poet. "Wash Away Your Sorrows" by Wasela Hiyate was originally published in *Grain*'s Spring 2002 issue and is used here with permission of the poet. Bowling, Tim. "Morenz," *The Thin Smoke of the Heart*. Montreal: MQUP, 2000. "Twelve O'Clock Chant" is excerpted from The Spice-Box of Earth by Leonard Cohen. Copyright © 1961 Leonard Cohen. Reprinted by permission of McClelland & Stewart, a division of Penguin Random House Canada Limited. "His Flute, My Ears" from *Love Medicine and One Song* by Gregory Scofield (Kegedonce Press, 2009) is used with permission of the poet.

Lipogram

"Her Other Language" by Nancy Mattson is used with permission of the poet. Excerpt from "Chapter E" from *Eunoia* by Christian Bök (Coach House Books, 2001) is used with permission of the poet and the publisher. "*L.*" from *Mobility of Light* (Wilfrid Laurier University Press, 2009) by Nicole Brossard and translated by Erin Mouré and Robert Majzels is used with permission of the poet and translators. "so'net 3" by Paul Dutton is used with permission of the poet. "Turnips Are" by bp Nichol is used with permission of the poet's estate. "Shuffles" from *The Afterlife of Trees* by Brian Bartlett (McGill-Queen's University Press, 2002) is used with permission of the poet and the publisher.

Palindrome

"Halfway World" from *The Secret Signature of Things* by Eve Joseph (Brick Books, 2010) is used with permission of the poet and publisher. "The Shoreline" by Joe Denham is used with permission of the poet. "ATM" from *Curio: Grotesques and Satires from the Electronic Age* by Elizabeth Bachinksy (Book-Thug, 2006) is used with permission of the poet and publisher. "Menorca #1" from *Spain is a State of Mind* by Patricia Young (The Alfred Gustav Press, 2013) is used with permission of the poet and the publisher. "Remembering. Autumn" from *Passing Stranger* by Pamela Galloway (Inanna Publications, 2014) is used with permission of the poet. "More" from *Lake of Two Mountains* by Arleen Paré (Brick Books, 2014) is used with permission of the poet and the publisher.

Pantoum

"Doug Hill" from *Meeting the Tormentors in Safeway* by Alexandra Oliver (Biblioasis, 2013) is used with permission of the poet and the publisher. "Vincent, in the Dream of Zundert" by Laura Ritland was originally published in *The Malahat Review* and is used here with the permission of the poet. "Lucie, *Lucie*" by Peter Garner is used with permission of the poet. "Labour Pantoum" from *How Do You Feel?* by Kirsten Emmott (Sono Nis Press, 1992) is used with permission of the poet. "In the Spring of No Letters" from *Shameless* by Marlene Cookshaw (Brick Books, 2002) is used with permission of the poet and the publisher. "Post-War Procession" from *Out to Dry in Cape Breton* by Anita Lahey (Signal Editions, 2006) is used with permission of the poet and the publisher. "Song" by Kayla Czaga from *For Your Safety Please Hold On*, Nightwood Editions, 2014, (www.nightwoodeditions.com). "Empty Chair" from *Dismantled Secrets* by Maxianne Berger (Wolsak & Wynn, 2008) is used with permission of the poet and the publisher.

Pas de Deux

"What We Heard About the Americans" and "What We Heard About the Canadians" from *Song and Spectacle* by Rachel Rose (Harbour Publishing, 2012) is used with permission of the poet and the publisher. "The Sea by the Wood" and "The Wood by the Sea" by Duncan Campbell Scott is reprinted from *Poets of the Confederation* (McClelland & Stewart, 1973)."What We Thought About the Chinese Mothers" and "What the Chinese Mothers Seemed to Think About Us" by Susan Olding originally appeared in *Desperately Seeking Susans* (Oolichan Books, 2012) and are used with permission of the poet. The poet thanks Rachel Rose as the originator of the form *pas de deux*. "Woods" from *A Reliquary and Other Poems* (Fitzhenry & Whiteside, 2013). Copyright © the estate of Daryl Hine, included by permission of the estate.

Prose Poem

Permission to use "Barker Fairley and the Blizzard" from *Gwendolyn MacEwen: Volume 2: The Later Years* by Gwendolyn MacEwen (Exile Editions, 1999) was provided by her family and estate. "Horses" from *The Tool Shed* by Glen Downie (Gaspereau Press, 2005) is used with permission of the poet. "blues" from *Instruments of Surrender* by Christine Wiesenthal (Buschek Books, 2001) is used with permission of the poet. "Habitat" from *Naked Trees* by John Terpstra (Wolsak & Wynn, 2012) is used with permission of the poet and the publisher. "Glossography of G" from *The Book of Marvels* by Lorna Crozier reprinted with permission from Greystone Books Ltd. "Sisyphean" from *Night-Eater* by Patricia Young (Quattro Books, 2012) is used with permission of the poet and the publisher. "Entry" from *Ink Monkey* by Diana Hartog (Brick Books, 2006) is used with permission of the poet and the publisher.

Rondeau

"In Flanders Fields" by John McCrae is reprinted from In Flanders Fields and Other Poems (Putnam, 1919). Excerpt from "Three Small Rooms" by Colin

Morton is used with permission of the poet. "Rondeau Redoublé" from Always Now by Margaret Avison (Porcupine's Quill, 2003) is used with permission of the poet's estate and the publisher. "Roundel to my Pipe" by Émile Nelligan and translated by P.F. Widdows is reprinted from The Poetry of Canada in Translation (Oxford University Press, 1970). "Triolets for Ken" from Crossing Salt Flats by Christopher Wiseman (Porcupine's Quill, 1999) is used with permission from the poet and the publisher. "Vuillard Interior" from Chameleon Hours copyright 2008 Elise Partridge. Reprinted by permission of House of Anansi Press Inc., Toronto. (www.houseofanansi.com) "Triolet for Afghanistan" by Leslie Timmins is used with permission of the poet. "Down" from Glasburyon by Mark Abley (Quarry Press, 1994) is used with permission of the poet. "In the slow spin of stars, a dancer turns" from Blue Sonoma by Jane Munro (Brick Books, 2013) is used with permission of the poet and the publisher.

Sestina

"Sestina: Whiskey Canyon" by Tanis MacDonald is used with permission of the poet. "The Lover's Sestina" from *Anywhere* by Bruce Meyer (Exile Editions, 2000) is used with permission of the poet. "Fiddle bid us" from *The Pemmican Eaters* by Marilyn Dumont (ECW Press, 2015) is used with permission of the poet and publisher. "In Juarez" from *Slow Moving Target* by Sue Wheeler (Brick Books, 2000) is used with permission of the poet and the publisher. "Ritual" by Sue Chenette first appeared in the autumn 2004 issue of *The Fiddlehead* and is used here with permission of the poet. "Sestina on a Train" by Al Purdy, *Beyond Remembering: Collected Poems*, edited by Sam Solecki, 2000, Harbour Publishing, (www.harbourpublishing.com).

Sonnet

"Meeting the Tormentors in Safeway" from *Meeting the Tormentors in Safeway* by Alexandra Oliver (Biblioasis, 2015) is used with permission of the poet and the publisher. "Apollo at Aberdeen" was originally published in *Climates* copyright © 1996 Herménégilde Chiasson, translation copyright © Jo-Anne Elder and Fred Cogswell. Reprinted with permission of Goose Lane Editions. Excerpt from "The Golden Lotus" from *The Golden Lotus* by Diana Brebner (Netherlandic Press, 1993) is used with permission of the poet's estate. "Head and Torso of the Minotaur" by John Reibetanz is used with permission of the poet. "In the box from the World Wildlife Fund" by Yvonne Blomer is used with permission of the poet. "Acoustics" from *Science Lessons: Poems* by W.H. New (Oolichan Books, 1996) is used with permission of the publisher. "Flirrup" from *Merrybegot* by Mary Dalton (Signal Editions, 2003) is used with permission of the poet. Excerpt from "SIGINT" from *On Malice* by Ken Babstock (Coach House

Books, 2014) is used with permission of the publisher. "Whisper Songs" from *Suddenly, So Much* by Sandy Shreve (Exile Editions, 2005) is used with permission of the poet.

Spoken Word

"Nelly Belly Swelly" by Lillian Allen is used with permission of the poet. "One" by Andrea Thompson is used with permission of the poet. "Drones" by Sheri-D Wilson is used with permission of the poet. "The Third Eye" Macpherson, Jay, *Poems Twice Told* © 1981, Oxford University Press Canada. Reprinted with permission of the publisher. "Bach Fugue" from *Wild Geese and Other Poems* by Barker Fairley (Penumbra Press, 1984) is used with permission of the publisher. "The Skater" by Sir Charles G.D. Roberts is reprinted from *The Oxford Book of Canadian Verse* (Oxford University Press, 1982). "Jaham Sings of the Fear of the Moon" from *Araby* by Eric Ormsby (Signal Editions, 2001) is used with permission of the poet. "Junco Partner" from *Parkway* by Peter Culley (New Star, 2013) is used with permission of the poet's estate and the publisher. "Tigers Know From Birth" by Anne Wilkinson is reprinted from *The Hangman Ties the Holly* (Macmillan, 1955). "The Second Hand" from *Selected Poems: The Vision Tree* by Phyllis Webb (Talonbooks, 1982) is used with permission of the publisher. "In Oak" from *Gathering Wild* by Marianne Bluger (Brick Books, 1987) is used with permission of the poet and the publisher. "The Broken Cup" from *Aurora* by Sharon Thesen (Talonbooks, 1995) is used with permission of the poet.

Stanza

"Barbed Wire" from *The Essential Richard Outram* by Richard Outram (Porcupine's Quill, 2011) is used with permission of the poet's estate and the publisher. "Keine Lazarovitch 1870–1959" is excerpted from *The Collected Poems of Irving Layton* by Irving Layton. Copyright © 1971 Irving Layton. Reprinted by permission of McClelland & Stewart, a division of Penguin Random House Canada Limited. "From the Hazel Bough" is excerpted from *Selected Poems of Earle Birney* by Earle Birney. Copyright © 1966 Earle Birney. Reprinted by permission of McClelland & Stewart, a division of Penguin Random House Canada Limited. "Alligator Pie" from *Alligator Pie* by Dennis Lee is used with permission of Harper Collins Canada. "Vagabond Song" by Bliss Carman is reprinted from *Canadian Poetry Vol. 1* (ECW Press, 1982). "Ebb Tide" by Marjorie Pickthall is reprinted from *Poetry by Canadian Women* (Oxford University Press, 1989). "The Train Dogs" by Pauline Johnson is reprinted from *Poetry by Canadian Women* (Oxford University Press, 1989). "Low Tide on the Grand Pré" by Bliss Carman is reprinted from *Canadian Poetry Vol. 1* (ECW Press, 1982). "Hollow" from *The Fly in Autumn* by David Zieroth (Harbour Publishing, 2009) is used with permission of the poet and publisher. "Water and Marble" from *The Hidden Room: Collected Poems* by P.K. Page (Porcupine's Quill, 1997) is used with permission of the publisher. "Drought" by Eric Duncan is reprinted from *The Poetry of the Canadian People 1720–1920: Two Hundred Years of Hard Work* (NC Press, 1976). "The City of the End of Things" by Archibald Lampman is reprinted from *The Oxford Book of Canadian Verse* (Oxford University Press, 1982). "Cell Sequencing" by Madeline Bassnett originally appeared in issue 28 of *The Fiddlehead* and is used here with permission of the poet.

Villanelle

"Villanelle" from *Trobairitz* by Catherine Owen (Anvil Press, 2012) is used with permission of the publisher. "The Ferry to South Baymouth" from *Anywhere* by Bruce Meyer (Exile Editions, 2000) is used with permission of the poet. "Little Miracle." Copyright © 1995 Molly Peacock, from *Cornucopia: New and Selected Poems* by Molly Peacock. Used by permission of W.W. Norton & Company, Inc. "A Wake" is excerpted from *Infinite Citizens of the Shaking Tent* by Liz Howard. Copyright © 2015 Liz Howard. Reprinted by permission of McClelland & Stewart, a division of Penguin Random House Canada Limited. "Ever" from *Nobel Gas, Penny Black* by David O'Meara (Brick Books, 2008) is used with permission of the poet and publisher. "Woods" by David Waltner-Toews is used with permission of the poet. "More of the Just" by Sandy Shreve is used with permission of the poet.

... and More

"Acrostic Lament" from *Jeremiah, Ohio* copyright 2008 by Adam Sol. Reprinted by permission of House of Anansi Press Inc., Toronto. (www.houseofanansi.com) "Queen Mary, She's My Friend" from *The Spaces in Between: Selected Poems 1965–2001* by Stephen Scobie (NeWest Press, 2003) is used with permission of the poet. "Riddle: These men dig fingers" by Cassidy McFadzean was originally published in Issue 69 of *Arc Poetry Magazine* and is used here with the permission of the poet. "How can you change 'rind' into 'dirt'?" by Barbara Nickel is used with the permission of the poet. "Particle Limericks" from *Animate Objects* by Alan Wilson (Turnstone Press, 1995) is used with permission of the publisher. "Recipe for Divertimento in D, K: 136" is excerpted from *Camber: Selected Poems, 1983–2000* by Don McKay. Copyright © 2004 Don McKay. Reprinted by permission of McClelland & Stewart, a division of Penguin Random House Canada Limited. Excerpt from "The Way Down." Macpherson, Jay, *Poems Twice Told* © 1981, Oxford University Press Canada. Reprinted with permission of the publisher. "The Hands" by David Daniel Moses is used with permission of the poet. "The Cherry Laurel" from *The Hundred Lives* by Russell Thornton

(Quattro Books, 2014) is used with permission of the poet. "The Ghost of His Hand" by Nancy Bennett is used with permission of the poet. "Reduce your eco-footprint" by Barbara Nickel is used with permission of the poet. "Blues" by bp Nichol is used with permission of the poet's estate.

INDEX OF TERMS

Primary references are indicated by bold numbers; references in footnotes are indicated by fn before the number.

Index of Poems

Index of Poets

H

J

K

L

M

N

O

P

Q

R

ACKNOWLEDGEMENTS

We are grateful to the numerous people who have helped us during our journey for both editions of this book. In addition to those who provided expertise, information and feedback for the first edition — Marianne Bluger, Charles Boname, George Elliott Clarke, Harvey DeRoo, Gary Geddes, Alice Korfman, Bruce Meyer, Nadeem Parmar, Robyn Sarah and Tom Wayman — we thank Lillian Allen, Terry-Ann Carter, Wayde Compton, Andrew Clarke, Zöe Landale, George McWhirter, Hilary Peach, Andrea Thompson and Sheri-D Wilson. The usual caveat, of course, applies — any errors are entirely our responsibility and no reflection on any of these generous colleagues and friends.

As before, special thanks to all the poets included here and to the many others who are writing wonderful poems that we just couldn't fit into the available space. We also deeply appreciate the thoughtful and detailed feedback we've had from teachers, writers and readers in response to the first edition. It encouraged us to write a second.

Our thanks also to Vici Johnstone who not only agreed to take on the distribution of the first edition of *In Fine Form*, but suggested publishing a second. Also to the staff at Caitlin — Michael Despotovic, Jakelene Plan and Demian Pettman, whose enthusiasm and care made bringing this book to fruition a pleasure.

Kate would especially like to thank the faculty of the Creative Writing and Journalism Department at Malaspina University-College (now Vancouver Island University) for their whole-hearted support for introducing formal poetry into the curriculum many years ago. Also thanks to John, who is my sonnet and my glosa.

Sandy thanks the two teachers extraordinaire who first nurtured her enduring love of form — Tom Trafford and Helen Beale; two poets who first introduced her to intriguing new forms — Kirsten Emmott and Gudrun Wight; and every poet who ever wrote a poem that left her breathless.

About the Editors

KIM GILLER

SANDY SHREVE has written, edited and co-edited seven books and two chap-books. Her most recent poetry collection is *Waiting for the Albatross* (Oolichan Books, 2015). Her previous books include *Suddenly, So Much* (Exile Editions, 2005) and *Belonging* (Sono Nis Press, 1997). Sandy's contributions to the literary arts include founding BC's Poetry in Transit program, as well as serving on a variety of committees and juries. Her poetry is widely anthologized and has won or been short-listed for several awards. Now retired, she worked in communications for fifteen years and, prior to that, as an office manager, secretary, union coordinator, library assistant and reporter. Born in Quebec and raised in Sackville, New Brunswick, she lived for some 40 years in Vancouver, British Columbia. She now makes her home on Pender Island in BC, where she is diving into a relatively new interest in photo art. www.shreve.shawwebspace.ca

BARRY PETERSON

KATE BRAID has edited, co-edited and written eleven books and two chap-books of poetry and non-fiction, many of them about working people including miners, fishermen, and artists Emily Carr, Georgia O'Keeffe and Glen Gould. Her poetry has won or been nominated for national, provincial and local prizes. Her most recent poetry book, *Rough Ground Revisited*, based on her 15 years as a construction carpenter, is a companion to her memoir, *Journeywoman: Swinging a Hammer in a Man's World*. For 12 years she also taught creative writing in Vancouver and Nanaimo, BC, including classes on how to write in form. In 2015 she won the Mayor of Vancouver's Arts Award in recognition of leadership and contributions to the Vancouver literary arts. She divides her time between the beauties of Vancouver and Pender Island. www.katebraid.com

Readers Notes

READERS NOTES

READERS NOTES

READERS NOTES

This text for this book is set in Bell MT.
Bell (sometimes known as John Bell) is a serif typeface designed in 1788 by Richard Austin. It is considered an early example of the Scotch Roman style, a style featuring stylish contrasts between thick and thin strokes and ball terminals on many letters. After a short initial period of popularity, the face fell into disuse until it was revived in the 1930s, after which it enjoyed an enduring acceptance as a text face. The initial success of the face was short lived however, as the introduction of lithography at the beginning of the nineteenth century caused taste in typefaces to change dramatically. Thus, while Bell's type was seldom seen after 1800 in England, it went on to become a favourite in the United States. Boston publisher Henry Houghton purchased the type in Europe for his Riverside Press but back in Boston the face was called copperplate.
In 1926 Stanley Morison came upon a sample of the type and arranged for its revival by Monotype Corporation that appeared in 1930.

The text was typeset by Vici Johnstone,
Caitlin Press, Spring 2016.